The Importance of Entrepreneurship in Fostering Economic Progress

Mohammed El Amine Abdelli
University of Brest, France

Naima Bentouir
Ain Temouchent University, Algeria

Esra Sipahi Döngül
Aksaray University, Turkey

IGI Global
PUBLISHER of TIMELY KNOWLEDGE

A volume in the Advances in Finance, Accounting, and Economics (AFAE) Book Series

Published in the United States of America by
IGI Global
Business Science Reference (an imprint of IGI Global)
701 E. Chocolate Avenue
Hershey PA, USA 17033
Tel: 717-533-8845
Fax: 717-533-8661
E-mail: cust@igi-global.com
Web site: http://www.igi-global.com

Library of Congress Cataloging-in-Publication Data

Names: Abdelli, Mohammed El Amine, editor. | Bentouir, Naima, DATE- editor. | Sipahi Döngül, Esra, editor.
Title: The importance of entrepreneurship in fostering economic progress / edited by Mohammed El Amine Abdelli, Naima Bentouir, and Esra Sipahi Döngül.
Description: Hershey, PA : Business Science Reference, [2023] | Includes bibliographical references and index. | Summary: "The book offers insights into recent developments in understanding the dynamics that support knowledge generation, diffusion, and commercialization through innovation and the role of the entrepreneur in the growth process. It discusses the impact of entrepreneurship on employment, the crucial role of technological innovation on economic growth, and the impact of the entrepreneurial economy on public policy. By exploring the regulation design influencing knowledge creation, ownership, entry barriers, labor mobility, and inefficient financial markets, this book offers relevant policy implications for policymakers seeking to design effective entrepreneurship policies to foster economic development, employment, and global competitiveness"-- Provided by publisher.
Identifiers: LCCN 2023025844 (print) | LCCN 2023025845 (ebook) | ISBN 9781668471272 (hardcover) | ISBN 9781668471289 (paperback) | ISBN 9781668471296 (ebook)
Subjects: LCSH: Economic development. | Technological innovations--Economic aspects. | Entrepreneurship.
Classification: LCC HD82 .I2975 2023 (print) | LCC HD82 (ebook) | DDC 338.9--dc23/eng/20230616
LC record available at https://lccn.loc.gov/2023025844
LC ebook record available at https://lccn.loc.gov/2023025845

This book is published in the IGI Global book series Advances in Finance, Accounting, and Economics (AFAE) (ISSN: 2327-5677; eISSN: 2327-5685)

British Cataloguing in Publication Data
A Cataloguing in Publication record for this book is available from the British Library.

Advances in Finance, Accounting, and Economics (AFAE) Book Series

ISSN:2327-5677
EISSN:2327-5685

MISSION

In our changing economic and business environment, it is important to consider the financial changes occurring internationally as well as within individual organizations and business environments. Understanding these changes as well as the factors that influence them is crucial in preparing for our financial future and ensuring economic sustainability and growth.

The **Advances in Finance, Accounting, and Economics (AFAE)** book series aims to publish comprehensive and informative titles in all areas of economics and economic theory, finance, and accounting to assist in advancing the available knowledge and providing for further research development in these dynamic fields.

COVERAGE

- Environmental And Social Accounting
- Applied Finance
- Health Economics
- Theoretical Issues in Economics, Finance, and Accounting
- Interest Rates and Annuities
- Fiscal Policy
- Evidence-Based Studies
- Borrowing and Lending
- Economics of Migration and Spatial Mobility
- E-Accounting

Titles in this Series

For a list of additional titles in this series, please visit:
http://www.igi-global.com/book-series/advances-finance-accounting-economics/73685

Circular Economy Implementation for Sustainability in the Built Environment
Nicoleta Cobîrzan (Technical University of Cluj-Napoca, Romania) Radu Muntean (Transilvania University of Brașov, Romania) and Raluca-Andreea Felseghi (Technical University of Cluj-Napoca, Romania)
Business Science Reference • copyright 2023 • 330pp • H/C (ISBN: 9781668482384) • US $250.00 (our price)

Management, Technology, and Economic Growth in Smart and Sustainable Cities
Jorge A. Ruiz-Vanoye (Universidad Politécnica de Pachuca, Mexico)
Business Science Reference • copyright 2023 • 320pp • H/C (ISBN: 9798369303733) • US $240.00 (our price)

Optimizing Energy Efficiency During a Global Energy Crisis
Meltem Okur Dinçsoy (Trakya University, Turkey) and Hamit Can (Trakya University, Turkey)
Business Science Reference • copyright 2023 • 408pp • H/C (ISBN: 9798369304006) • US $240.00 (our price)

Theory and Practice of Illegitimate Finance
Abdul Rafay (University of Management and Technology, Pakistan)
Business Science Reference • copyright 2023 • 389pp • H/C (ISBN: 9798369311905) • US $295.00 (our price)

The Sustainable Fintech Revolution Building a Greener Future for Finance
Kuldeep Singh (Faculty of Management Studies, CMS Business School, Jain University (Deemed), Bengaluru, India) Rebecca Abraham (Huizenga College of Business and Entrepreneurship, Nova Southeastern University, Fort Lauderdale, USA) and Prasanna Kolar (Koneru Lakshmaiah Education Foundation, India)
Business Science Reference • copyright 2023 • 358pp • H/C (ISBN: 9798369300084) • US $250.00 (our price)

For an entire list of titles in this series, please visit:
http://www.igi-global.com/book-series/advances-finance-accounting-economics/73685

IGI Global
PUBLISHER of TIMELY KNOWLEDGE

701 East Chocolate Avenue, Hershey, PA 17033, USA
Tel: 717-533-8845 x100 • Fax: 717-533-8661
E-Mail: cust@igi-global.com • www.igi-global.com

Table of Contents

Detailed Table of Contents

to foster economic growth. Despite its advantageous geographical position for solar energy utilization, Turkey's solar water heating system sector has yet to capitalize on its potential fully. Hence, there is a need to expand entrepreneurship in solar water heating systems. Consequently, attaining national and sustainable development goals can be facilitated alongside promoting regional development. This chapter examines the impact of entrepreneurship in the solar water heating system industry on economic growth, with a specific focus on Turkey's position in this sector. The evaluation is conducted by drawing upon relevant research. The chapter examines the various aspects that could potentially influence the development of entrepreneurship in the solar water heating system industry. It also proposes potential solutions to improve the prospects of solar water heating system entrepreneurship.

Preface

There is still a lack of a clear grasp of entrepreneurship and growth components. Furthermore, the relationship between the microeconomic foundations of development and the macroeconomic outcome remains too crudely modeled to capture the full breadth of these complex and opposing processes. For example, the three primary sources of growth in any economy are increases in production inputs, improvements in the efficiency of input allocation across economic activities, innovation, which develops new products, devises new applications for existing products, and increases the efficiency of input utilization.

Large businesses are increasingly taking over investment in innovation in industrialized countries, running R&D departments and making technological change a routine bureaucratic process. In research on the impact of technological innovation on growth, the function of new firm creation has been generally disregarded. Innovation has been a crucial engine of economic growth and job creation. These aspects of new venture competitiveness and performance, such as growth and survival, the industry and how it evolves, and the location and influence of entrepreneurial activity, require further study. Furthermore, the importance of entrepreneurship in fostering inventive activity and economic progress is emphasized in these chapters. Finally, the entrepreneurial economy's impact on public policy is explored, and the vital role of entrepreneurship policy in economic development, employment, and global competitiveness.

The primary goal of this book is to illuminate recent developments in our understanding of the dynamics that support knowledge generation, diffusion, and commercialization through innovation and the role of the entrepreneur in the growth process. The regulation design influencing knowledge creation, ownership, entry barriers, labor mobility, and (inefficient) financial markets are particularly relevant policy implications. We presuppose that knowledge is efficiently disseminated through the entry. Incentives that motivate systems to turn information into social and beneficial requirements must be matched by knowledge generation.

CHAPTERS OVERVIEW

Chapter 1: Digital Entrepreneurship Towards Changing Consumer Preferences

The chapter emphasizes the importance of digital entrepreneurs being prepared for sustainable innovations and identifying emerging opportunities in the business world, as digitalization leads to rapid and transformative change, including the concept of "digital entrepreneurship."

Chapter 2: Are Technical Graduates Best Suited for Entrepreneurship? Examining Entrepreneurial Attitude as a Moderator Between Their Characteristics and Intention

This study investigates the lack of entrepreneurial attitude among technical/engineering students in Chhattisgarh state. It examines the moderating effect of entrepreneurial attitude dimensions like success, innovation, personal control, and self-esteem on the relationship between entrepreneurial characteristics and self-employment intention. The results show that entrepreneurial attitude dimensions significantly influence these factors.

Chapter 3: Driving Economic Development – Unveiling the Transformative Power of Women Entrepreneurs in Algeria

This study examines the impact of empowering women in entrepreneurship on Algeria's economic growth, focusing on the role of Algerian women in economic development. Five variables were analyzed: GDP, business women's ownership, women in the industrial sector, women in forced labor, and women's unemployment. The findings highlight the need for women's empowerment and its potential benefits for economic growth.

Chapter 4: Unlocking Algeria's Economic Potential – The Entrepreneurship's Effect on Growth

The chapter discusses the role of entrepreneurship education in promoting employment, productivity, economic growth, innovation, and competitiveness. It assesses the impact of entrepreneurship on Algeria's economic development using ARDL data from 2006 to 2020. Results show consistent long-term relationships between variables, with higher education, new job intensity, and school enrollment positively impacting GDP growth.

Chapter 5: The Legal Framework Start-Ups in Algeria – Applications and Solutions

The department aims to enhance the theoretical and practical understanding of the start-up industry by analyzing key elements and drivers. It reviews multiple models, including the 3M model, which is crucial for Algeria's startup ecosystem. The review also examines the complex interactions between conceptual frameworks, legal definitions, and practical applications.

Chapter 6: The Effect of Entrepreneurship on the Achievement of Business Performance – Approach Through the Psychological Traits of the Entrepreneurs: Case Study of Algerian SMEs

The chapter analyzes the entrepreneurial orientation (ROI) of 101 Algerian manufacturing SMEs and its impact on business performance. Results show low direction and significant relationships between proactivity, risk-taking dimensions, and performance. The study suggests that Algerian entrepreneurs need success and entrepreneurial self-efficacy to develop entrepreneurial skills.

Chapter 7: Entrepreneurship Education – A Sustainable Strategy for Economic Development in Nigeria

Economic development is a top priority in all aspects of a country's economy, including education, which can promote growth and development through entrepreneurial education, focusing on individual well-being and resource allocation.

Chapter 8: A Review of the Promotion of Entrepreneurship in the Solar Water Heating Industry in Turkey

The chapter evaluates the role of solar water heating system entrepreneurship in Turkey's economic growth and its position in the field. It discusses factors affecting SWHS entrepreneurship promotion and suggests solutions to enhance its potential for national and sustainable development.

IN SUMMARY

The Importance of Entrepreneurship in Fostering Economic Progress deeply examines entrepreneurship issues' effects on economic development and the global dynamic world. Entrepreneurship is increasingly recognized for individual success stories and as a critical driver of societal and economic transformations. The book discusses the latest developments in understanding what environment entrepreneurship shapes commercialization and economic growth.

The impact of entrepreneurship on growth and the critical role of technological innovation, Education, and Legal issues in economic development are focal points of this study. Simultaneously, it comprehensively addresses the effects of the entrepreneurial economy on public policy, offering insights into how effective entrepreneurship policies can be designed. This book explains how entrepreneurship is vital for economic development, entry barriers, labor mobility, and financial markets.

This book provides a valuable solution to understanding how entrepreneurship shapes economic progress. We hope this book will be a valuable resource for academics, students, and researchers seeking a deeper understanding of entrepreneurship's contribution to growth.

Mohammed El Amine Abdelli
University of Brest, France

Naima Bentouir
Ain Temouchent University, Algeria

Esra Sipahi Döngül
Aksaray University, Turkey

Section 1

Environmental Entrepreneurship and Economics: Education, Digitalisation

Chapter 1
Digital Entrepreneurship Towards Changing Consumer Preferences

Asu Yaşar Tabanlı
https://orcid.org/0000-0002-0675-6672
İzmir Katip Çelebi University, Turkey

Alper Işın
İzmir Katip Çelebi University, Turkey

Atilla Akbaba
https://orcid.org/0000-0002-9434-2145
İzmir Katip Çelebi University, Turkey

ABSTRACT

As the phenomenon of digitalization leads to diverse consequences through rapid and transformative change, it is important for entrepreneurs to be ready for sustainable innovations and identify emerging opportunities in the business world. Business models in entrepreneurship are faced with a major transformation from single new developments to completely digital environments with digitalization. Besides the creation of new businesses from the opportunities contributed by digitalization, available branches, and businesses establish "digital entrepreneurship" as a new type of entrepreneurial activity by transfer from offline commerce to online business.

DOI: 10.4018/978-1-6684-7127-2.ch001

INTRODUCTION

As the phenomenon of digitalisation leads to diverse consequences through rapid and transformative change, it is important for entrepreneurs to be ready for sustainable innovations and identify emerging opportunities in the business world. Business models in entrepreneurship are faced with a major transformation from single new developments to completely digital environments with digitalisation. Besides the creation of new businesses from the opportunities contributed by digitalisation, available branchs and businesses establish "digital entrepreneurship" as a new type of entrepreneurial activity by transfer from offline commerce to online business (Kraus, Palmer, Kailer, Kallinger, & Spitzer, 2019: 354).

Key elements of entrepreneurship to overcome the Covid-19 crisis include innovation, risk-taking and being active in the market (Ratten, 2020: 508). Initially, entrepreneurship was adversely affected by Covid-19 as with other economic factors. Although many businesses did not survive after the significant decline in demand, there were businesses that turned this situation into an opportunity (Galindo-Martín, Castaño-Martínez, & Méndez-Picazo, 2021: 345-346). In addition to the importance of being practical and taking risks in the market, the innovativeness of the initiatives create a sustainability both for the time of the pandemic and after.

Entrepreneurship

People need land, labour and capital to produce goods and services that maintain and enhance their lives. But land, labour and capital produce nothing until they are activately employed. They need to be guided and focused by an entrepreneurial mind to create value. Entrepreneurship is the unseen factor of production as a dynamic process that adds value to society, business and the environment (Butler, 2020: 5; Kuratko, O'Connor & Frederick, 2018: 10). Entrepreneurship, in its most general form, is the ability to sort resources to capture new business opportunities. Entrepreneurship, defined in this broad sense, is central to the functioning of market economies (OECD, 1998: 11,41). Entrepreneurship itself is a "meta-economic" event that deeply affects and shapes the economy without being a part of the economy (Drucker, 1985: 13).

Entrepreneurship creates an environment that enables more entrepreneurship (Holcombe, 1998: 51). There must exist two conditions to development of entrepreneuship: freedom –freedom to establish an economic initiative, and freedom to be creative and innovative with this initiative- and prosperity –the convenient economic conditions that give an entrepreneurial organization the opportunity to gain and grow (Dollinger, 2008: 12).

Tekin (2019), divided entrepreneurship into two as traditional and contemporary. While dividing the traditional types of entrepreneurship into subheadings as (1) original entrepreneurship, (2) intrapreneurship, (3) corporate entrepreneurship, (4) entrepreneurial entrepreneurship, (5) professional entrepreneurship, (6) opportunity entrepreneurship, (7) follower entrepreneurship, (8) public entrepreneurship, (9) creative entrepreneurship and (10) strategic entrepreneurship. Tekin (2019), also listed the current types of entrepreneurship as (1) women's entrepreneurship, (2) social entrepreneurship, (3) virtual entrepreneurship, (4) technological (techno) entrepreneurship, (5) environmentalist (eco) entrepreneurship, and (6) academic entrepreneurship (Tekin, 2019). Digital entrepreneurship, which is growing rapidly in its field, creates a confusion in academic research with its dynamic terminology. For instance, at the beginning of the field in 2000-2001, it was called 'internet entrepreneurship', around 2004 it was called e- and cyber entrepreneurship, while now digital entrepreneurship is used (Zaheer, Breyer, & Dumay, 2019). Tajvidi, R., & Tajvidi, M. (2021), aimed to explore cyber entrepreneurship in the food industry and the opportunities it offers for entrepreneurs in epidemics such as Covid-19 in their studies. They wrote this entrepreneurship, which has emerged as a new genre in the digital age, using the concept of cyber entrepreneurship. Accordingly, even if titles are given with different names in the literature, the same concepts are mentioned in the content of the studies.

Digital Entrepreneurship

The digital world offers entrepreneurs a vast universe of new resources to tap into, from exponentially growing collections of open data, content, code and services to online contributions from users and communities around the world. The power of the cloud, big data, social media, mobile technology and artificial intelligence has increased significantly while costs have fallen. The development of digital technology also encourages entrepreneurship (Allen, 2019).

Digital technology, transforms the process of delivering a live product or service in front of a real customer (Allen, 2019). Emerging digital technologies herald a new era in entrepreneurship, in which traditional ways and forms of pursuing entrepreneurial opportunities are increasingly being questioned, affecting and reshaping a firm's ability to change its business models, operating models and culture (Nambisan, 2017: 1047; Ghosh, Hughes, M., Hughes, P., & Hodgkinson, 2021: 189).

Digital entrepreneurship and traditional entrepreneurship differ from each other in terms of how they are marketed, the product itself as a good or service, and the workplace (Hull, Hung, Hair, Perotti, & DeMartino, 2007). Digital entrepreneurship encompasses all new initiatives and the transformation of existing businesses by creating and using new digital technologies (EU, 2018: 2). Digital entrepreneurship requires taking advantage of new means-ends connections based on the material possibilities of the Internet, new media and IT (information technology) in general, including global geographical access, 24x7 accessibility and increasing interaction across time and space as more people gain broadband internet access (Davidson & Vaast, 2010: 4).

Hull et al. (2007) divided digital entrepreneurship into three types: (1) *mild digital entrepreneurship*, (2) *moderate digital entrepreneurship* and (3) *extreme digital entrepreneurship*. The differences between traditional and digital entrepreneurship and the three types of digital entrepreneurship can be seen in the context of ease of entry, ease of production and storage, ease of distribution in the digital marketplace, digital workplace, digital products, digital service and digital commitment (Hull, Hung, Hair, Perotti, & DeMartino, 2007).

E-Commerce

The Internet has facilitated commercial activities all over the world by using information and communication technologies (ICT) and has doubled the trade volume (Gökmen, 2012). Although e-commerce is a new concept, it has been one of the most important scientific achievements of the 20th century. E-commerce has resulted in a revolution in the distribution system. It transcends the boundaries of time and space, changes trade patterns, improves the circulation of goods, capital and information, and make businesses more competitive by effectively lowers the cost of production. In short, e-commerce has enabled traditional commerce to achieve larger, faster, better and more economical results (Qin, Chang, Li, & Li, 2014: 1).

E-commerce, in a broad sense, means doing business through electronic means, mainly the Internet, selling goods and services delivered offline, as well as products that can be "digitized" and delivered online, such as computer software (Coppel, 2000: 4; Gökmen, 2012). E-commerce technology has helped businesses and companies to sell their products and services worldwide and easily, but also helps customers make purchases whenever and wherever they want (Babenko, Kulczyk, Perevosova, Syniavska and Davydova, 2019: 5). The globalization of companies is explained as a key factor in the spread of e-commerce. Large global companies are expected to use technologies such as e-commerce more intensively, which will enable them to maintain or expand their market shares and work more efficiently, as they are more faced with foreign competition (Babenko, Kulczyk, Perevosova, Syniavska, & Davydova, 2019: 4).

Above, a graph has been created with the data of the Ministry of Commerce E-commerce Information Platform on the Number of Businesses Engaged in E-Commerce. E-Commerce Information Platform shared these numbers as 68,457 for the whole year of 2019, 256,861 for the whole year of 2020, 321,742 for the

Figure 1. Number of businesses engaged in e-commerce (Ministry of Commerce E-Commerce Information Platform)

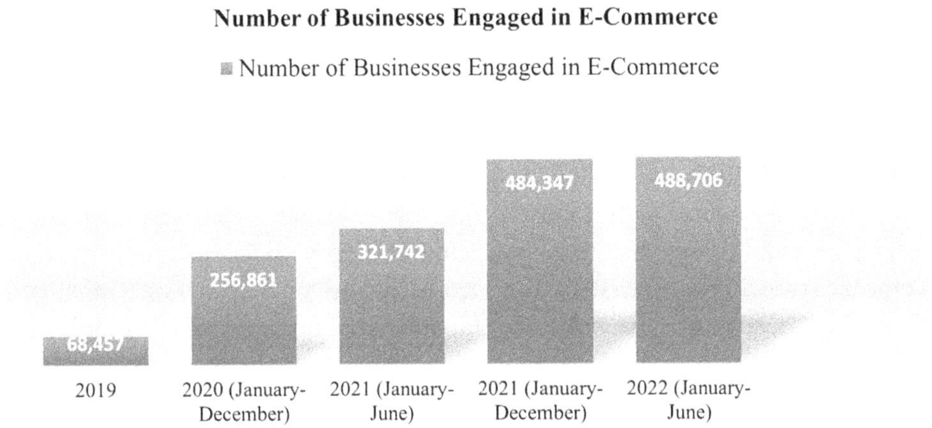

first 6 months of 2021, 484,347 for the whole year of 2021, and 488,706 for the first 6 months of 2022. In the light of the data, it is seen that the Covid-19 pandemic caused a jump on the number of e-commerce businesses from 2019 to 2020. This number, which is progressing on an increasing course, has only increased by 4,359 between the whole of 2021 and the first 6 months of 2022.

Figure 2. Distribution of e-commerce volume by sectors (Ministry of Commerce E-Commerce Information Platform)

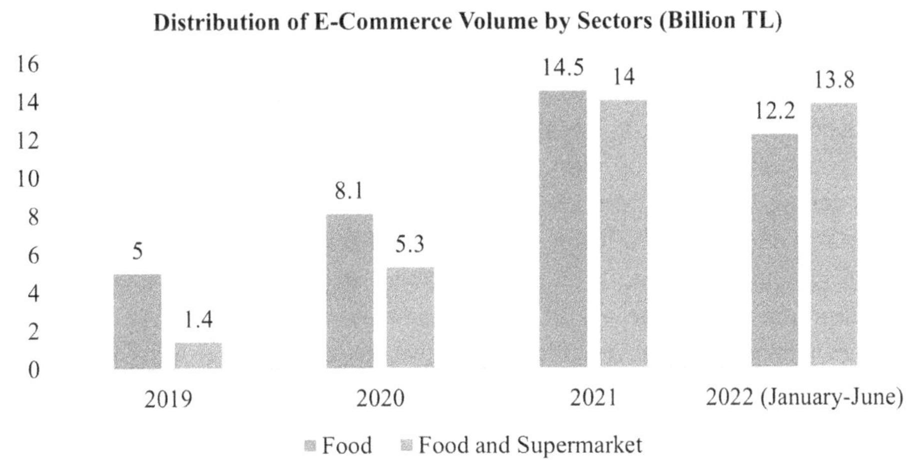

Above, a graph has been created with the Ministry of Commerce E-commerce Information Platform's data on the Distribution of E-Commerce Volume by Sector, specifically for food and food and supermarkets. According to the data shared by the E-Commerce Information Platform, it can be interpreted that the food sector was in a good place in terms of e-commerce volume before the Covid-19 pandemic. Of course, with the pandemic, this place has increased exponentially and experienced its best volume in 2021. However, it is also observed that a decrease occurred for the first 6 months of 2022 compared to the previous year. Again, in the light of the data, it is seen that the volume of the food and supermarket sector, which is another sector, had a quite small volume before the pandemic compared to the volume of the food sector. The situation between these two sectors changed only in the first 6 months of 2022 with the increase in the volume of the food and supermarket sector. It is seen that the food and supermarket sector experienced its best volume in 2021, as well as the food sector volume. In this direction, there have been consumers who have adopted the restrictions required by the pandemic and have turned online shopping into a habit. Entrepreneurs and businesses, seeing the density of these consumers, have focused on these sectors. It can be concluded that entrepreneurs or businesses may have withdrawn from the market according to changing consumer demands with the relaxation of restrictions as the reason for the decline in these volumes in the two sectors in the first 6 months of 2022. But still, there has not been a dramatic decline. This leads to the inference that the two sectors have gained a place in the online shopping environment.

Online Shopping

Nowadays, people live in a digital environment. The changing lifestyles of individuals have changed the way they shop from traditional to digital, and shopping has also been shifted to online shopping (Daroch, Nagrath, & Gupta, 2021: 39). This situation has been faster during the pandemic period, due to the closure of some fixed retail stores, online shopping has become the only way to meet the consumer's consumption needs (Koch, Frommeyer, & Schewe, 2020: 1).

The potential benefits of online shopping for consumers include convenience, various options, low price, original services, personal attention and easy access to information (Zhou, Dec, & Zhang, 2007: 41). The decision and compliance process involved in consumers' online shopping is about steps from initial awareness to potential online sales. The result of the adaptation process experienced by the consumer and the perceived advantages/disadvantages after the purchase will affect whether the online consumer will repurchase online (Kornum, & Bjerre, 2005: 2).

The development of online retailing means an almost limitless choice of products and services where the consumer benefits from product customization, real-time interactive communication and fast delivery. Although the food industry is a saturated market, retailers have begun to offer additional online services to maintain their competitiveness (Yeo, Goh, & Rezaei, 2017: 150). In fact, it is known that the online food market was an active market even before the pandemic. There have been initiatives that have seen the development of the digital age and taken action beforehand.

Looking at the main online food ordering platforms in Türkiye, 'Yemek Sepeti' founded in 2000, 'Getir Yemek' launched in 2019, 'Trendyol Yemek' that started serving in September 2020, 'Fuudy' in July 2020, 'Migros Yemek' in 2022 (Migros Basın Bülteni, 2022) entered the market. When it comes to online grocery ordering platforms, Türkiye's first food e-commerce site 'Migros Sanal Market' in 1997, 'Migros Hemen' in 2019 (Migros Faaliyet Raporu, 2020), 'Hepsi Express' in 2019, 'Trendyol Market' in June 2020, 'Maximum Pazarama' in April 2021, 'Fuudy' in October 2021 started operations (Rekabet Kurumu, 2022). In the light of these data, it is seen that initiatives for online food and grocery order platforms have increased with the pandemic. Before the pandemic companies, providing services outside of these sectors, saw the demand in the market and took action. Companies such as Migros and Trendyol, which did not provide any service before, especially in the food sector, can be given as examples. Likewise, this situation is also seen in market orders. Although the Covid-19 epidemic has passed, there has been no rupture from these platforms. In fact that it can be interpreted that the market is active, as in the example of Migros established 'Migros Yemek' in 2022.

Consumer Purchasing Preferences/Behaviors

The rapid spread of electronic commerce (e-commerce) or mobile commerce (m-commerce) has changed people's food consumption patterns and more and more consumers have considered purchasing food online (Li, Yao, Osman, Zainudin, & Sabri, 2022: 1). The unexpected changes brought about by the Covid-19 pandemic have led to numerous discontinuous changes in consumers' preferences and related behaviors (Bivona, & Cruz, 2021: 3638, 3639). Globally, the Covid-19 pandemic has driven both business and consumers to digitalisation. Consumers have started to spend more time in digital environments under strict quarantine restrictions, and this has reshaped their shopping habits. In the research conducted by Gu, Ślusarczyk, Hajizada, Kovalyova, & Sakhbieva (2021), they revealed the analysis of web traffic during the coronavirus pandemic. In this analysis, visits to online supermarkets have achieved a bounce during this period. As a result, they concluded that online shoppers showed their commitment to daily shopping and that the pandemic created a continuous buying behavior (Gu, Ślusarczyk, Hajizada, Kovalyova, & Sakhbieva, 2021).

Keen, Wetzels, De Ruyter, & Feinberg (2004) obtained findings related to the structure of consumer decision-making process in their study. Based on these findings, they concluded that traditional retail stores may have a great advantage over the Internet. But Keen et al. (2004), also stated that the consumer decision structure is not a stationary structure, but depends on a certain place and time (Keen, Wetzels, De Ruyter, & Feinberg, 2004). In the times when the Internet has just become widespread, consumers have continued along a line that does not deviate from the traditional one due to both the trust factor and the lack of knowledge about shopping on the Internet. However, this perception has changed in the process up to today and it still continues to change. Especially with the Covid-19 pandemic, even the consumer, who had not previously shopped on any Internet environment, has directed his/her purchasing preference towards this side due to the concern caused by the virus. In fact that even after the pandemic is over, this buying behavior has become a habit for the consumer.

Li, Yao, Osman, Zainudin, & Sabri (2022), examined 40 articles published from 2020 to the present, and basically created eight themes related to the factors affecting consumer behavior in using food delivery services: (1) technical and utilitarian factors, (2) system-related features, (3) emotional and hedonic factors, (4) individual characteristics, (5) service quality, (6) risk-related factors, (7) social factors, and (8) food-related features.

Customers are interested in technology that can provide convenience by saving time and effort (Yeo, Goh, & Rezaei, 2017). That is, online food consumers' attitudes are determined by how easy it is to order and purchase food through retailers' websites (Nguyen, T. T. H., Nguyen, N., Nguyen, T. B. L., Phan, T. T. H., Bui, L. P., & Moon, H. C., 2019). When using online food ordering platforms, customers' preferences may vary as they expect to receive their food as soon as possible (Saqib, & Shah, 2023). This digital age has brought with it the problem of focusing, especially with the effect of the pandemic. Therefore, sites that are user-friendly and able to process the customer's request as quickly as possible will enable them to complete a transaction quickly, which is beneficial for both the customer and marketers (Yeo, Goh, & Rezaei, 2017).

CONCLUSION

Increasing competition on a global basis encourages the changes in the demands and needs of consumers and the ease of access to various resources, the creation of virtual jobs in the global business world or the partial virtualization of some of the traditional business activities and structures (cyber business, digital business and e-business). In this way, they will be able to easily adapt to various changes in the global job market and other challenging contexts thanks to their flexible and agile organizational structures (Gökmen, 2012). The Covid-19 pandemic is one of the most important and influential crises that caused these changes. As a result of this crisis, there were companies that easily adapted to the restrictions required by the epidemic.

The high penetration of social media and digital marketing has led to a reduction in the cost of attracting new customers to companies at the global, national and local levels (Gu, Ślusarczyk, Hajizada, Kovalyova, & Sakhbieva, 2021). Although this penetration was a process that continued its existence before the pandemic, it has increased with the pandemic. Especially the change in people's online shopping behavior has helped companies to understand the importance of this digital market. In particular, it is seen in the shift or intensification of both virtual and traditional retail shopping services towards digital in this food and supermarket market.

REFERENCES

Allen, J. P. (2019). *Digital Entrepreneurship*. Routledge. doi:10.4324/9780429506567

Babenko, V., Kulczyk, Z., Perevosova, I., Syniavska, O., & Davydova, O. (2019). Factors of the development of international e-commerce under the conditions of globalization. In *SHS Web of Conferences* (*Vol. 65*, p. 04016). EDP Sciences. 10.1051hsconf/20196504016

Bivona, E., & Cruz, M. (2021). Can business model innovation help SMEs in the food and beverage industry to respond to crises? Findings from a Swiss brewery during COVID-19. *British Food Journal*, *123*(11), 3638–3660. doi:10.1108/BFJ-07-2020-0643

Butler, E. (2020). Entrepreneurship: A Primer. American Institute for Economic Research Coppel, J. (2000). E-Commerce: Impact and policy challenges. *OECD Ec. Dep. Work. P.*, *252*, 45–60.

Daroch, B., Nagrath, G., & Gupta, A. (2021). A study on factors limiting online shopping behaviour of consumers. *Rajagiri Management Journal*, *15*(1), 39–52. doi:10.1108/RAMJ-07-2020-0038

Davidson, E., & Vaast, E. (2010). Digital Entrepreneurship and its Sociomaterial Enactment. *43rd Hawaii International Conference on System Sciences*, 1-10.

Dollinger, M. J. (2008). *Entrepreneurship*. Marsh Publications.

Drucker, P. F. (1985). *Innovation and Entrepreneurship: Practice and Principles*. Harper & Row.

EU. (2018). *ENTR/E4-Fuelling Digital Entrepreneurship in Europe*. Background Paper; European Commission 2018; EU Commission Strategic Policy Forum on Digital Entrepreneurship. Available online: http://ec.europa.eu/DocsRoom/documents/5313/attachments/1/translations

Galindo-Martín, M. Á., Castaño-Martínez, M. S., & Méndez-Picazo, M. T. (2021). Effects of the Pandemic Crisis on Entrepreneurship and Sustainable Development. *Journal of Business Research*, *137*, 345–353. doi:10.1016/j.jbusres.2021.08.053 PMID:34602680

Ghosh, S., Hughes, M., Hughes, P., & Hodgkinson, I. (2021). Corporate digital entrepreneurship: Leveraging industrial internet of things and emerging technologies. *Digital Entrepreneurship*, 183-207.

Gökmen, A. (2012). Virtual business operations, e-commerce & its significance and the case of Turkey: Current situation and its potential. *Electronic Commerce Research*, *12*(1), 31–51. doi:10.100710660-011-9084-2

Gu, S., Ślusarczyk, B., Hajizada, S., Kovalyova, I., & Sakhbieva, A. (2021). Impact of the covid-19 pandemic on online consumer purchasing behavior. *Journal of Theoretical and Applied Electronic Commerce Research*, *16*(6), 2263–2281. doi:10.3390/jtaer16060125

Holcombe, R. G. (1998). Entrepreneurship and Economic Growth. *The Quarterly Journal of Austrian Economics*, *1*(2), 45–62. doi:10.100712113-998-1008-1

Hull, C. E. K., Hung, Y. T. C., Hair, N., Perotti, V., & DeMartino, R. (2007). Taking advantage of digital opportunities: A typology of digital entrepreneurship. *International Journal of Networking and Virtual Organisations*, *4*(3), 290–303. doi:10.1504/IJNVO.2007.015166

Keen, C., Wetzels, M., De Ruyter, K., & Feinberg, R. (2004). E-tailers versus retailers: Which factors determine consumer preferences. *Journal of Business Research*, *57*(7), 685–695. doi:10.1016/S0148-2963(02)00360-0

Koch, J., Frommeyer, B., & Schewe, G. (2020). Online shopping motives during the COVID-19 pandemic—Lessons from the crisis. *Sustainability (Basel)*, *12*(24), 10247. doi:10.3390u122410247

Kornum, N., & Bjerre, M. (Eds.). (2005). *Grocery E-Commerce: Consumer behaviour and business strategies*. Edward Elgar Publishing. doi:10.4337/9781781008317

Kraus, S., Palmer, C., Kailer, N., Kallinger, F. L., & Spitzer, J. (2019). Digital entrepreneurship: A research agenda on new business models for the twenty-first century. *International Journal of Entrepreneurial Behaviour & Research*, *25*(2), 353–375. doi:10.1108/IJEBR-06-2018-0425

Kuratko, D. F., O'Connor, A., & Frederick, H. (2018). *Entrepreneurship: Theory/ Process/ Practice*. Cengage Learning Australia.

Li, Y., Yao, P., Osman, S., Zainudin, N., & Sabri, M. F. (2022). A Thematic Review on Using Food Delivery Services during the Pandemic: Insights for the Post-COVID-19 Era. *International Journal of Environmental Research and Public Health*, *19*(22), 15267. doi:10.3390/ijerph192215267 PMID:36429983

Migros Faaliyet Raporu. (2020). https://www.migroskurumsal.com/userfiles/image/pdf/migros-tr-20.pdf

Migros Yemek Basın Bülteni. (2022). https://migroskurumsalstr.blob.core.windows.net/migroskurumsalstr/migros-yemek-basin-bulte ni-10-06-2022-637908068272354200.pdf

Nambisan, S. (2017). Digital Entrepreneurship: Toward a Digital Technology Perspective of Entrepreneurship. *Entrepreneurship Theory and Practice*, *41*(6), 1029–1055. doi:10.1111/etap.12254

Nguyen, T. T. H., Nguyen, N., Nguyen, T. B. L., Phan, T. T. H., Bui, L. P., & Moon, H. C. (2019). Investigating consumer attitude and intention towards online food purchasing in an emerging economy: An extended tam approach. *Foods*, *8*(11), 576. doi:10.3390/foods8110576 PMID:31731668

OECD. (1998). *Fostering Entrepreneurship, The OECD Jobs Strategy*. OECD.

Qin, Z., Chang, Y., Li, S., & Li, F. (2014). *E-commerce Strategy*. Springer. doi:10.1007/978-3-642-39414-0

Ratten, V. (2020). Coronavirus (covid-19) and entrepreneurship: Changing life and work landscape. *Journal of Small Business and Entrepreneurship*, *32*(5), 503–516. doi:10.1080/08276331.2020.1790167

Rekabet Kurumu. (2022). *Rekabet Kurulu Kararı*. https://www.rekabet.gov.tr/Karar?kararId=b6684eb6-1ca3-4551-945e-7487d0930393

Saqib, N., & Shah, G. B. (2023). Business Model Innovation Through Digital Entrepreneurship: A Case of Online Food Delivery Start-Up in India. *International Journal of E-Entrepreneurship and Innovation*, *13*(1), 1–20. doi:10.4018/IJEEI.315294

Tajvidi, R., & Tajvidi, M. (2021). The growth of cyber entrepreneurship in the food industry: Virtual community engagement in the COVID-19 era. *British Food Journal*, *123*(10), 3309–3325. doi:10.1108/BFJ-06-2020-0559

Tekin, E. (2019). *Girişimcilik ve Sosyal Sermaye*. Eğitim Yayınevi.

Ticaret Bakanlığı E-ticaret Bilgi Platformu Genel İstatistikler. (n.d.). https://www.eticaret.gov.tr/istatistikler

Yeo, V. C. S., Goh, S. K., & Rezaei, S. (2017). Consumer experiences, attitude and behavioral intention toward online food delivery (OFD) services. *Journal of Retailing and Consumer Services*, *35*, 150–162. doi:10.1016/j.jretconser.2016.12.013

Zaheer, H., Breyer, Y., & Dumay, J. (2019). Digital entrepreneurship: An interdisciplinary structured literature review and research agenda. *Technological Forecasting and Social Change*, *148*, 119735. doi:10.1016/j.techfore.2019.119735

Zhou, L., Dai, L., & Zhang, D. (2007). Online shopping acceptance model-A critical survey of consumer factors in online shopping. *Journal of Electronic Commerce Research*, *8*(1).

Chapter 2
Are Technical Graduates Best Suited for Entrepreneurship?
Examining Entrepreneurial Attitude as a Moderator Between Characteristics and Intention

Pushkar Dubey
Pandit Sundarlal Sharma (Open) University, Chhattisgarh, India

Kailash Kumar Sahu
Pandit Sundarlal Sharma (Open) University, Chhattisgarh, India

Parul Dubey
https://orcid.org/0000-0001-8903-6664
G.H. Raisoni College of Engineering and Technology, Nagpur, India

ABSTRACT

Converting technical students into entrepreneurs is not a new concept, but now it is a necessary one to effectively address the unemployment issue. The present study explores the moderation effect of entrepreneurial attitude dimensions (i.e., achievement, innovation, personal control, and self-esteem) in the link between entrepreneurial characteristics and self-employment intention among technical undergraduates studying in different government and private technical institutions of Chhattisgarh state. Authors incorporated stratified random sampling method for collecting primary data. About 1245 questionnaires were sent to the technical students in which 1000 questionnaires were returned usable for analysis. Analysis revealed that the entrepreneurial attitude dimensions (i.e., achievement, innovation, personal control, and self-esteem) were found statistically significant moderator in the link between entrepreneurial characteristics and self-employment intention

DOI: 10.4018/978-1-6684-7127-2.ch002

among technical undergraduates of Chhattisgarh state. However, the interaction effect was found to be negative.

1. INTRODUCTION

India boasts the youngest population among major global economies. However, the challenge lies not just in job creation but also in equipping its youth with the necessary employability skills. Rao (2017) suggests that student entrepreneurship can offer a dual solution by both upskilling students and fostering job creation. While the influence of entrepreneurship in shaping modern engineering education and guiding potential entrepreneurs' career trajectories remains largely unexplored, an increasing number of engineering students are being introduced to entrepreneurial programs. Despite this, only a handful of studies have delved into how entrepreneurial attitudes shape their learning or assess their professional competency. It's noteworthy that incorporating entrepreneurship within engineering curricula is a relatively recent initiative, aimed at nurturing engineers to also consider entrepreneurial paths (Standish-Kuon & Rice, 2002).

Given India's rapid population growth, there's an urgent need to create jobs for its youth at an accelerated pace. Bhagchandani (2017) discussed this in his article, "How India can up its start-up game by bolstering student entrepreneurship," drawing insights from India's diverse experiences. He highlighted the critical need for adequate support, mentorship, and guidance for budding entrepreneurs and innovators. Despite the steady rise in incubators, support remains scarce at the grassroots level and is largely limited to major urban centers. Bhagchandani further noted that while India has the potential to be a global start-up hub, it still lacks the vital components for a robust start-up ecosystem.

Bhagchandani further delved into the symbiotic relationship between premier universities and the flourishing entrepreneurship ecosystems they foster, drawing a parallel between Stanford University and Silicon Valley. He emphasized the direct benefits these institutions offer potential entrepreneurs: (i) Universities grant budding entrepreneurs access to vital resources such as experimental labs, valuable connections, and seasoned mentors who provide practical insights; (ii) University students possess both the foundational knowledge needed to kickstart businesses and ample time to refine potential business ideas; and (iii) at this juncture in their lives, students typically have a lower risk threshold. Consequently, if an entrepreneurial venture does not succeed, they have the resilience and opportunity to regroup and try again. At last, Bhagchandani advocated for greater student engagement in entrepreneurship and innovation-focused endeavors. He projected that if even 20% of these engaged students, which translates to just 1% of the entire student body, become successful entrepreneurs, they could be the linchpin in addressing India's employment challenges. This would swiftly position India as a rapidly advancing knowledge-based economy.

Addressing the job crisis, particularly youth unemployment, is a primary concern for governments today. Entrepreneurship emerges as a potent solution to this challenge. With this perspective, the current study examines how entrepreneurial attitudes moderate the relationship between entrepreneurial traits and the intention to pursue self-employment, focusing on engineering undergraduates from various technical institutions in Chhattisgarh state.

2. THEORETICAL GROUNDING

2.1 Entrepreneurial Characteristics

Numerous studies, both in India and internationally, have considered individual characteristics as a vital component. Morrison (2000) asserted that socio-cultural attributes and an individual's experience significantly influence their decision to pursue entrepreneurship. Factors such as technical expertise, managerial and entrepreneurial experience play pivotal roles in shaping entrepreneurial intentions and behaviors (Lamont 1972; Cooper, Dunkenberg & Woo, 1988; Ronstadt, 1988). Moreover, those with a higher propensity for risk often show a stronger inclination towards entrepreneurship. This sentiment is echoed in various studies, indicating that individuals with higher risk tolerance tend to have firmer entrepreneurial intentions (Luthje & Franke, 2003; Segal, Borgia & Schoenfeld, 2005; Nabi, Liñán, Ertuna & Gurel, 2011). Additionally, a conducive educational environment can foster students' entrepreneurial aspirations and emphasize key entrepreneurial traits (Michelle & Tendai, 2016). Chen, Greene, and Crick (1998) emphasized the importance of sustained efforts to shift students' perceptions about their entrepreneurial abilities. To achieve this, entrepreneurship courses should not only cultivate traits like risk-taking and innovativeness but also bolster students' confidence in their entrepreneurial prowess.

2.2 Entrepreneurial Attitude

Attitude has long been recognized as a fundamental step in the entrepreneurial journey (Asenjo & Barberá, 2013). Defined as a person's learned inclination to react either positively or negatively to a specific action (Ajzen, 1987), attitudes can be molded by past experiences or perceptions developed throughout one's life (Kuehn, 2008). An attitude towards entrepreneurship essentially reflects an individual's personal aspiration to become an entrepreneur (Kolvereid & Meon, 1997). According to the theory of planned behavior, a favorable attitude towards a particular action can boost the intention to manifest that behavior (Armitage & Conner, 2001). A positive mindset, amplified by acquiring entrepreneurial skills, can greatly elevate a person's drive to initiate a business venture (Krueger, Michael & Carsrud, 2000). A multitude of research emphasizes the positive link between attitude and behavioral intentions (Kolvereid & Meon, 1997; Krueger, Michael &Carsrud, 2000; Autio et al., 2001; Van Gelderen et al., 2008; Bodewes et al., 2010; Tegtmeier, 2012; Yang, 2013). Furthermore, prior studies have illustrated that elements like personality traits, beliefs, attitudes, and formative learning experiences play a direct role in shaping entrepreneurial ambitions (Zhao, Seibert & Hills, 2005).

2.3 Self-Employment Intention

Self-employment intention refers to an individual's willingness, engagement, or intention to initiate a business venture (Krueger & Carsrud, 1993; Luthje & Franke, 2003; Drennan et al., 2005; Souitaris et al., 2007). This intention, stemming from a conscious mindset, gears one's focus towards entrepreneurial actions such as launching a new business (Moriano et al., 2012). The topic has been extensively explored, especially regarding graduate entrepreneurship in universities (Wang & Wong, 2004; Van Gelderen et al., 2008; Iakovleva et al., 2011). The literature indicates that a favorable entrepreneurial attitude is instrumental in boosting such intentions (Robinson et al., 1991; Phan et al., 2002; Luthje & Franke, 2003). Pretheeba (2014) examined the entrepreneurial intentions of business and engineering students in Sri Lanka, focusing on key determinants like attitude towards entrepreneurship, subjective norms, and perceived behavioral control. Interestingly, both groups of students shared similar views on the appeal of ventures and societal pressures regarding specific behaviors. The theory of planned behavior recognizes these three factors—attitude, subjective norms, and perceived control—as pivotal in shaping intentions (Tiwari, Bhat & Tikoria, 2017). Notably, in India, societal perceptions play a crucial role in influencing entrepreneurial intentions, particularly among women (Srivastava & Misra, 2017).

2.4 Applied Factors

(a) Entrepreneurial Characteristics (EC)

Entrepreneurial characteristics represent the amalgamation of traits and skills an individual develops over time and through diverse experiences. These encompass ambiguity tolerance, autonomy, internal locus of control, propensity for risk-taking, adeptness in planning and organizing, and proficiency in social networking.

(b) Self-Employment Intention (SEI)

The concept of self-employment intention varies in its definition. It can be perceived as the drive to initiate a new business (Zhao, Hills, and Seibert, 2005), the ambition to own an enterprise (Crant, 1996), or the aspiration to be self-employed (Douglas and Shepherd, 2002).

(c) Entrepreneurial Attitude (EA)

Attitude, as defined by Ajzen (1987), is an individual's ingrained tendency to respond positively or negatively to a specific action, influenced by their past experiences and accumulated perceptions (Kuehn, 2008). Mitchell et al. (2003) depict entrepreneurial attitude as an individual's perspective on adaptability, capabilities, and actions within the entrepreneurial journey.

(d) Achievement (A)

Achievement embodies the sentiment of realizing one's goals in the entrepreneurial landscape. As McClelland suggested, the motivation for achievement is a cornerstone of entrepreneurial behavior (Chell 2008).

(e) Innovation (I)

Innovation is the art of introducing novel products, methods, markets, or establishing a fresh organizational paradigm. It's about recognizing and executing business endeavors in distinctive manners (Kirton, 1978; Drucker, 1985).

(f) Personal Control (PC)

This pertains to an individual's sense of authority and sway over their business outcomes. A pronounced internal sense of personal control often fosters a positive entrepreneurial attitude (Robinson et al., 1991).

(g) Self-Esteem (SE)

Those who are confident in their skillset and abilities, believing them sufficient for entrepreneurial success, are naturally inclined to invest the required effort (Douglas and Shepherd, 2000).

2.5 Research Question

The core research query of this study seeks to determine if dimensions of entrepreneurial attitude, specifically achievement, innovation, personal control, and self-esteem, influence the relationship between entrepreneurial characteristics and the self-employment intentions of engineering students from both government and private technical institutions in Chhattisgarh state.

3. RESEARCH METHODOLOGY

3.1 Conceptual Model

In pursuit of addressing the research question, we have formulated a conceptual model, as illustrated in Figure 1.

Figure 1. Conceptual model

3.2 Hypotheses

H1. Achievement moderates the link between EC and SEI among engineering undergraduate students.
H2. Innovation moderates the link between EC and SEI among engineering undergraduate students.
H3. Personal control moderates the link between EC and SEI among engineering undergraduate students.
H4. Self-esteem moderates the link between EC and SEI among engineering undergraduate students.
H5. Entrepreneurial attitude moderates the link between EC and SEI among engineering undergraduate students.

3.3 Sampling and Data Collection

In this study, we employed a correlational research design. We targeted technical students in their third and fourth years from various government and private institutions. Of the 1245 questionnaires distributed, we received 1000 usable responses, resulting in an approximate response rate of 80.32%. Data collection spanned from November 2019 to March 2020.

Table 1. Description of primary data

Gender		Locality		Institution		Total
Male	Female	Rural	Urban	Government	Private	1000
429	571	434	566	236	764	

3.4 Research Instrument

The meticulous design, development, and refinement of the research instrument are crucial to collecting accurate primary data. In line with this, the authors embarked on a systematic approach to craft and validate the instrument for this study.

Initially, an exhaustive review of prior literature was conducted, leading to the identification of eleven relevant constructs pertaining to the study objectives. These were either adopted as is or with certain modifications based on their relevance. To ensure content accuracy and gain deeper insights, these constructs were then reviewed by four domain experts. Their feedback led to minor changes in some items.

Subsequently, a pilot study with 50 participants was carried out to further assess the content validity. Since no significant modifications were suggested by the participants, the instrument was finalized with 47 items.

The final questionnaire comprised:

- Entrepreneurial attitude dimensions such as achievement (6 items), innovation (6 items), personal control (5 items), and self-esteem (6 items), sourced from Ismail et al. (2013).
- Entrepreneurial characteristics dimensions like ambiguity tolerance, self-sufficiency, locus of control, risk-taking propensity (all with 3 items each) drawn from Bezzina (2010). Additionally, planning and organizing ability (3 items) and social networking (3 items) were adapted from Schmidt and Bohnenberger (2009), Rocha and Freitas (2014), and Moraes et al. (2018).
- Lastly, the dimension of self-employment intention, with 6 items, was also adapted from Ismail et al. (2013).

3.5 Scale Validation

In this study, we employed the partial least square confirmatory factor analysis to assess the reliability and validity of the primary data, as detailed in Tables 2 and 3.

3.5.1 Reliability Measures

Internal consistency is gauged using Cronbach's alpha, which should ideally exceed 0.7 as suggested by Nunnally (1978). Our study's analysis confirms a Cronbach's alpha value surpassing 0.7, as seen in Table 2. Rho A, another indicator for reliability, should also exceed 0.7. In our study, all constructs exhibited Rho A values greater than 0.7, as detailed in Table 2.

3.5.2 Convergent Validity

Convergent validity assesses the agreement among multiple items within a scale (Fornell and Bookstein, 1982; Barclay et al., 1995). Composite reliability (CR) values exceeding 0.7 indicate satisfactory internal consistency reliability (Bagozzi and Yi, 1988; Hair et al., 2010). As displayed in Table 2, all constructs in our study achieved a composite reliability value above 0.7.

The Average Variance Extracted (AVE) serves as an indicator of a scale's convergent validity. Ideally, AVE values should exceed 0.7 for a satisfactory measure (Hu et al., 2004; Henseler et al., 2009). As presented in Table 2, all constructs in this study met this threshold, with AVE values surpassing 0.7.

Table 2. Measurement results

Factors	Cronbach Alpha	Rho A	CR	AVE
Achievement (A)	0.857	0.887	0.861	0.52
Innovation (I)	0.882	0.884	0.881	0.554
Personal Control (PC)	0.844	0.846	0.844	0.52
Self Esteem (SE)	0.716	0.733	0.715	0.503
Self-Employment Intention (SEI)	0.812	0.827	0.817	0.531
Ambiguity Tolerance (AT)	0.782	0.786	0.777	0.516
Self Sufficiency (SS)	0.765	0.774	0.77	0.504
Locus of Control (LoC)	0.702	0.705	0.786	0.526
Risk-Taking Propensity (RTP)	0.738	0.74	0.739	0.586
Planning (P)	0.781	0.786	0.783	0.519
Social Networking (SN)	0.725	0.726	0.724	0.557
Entrepreneurial Attitude (EA)	0.944	0.951	0.946	0.539
Entrepreneurial Characteristics (EC)	0.893	0.897	0.894	0.521

3.5.3 Discriminant Validity

Discriminant validity ensures that constructs are distinct from one another. For robust construct validity, the value for discriminant validity should exceed 0.5. As delineated in Table 3, all seven constructs in the study surpass this benchmark. Thus, the study's measurement model can be deemed satisfactory.

Table 3. Discriminant validity

	A	AT	I	LOC	PC	POA	RTP	SEI	SE	SS	SN
A	**0.988**										
AT	0.887	**0.824**									
I	0.846	0.821	**0.917**								
LOC	0.721	0.718	0.744	**0.973**							
PC	0.759	0.778	0.841	0.962	**0.925**						
POA	0.693	0.66	0.714	0.865	0.721	**0.97**					
RTP	0.659	0.65	0.709	0.785	0.702	0.804	**0.832**				
SEI	0.491	0.562	0.59	0.707	0.621	0.647	0.744	**0.877**			
SE	0.635	0.63	0.613	0.776	0.656	0.734	0.697	0.738	**0.742**		
SS	0.466	0.556	0.564	0.703	0.613	0.642	0.663	0.697	0.619	**0.833**	
SN	0.448	0.493	0.51	0.571	0.557	0.617	0.546	0.656	0.551	0.636	**0.597**

3.6 Data Analysis

The study utilized the licensed version of SPSS v25 and the trial version of Smart PLS 3 for primary data analysis.

4. ANALYSIS AND RESULTS

The study examined how individual facets of entrepreneurial attitude—namely achievement, innovation, personal control, and self-esteem—moderate the relationship between entrepreneurial characteristics and the intention for self-employment.

A. Moderating Effect of Achievement (Testing of H1)

The study sought to understand the moderating effect of the achievement component within entrepreneurial attitudes on the relationship between entrepreneurial characteristics and the intention for self-employment. Using standardized values (z-score) for achievement, entrepreneurial characteristics, and self-employment intention, the results showcased in Table 4 revealed that achievement and entrepreneurial characteristics accounted for 49.5% of the variance (R2 = 0.495, F (2,997) = 487.99, p< 0.01). Introducing an interaction term (Achievement x Entrepreneurial Characteristics) in the second model contributed an additional 2.3% (ΔF (1,996) = 47.015, p <0.01) to the variance explanation for self-employment intention. This suggests that as achievement and entrepreneurial characteristics increase, the intensity of their relationship with self-employment intention diminishes.

Table 4. Moderating effect of achievement between entrepreneurial characteristics and entrepreneurial intention

Achievement		
Predictors	**Model 1**	**Model 2**
	β	**β**
Z score (Achievement)	0.258	0.223
Z score (Entrepreneurial Characteristics)	0.527	0.484
A x E.C.		-0.166
R^2	0.495	0.517
ΔR^2	0.495	0.023
ΔF	$F_{(2,997)} = 487.99^{**}$	$F_{(1,996)} = 47.015^{**}$
***p < 0.05, **p< 0.01**		

B. Moderating Effect of Innovation (Testing of H2)

The study examined the moderating influence of the innovation aspect within entrepreneurial attitudes on the connection between entrepreneurial characteristics and the intent for self-employment. Utilizing standardized values (z-score) for innovation, entrepreneurial characteristics, and self-employment intention, the findings presented in Table 5 demonstrated that innovation and entrepreneurial characteristics accounted for 47.4% of the total variance (R2 = 0.474, F (2,997) = 449.692, p < 0.01). When the interaction term (Innovation x Entrepreneurial Characteristics) was introduced in the subsequent model, it contributed an additional 3.8% (ΔF (1,996) = 78.003, p < 0.01) to the variance explanation of the self-employment intention. This suggests that as both innovation and entrepreneurial characteristics rise, their correlation with the intention towards self-employment becomes less pronounced.

Table 5. Moderating effect of innovation between entrepreneurial characteristics and entrepreneurial intention

Innovation		
Predictors	**Model 1**	**Model 2**
	β	**β**
Z score (Innovation)	0.198	0.169
Z score (Entrepreneurial Characteristics)	0.554	0.498
I x E.C.		-0.210
R^2	0.474	0.512
ΔR^2	0.474	0.038
ΔF	$F_{(2,997)} = 449.692^{**}$	$F_{(1,996)} = 78.003^{**}$
***p < 0.05, ** p< 0.01**		

C. Moderating Effect of Personal Control (Testing of H3)

The study assessed the moderating role of the personal control facet of entrepreneurial attitude in the relationship between entrepreneurial characteristics and the intent to be self-employed. Using standardized values (z-score) for personal control, entrepreneurial characteristics, and self-employment intention, the findings, as shown in Table 6, revealed that personal control alongside entrepreneurial characteristics accounted for 46.5% of the overall variance (R2 = 0.465, F (2,997) = 434.080, p < 0.01). Introducing the interaction term (Personal Control x Entrepreneurial

Table 6. Moderating effect of personal control between entrepreneurial characteristics and entrepreneurial intention

Personal Control		
Predictors	Model 1	Model 2
	β	β
Z score (Personal Control)	0.166	0.119
Z score (Entrepreneurial Characteristics)	0.568	0.548
PC x E.C.		-0.148
R^2	0.465	0.484
ΔR^2	0.465	0.018
ΔF	$F_{(2,997)} = 434.080^{**}$	$F_{(1,996)} = 34.835^{**}$
** p < 0.05, ** p< 0.01*		

Characteristics) in the subsequent model contributed an additional 1.8% (ΔF (1,996) = 34.835, p < 0.01) to the variance explanation for self-employment intention. This implies that as both personal control and entrepreneurial characteristics amplify, their association with self-employment intent weakens.

D. Moderating Effect of Self-Esteem (Testing of H4)

The study explored the moderating influence of the self-esteem aspect of entrepreneurial attitude on the connection between entrepreneurial traits and the intent to pursue self-employment. Using standardized values (z-score) of self-esteem, entrepreneurial characteristics, and self-employment intention, the findings depicted in Table 7 showed that self-esteem combined with entrepreneurial traits accounted for 49.8% of the overall variance (R2 = 0.498, F (2,997) = 493.92, p < 0.01). When the interaction term (Self-esteem x Entrepreneurial Characteristics) was integrated into the subsequent model, it contributed an additional 0.05% (ΔF (1,996) = 9.772, p < 0.01) to the explained variance for the intention to be self-employed. This suggests that as both self-esteem and entrepreneurial traits rise, their correlation with the inclination toward self-employment diminishes.

E. Moderating Effect of Attitude (Testing of H5)

The study investigated the moderating role of entrepreneurial attitude on the relationship between entrepreneurial traits and the desire for self-employment. By using standardized values (z-score) for attitude, entrepreneurial characteristics, and self-employment intention, the findings showcased in Table 8 demonstrated that

Table 7. Moderating effect of self-esteem between entrepreneurial characteristics and entrepreneurial intention

Self-Esteem		
Predictors	**Model 1**	**Model 2**
	B	**β**
Z score (Self-Esteem)	0.268	0.265
Z score (Entrepreneurial Characteristics)	0.519	0.500
SE x E.C.		-0.073
R^2	0.498	0.503
ΔR^2	0.498	0.005
ΔF	$F_{(2,997)} = 493.926^{**}$	$F_{(1,996)} = 9.772^{**}$
p < 0.05, **p< 0.01		

the combined influence of attitude and entrepreneurial traits accounted for 49.5% of the total variance (R2 = 0.495, F (2,997) = 489.494, p < 0.01). Introducing the interaction term (Attitude x Entrepreneurial Characteristics) in the subsequent model led to a 2.1% increase (ΔF (1,996) = 43.059, p < 0.01) in the explained variance regarding the intention for self-employment. This suggests that as both entrepreneurial attitude and characteristics increase, their combined impact on the propensity for self-employment slightly diminishes.

Table 8. Moderating effect of entrepreneurial attitude between entrepreneurial characteristics and entrepreneurial intention

Entrepreneurial Attitude		
Predictors	**Model 1**	**Model 2**
	β	**β**
Z score (Entrepreneurial Attitude)	0.283	0.249
Z score (Entrepreneurial Characteristics)	0.489	0.452
EA x E.C.		-0.158
R^2	0.495	0.516
ΔR^2	0.495	0.021
ΔF	$F_{(2,997)} = 489.494^{**}$	$F_{(1,996)} = 43.059^{**}$
p < 0.05, **p< 0.01		

6. DISCUSSION AND FINDINGS

The examined hypotheses (H1 to H5) investigate various factors that moderate the relationship between entrepreneurial characteristics and self-employment intentions among engineering undergraduates. These factors include achievement, innovation, personal control, self-esteem, and overall entrepreneurial attitude. A recurring theme across these hypotheses is the counterintuitive finding that when these factors are present alongside strong entrepreneurial traits, there's often a decline in self-employment intentions. The discussions probe potential reasons behind these unexpected results, suggesting a range of interpretations and strategies to better align these factors with fostering entrepreneurial aspirations. Through these hypotheses, we gain insight into the nuanced interplay between inherent characteristics, cultivated attitudes, and career intentions among budding engineers.

The results of the examined hypothesis (H1) suggest that achievement does play a moderating role in the relationship between entrepreneurial characteristics and self-employment intention. This moderation effect was not only statistically significant but was also negative. This implies that when students possess entrepreneurial characteristics and pair these with a strong achievement orientation, their intention towards self-employment surprisingly diminishes. This underscores the counterintuitive nature of the result; one might expect that those with both strong entrepreneurial characteristics and a high achievement mindset would be more inclined towards self-employment. Yet, the data suggests otherwise.

The negative moderation effect of achievement on the connection between entrepreneurial traits and self-employment intention raises several intriguing questions. Does a high achievement attitude redirect students towards more traditional or stable job roles, given the perceived risks associated with entrepreneurship? Or does it indicate a preference for intrapreneurial roles within established firms, where they can exhibit entrepreneurial behaviors but within the safety net of a structured organization? Regardless of the reasons behind this relationship, it is evident that there's a crucial need to carefully cultivate the entrepreneurial spirit in engineering undergraduates. By doing so, educators and mentors can better shape their achievement mindset, ensuring it complements, rather than diminishes, their entrepreneurial aspirations. This nuanced approach can be pivotal in directing their career choices, especially if the goal is to encourage more self-driven entrepreneurial ventures among this cohort.

The outcomes of the tested hypothesis (H2) suggest that innovation acts as a significant moderating force between entrepreneurial characteristics and the intention towards self-employment. Interestingly, this moderation effect was negative. This implies that while students with entrepreneurial characteristics might typically lean towards self-employment, when this is combined with a strong innovation mindset, their inclination surprisingly drops.

This raises a fascinating perspective. Could it be that students with a high innovation mindset are attracted to environments where they can leverage existing structures and resources, such as R&D departments in large firms, to bring their innovative ideas to fruition? Perhaps these students see the potential for greater impact through innovation within existing organizations, rather than starting afresh on their own. Another angle to consider is the perceived risks associated with entrepreneurship. It is possible that students with strong innovative ideas might fear the uncertainties of self-employment, suspecting that they might not have the adequate resources or platforms to realize their innovative visions independently. Therefore, for the objective of encouraging self-employment, it is imperative to not only foster the entrepreneurial spirit in engineering undergraduates but also to equip them with tools and confidence to innovate independently. Institutions should provide more comprehensive entrepreneurial training that integrates innovation and business acumen, assuring students that they can indeed bring their innovative visions to life within the realm of self-employment. Moreover, highlighting successful case studies of innovators-turned-entrepreneurs can serve as motivational tools, pushing students to bridge the gap between innovation and entrepreneurship.

The outcomes of the tested hypothesis (H3) reveal that the personal control factor acts as a significant moderator between entrepreneurial characteristics and self-employment intention among engineering undergraduates. Yet, counterintuitively, this effect was negative. This suggests that when the entrepreneurial spirit of engineering undergraduates is aligned with a strong sense of personal control, there's an unexpected decline in their inclination towards self-employment.

One possible interpretation is that these undergraduates, when feeling a heightened sense of control over their career trajectories, might perceive more traditional employment routes as offering greater stability and predictability. They might associate this control with the ability to guide their career in established firms where structures and systems are already in place, rather than venturing into the uncertainties of entrepreneurship. Alternatively, engineering undergraduates with a strong personal control attitude may seek roles within larger organizations where they can influence change and play a lead role, seeing these as safer environments to exert their control and make a tangible impact, rather than the volatile world of startups and self-employment. Given this, if the goal is to increase the intention towards self-employment among these students, it is imperative to address this paradox. Institutions and mentors should strive to redefine what personal control can mean within the entrepreneurial context. Workshops, case studies, and mentoring can underscore that entrepreneurship, in fact, offers the ultimate form of personal control: the ability to shape one's venture from the ground up. By aligning the concept of personal control with the independence and agency offered by entrepreneurship, there's a potential to shift these perceptions and foster greater self-employment aspirations among engineering undergraduates.

The findings from the tested hypothesis (H4) indicate that self-esteem acts as a noteworthy moderator between entrepreneurial characteristics and self-employment intentions among engineering undergraduates. However, this effect was negatively skewed. This means that engineering students possessing strong entrepreneurial traits, when imbued with higher self-esteem, surprisingly show a reduced inclination towards self-employment.

This is an intriguing observation. A plausible explanation could be that those with high self-esteem might feel they have more to offer in well-established, recognized roles within existing organizations, where their contributions can be readily seen and valued. For such individuals, the risk and uncertainty of entrepreneurship might appear as a potential threat to their self-worth, especially if the venture does not succeed. Alternatively, those with high self-esteem might see themselves as assets to larger teams or organizations, where their skills can be amplified by working in synergy with others. They may equate self-employment with isolation, feeling that the challenges of entrepreneurship might not provide the collaborative and affirming environment they seek. Therefore, to encourage self-employment among this group, it is essential to redefine how self-esteem aligns with entrepreneurial ventures. Universities and mentors should emphasize that the entrepreneurial journey, with its challenges and uncertainties, can be a powerful tool for personal growth and self-affirmation. Real-life success stories of entrepreneurs who have overcome challenges can instill confidence in these students. It's vital to illustrate that self-employment can be an avenue where one's high self-esteem can be both tested and amplified, rather than diminished.

The analysis of the tested hypothesis (H5) reveals that an overall entrepreneurial attitude indeed serves as a significant moderator between entrepreneurial characteristics and self-employment intentions among engineering undergraduates. Yet, intriguingly, this moderation effect is negative. This suggests that even though engineering students might possess entrepreneurial traits, when these traits are paired with a broader entrepreneurial attitude, there's a paradoxical decline in their drive towards self-employment.

This counterintuitive outcome may suggest a few insights. Perhaps students with an overarching entrepreneurial attitude appreciate the complexities and challenges of the entrepreneurial journey more acutely. Having a well-rounded perspective might make them more cautious, leading them to opt for roles where they can exhibit entrepreneurial behaviors but within the relative safety of established organizations. Another perspective could be that these students, armed with both entrepreneurial characteristics and a holistic entrepreneurial attitude, are more discerning about when and how to take the plunge into self-employment. They may choose to bide their time, gather more experience, and only venture into self-employment when they feel fully equipped. Therefore, to increase the self-employment drive among these students, it's crucial to provide a supportive ecosystem that complements their comprehensive entrepreneurial attitude. Educational institutions and mentors should offer platforms where students can test their entrepreneurial skills in real-world scenarios, perhaps through incubation centers or live projects. This allows them to confront and understand the challenges, build resilience, and affirm their capability to thrive in entrepreneurial ventures. Equally essential is to offer mentorship and success stories that showcase the journey, not just the destination, thereby preparing and inspiring them for their entrepreneurial path.

In essence, while these findings shine light on the intricate dynamics between various attitudes and entrepreneurial characteristics, they also bring to the fore the complex, and sometimes counterintuitive, pathways to self-employment intentions. There's a need to delve deeper into the interplay of these factors, ensuring students are not only equipped with the right characteristics but also the right attitudes to navigate the world of entrepreneurship.

7. CONTRIBUTION OF THE STUDY

The current research offers significant insights into the realm of management studies. It delves deeply into the entrepreneurial characteristics of technical students and examines how these traits influence their inclination towards self-employment, emphasizing their entrepreneurial attitudes. While prior studies have touched upon the entrepreneurial potential of technical undergraduates, there's an emerging concern in developing countries like India. The country faces a surge in engineering graduates, leading to a disparity where job creation doesn't match the increasing number of degree holders. This study posits that channeling these graduates towards entrepreneurship could be a viable solution to the looming unemployment crisis, especially in India.

Interestingly, the results reveal a nuanced scenario. While technical undergraduates exhibit the necessary entrepreneurial characteristics and attitudes that could potentially foster self-employment intentions, currently, these aren't translating positively. To pivot this trend towards a positive trajectory, the study suggests several transformative steps: firstly, creating a conducive environment for nurturing technical students; secondly, fostering an entrepreneurial culture where innovation is discussed and celebrated; and lastly, garnering active support from the government and relevant authorities, including financial backing.

Unemployment, an ever-present specter haunting developing nations like India, is more than just an economic issue. It is the catalyst for various societal challenges, from poverty and illiteracy to issues like the dowry system. Addressing unemployment isn't merely a governmental responsibility but a societal imperative. Research underscores the inherent entrepreneurial capabilities of technical students. If harnessed, these can lead to a wave of new entrepreneurs, benefiting not just the economy but society at large. For this potential to be realized, a concerted effort by educational institutions, government bodies, and authorities is paramount.

In essence, entrepreneurs are pivotal to societal progression. With a vast pool of technically skilled undergraduates, the potential for entrepreneurial growth is immense. Instead of merely seeking employment, these students have the capability to be job creators. The study's findings affirm that with the right support, opportunities, and encouragement, these budding entrepreneurs can spearhead a new era of innovation and job creation, steering societies towards prosperity and harmony.

8. CONCLUSION

Entrepreneurship stands as a foundation for economic progression, fostering wealth creation and growth on multiple scales, from the individual to the international (Obembe et al., 2014). However, not everyone is cut out for the entrepreneurial journey. Only those equipped with the right blend of characteristics and attitude are best suited for this path, with technical undergraduates often emerging as prime candidates, as multiple studies indicate. This study delves into how entrepreneurial attitudes and their underlying characteristics influence the self-employment intentions of technical undergraduates in Chhattisgarh state. While the results affirm a significant interaction between entrepreneurial attitudes and their characteristics, it intriguingly reveals a negative impact on the self-employment aspirations of these students. This underscores an urgent need to refine and nurture the entrepreneurial mindset of these undergraduates, given that they appear to grapple with fully developing the right entrepreneurial perspective to initiate or plan a new venture. Given the implications for societal and economic advancement, it's imperative for governmental bodies, educational institutions, and other relevant authorities to step in. Recognizing the gravity of the situation and the potential long-term ramifications, they should consider reforms or introduce new policies aimed at fostering the right entrepreneurial spirit and attitude among technical undergraduates.

8.1 Future Research Avenues

Future researchers could delve into the myriad policies aimed at enhancing entrepreneurial attitudes, conducting longitudinal studies to assess their impacts across various stages. This approach would provide a more comprehensive understanding of their efficacy.

8.2 Limitations

The conclusions drawn were based on cross-sectional data. However, employing longitudinal data, by collecting information at multiple intervals during their engineering studies, would offer a more nuanced understanding of students' evolving inclinations towards entrepreneurship at different stages.

ACKNOWLEDGMENT

This research is a part of a project sponsored by the Indian Council of Social Sciences Research (ICSSR), New Delhi, through the IMPRESS scheme. The author extends heartfelt gratitude to ICSSR, New Delhi, for their generous support and resources that made this study possible.

REFERENCES

Ajzen, I. (1987). Attitudes, traits, and actions: Dispositional prediction of behavior in personality and social psychology. *Advances in Experimental Social Psychology*, *20*(1), 1–63.

Armitage, C. J., & Conner, M. (2001). Efficacy of the theory of planned behaviour: A meta-analytic review. *British Journal of Social Psychology*, *40*(4), 471–499. doi:10.1348/014466601164939 PMID:11795063

Asenjo, M. P. F., & Barbera, J. P. (2013). Assessing the impact of higher education on entrepreneurial intention. *History and Social Communication*, *18*(11), 377–386.

Autio, E. H., Keeley, R., Klofsten, M. G. C., Parker, G., & Hay, M. (2001). Entrepreneurial intent among students in Scandinavia and in the USA. *Enterprise and Innovation Management Studies*, *2*(2), 145–160. doi:10.1080/14632440110094632

Bagozzi, R. P., & Yi, Y. (1988). On the evaluation of structural equation models. *Journal of the Academy of Marketing Science*, *16*(1), 74–94. doi:10.1007/BF02723327

Barclay, D., Higgins, C., & Thompson, R. (1995). The Partial Least Squares (PLS) approach to casual modeling: Personal computer adoption and use as an illustration. *Technology Studies, Special Issue on Research Methodology*, *2*(2), 285–309.

Bezzina, F. (2010). Characteristics of the Maltese entrepreneur. *The International Journal of the Arts in Society*, *3*(7), 292–312.

Bhagchandani, R. (2017). *How India can up its startup game by bolstering student entrepreneurship.* Retrieved Date 05 September 2018 from https://yourstory.com/2017/01/india-startup-game-bolstering-student-entrepreneurship

Chell, E. (2008). *The Entrepreneurial Personality: A Social Construction* (2nd ed.). Routledge. doi:10.4324/9780203938638

Chen, C. C., Greene, P. G., & Crick, A. (1998). Does entrepreneurial self-efficacy distinguish entrepreneurs from managers? *Journal of Business Venturing*, *13*(4), 295–316. doi:10.1016/S0883-9026(97)00029-3

Cooper, A. C., Dunkelberg, W. C., & Woo, C. Y. (1988). Survival and failure: A longitudinal study. *Frontiers of Entrepreneurship Research*, *1*, 225-237.

Crant, J. M. (1996). The proactive personality scale as a predictor of entrepreneurial intentions. *Journal of Small Business Management*, *34*(3), 42–49.

Douglas, E. J., & Shepherd, A. D. (2002). Self-employment as a career choice: Attitudes, entrepreneurial intentions, and utility maximization. *Entrepreneurship Theory and Practice*, *26*(3), 81–90. doi:10.1177/104225870202600305

Douglas, E. J., & Shepherd, D. A. (2000). Entrepreneurship as a utility maximizing response. *Journal of Business Venturing*, *15*(3), 231–251. doi:10.1016/S0883-9026(98)00008-1

Drennan, J., Kennedy, J., & Renfrow, P. (2005). Impact of childhood experiences on the development of entrepreneurial intentions. *International Journal of Entrepreneurship and Innovation*, *6*(4), 231–238. doi:10.5367/0000000005775179801

Drucker, P. F. (1985). Principles of successful innovation. *Research Management*, *28*(5), 10–12. doi:10.1080/00345334.1985.11756915

Fornell, C., & Bookstein, F. L. (1982). Two structural equation models: LISREL and PLS applied to consumer exit-voice theory. *JMR, Journal of Marketing Research*, *19*(4), 440–452. doi:10.1177/002224378201900406

Hair, J. F., Black, W. C., Babin, B. J., & Anderson, R. E. (2010). *Multivariate data analysis: International version*. Pearson.

Henseler, J., Ringle, C. M., & Sinkovics, R. R. (2009). *The use of partial least squares path modeling in international marketing*. New Challenges to International Marketing. doi:10.1108/S1474-7979(2009)0000020014

Hu, X., Lin, Z., Whinston, A. B., & Zhang, H. (2004). Hope or hype: On the viability of escrow services as trusted third parties in online auction environments. *Information Systems Research*, *15*(3), 236–249. doi:10.1287/isre.1040.0027

Ismail, N., Jaffar, N., & Hooi, T. S. (2013). Using EAO model to predict the self-employment intentions among the Universities' Undergraduates in Malaysia. *International Journal of Trade, Economics and Finance*, *4*(5), 282–287. doi:10.7763/IJTEF.2013.V4.302

Kirton, M. (1978). Field dependence and adaption-innovation theories. *Perceptual and Motor Skills*, *47*(3), 1239–1245. doi:10.2466/pms.1978.47.3f.1239 PMID:745906

Kolvereid, L., & Moen, Ø. (1997). Entrepreneurship among business graduates: Does a major in entrepreneurship make a difference? *Journal of European Industrial Training*, *21*(4), 154–160. doi:10.1108/03090599710171404

Krueger, N. F., & Carsrud, A. L. (1993). Entrepreneurial intentions: Applying the theory of planned behaviour. *Entrepreneurship and Regional Development*, *5*(4), 315–330. doi:10.1080/08985629300000020

Krueger, N. F. Jr, Reilly, M. D., & Carsrud, A. L. (2000). Competing models of entrepreneurial intentions. *Journal of Business Venturing*, *15*(5&6), 411–432. doi:10.1016/S0883-9026(98)00033-0

Kuehn, K. W. (2008). Entrepreneurial intentions research: Implications for entrepreneurship education. *Journal of Entrepreneurship Education*, *11*, 87.

Luthje, C., & Franke, N. (2003). The 'making'of an entrepreneur: Testing a model of entrepreneurial intent among engineering students at MIT. *Research Management*, *33*(2), 135–147.

Michelle, K., & Tendai, C. (2016). The association of entrepreneurship education and entrepreneurial intention among university students in the Eastern Cape Province of South Africa. *International Journal of Educational Sciences*, *12*(3), 200–211. doi:10.1080/09751122.2016.11890427

Mitchell, R. K., Busenitz, L., Lant, T., McDougall, P. P., Morse, E. A., & Smith, J. B. (2003). Toward a theory of entrepreneurial cognition: Rethinking the people side of entrepreneurship research. *Entrepreneurship Theory and Practice*, *27*(2), 93–104. doi:10.1111/1540-8520.00001

Moraes, G. H. S. M. D., Iizuka, E. S., & Pedro, M. (2018). Effects of entrepreneurial characteristics and university environment on entrepreneurial intention. *RAC. Revista de Administração Contemporânea*, *22*(2), 226–248. doi:10.1590/1982-7849rac2018170133

Moriano, J. A., Gorgievski, M., Laguna, M., Stephan, U., & Zarafshani, K. (2012). A cross-cultural approach to understanding entrepreneurial intention. *Journal of Career Development*, *39*(2), 162–185. doi:10.1177/0894845310384481

Morrison, A. (2000). Entrepreneurship: What triggers it? *International Journal of Entrepreneurial Behaviour & Research*, *6*(2), 59–71. doi:10.1108/13552550010335976

Nabi, G., Liñán, F., Ertuna, Z. İ., & Gurel, E. (2011). The moderating role of higher education on entrepreneurship. *Education + Training*, *53*(5), 387–402. doi:10.1108/00400911111147703

Nunnally, J. C. (1978). An overview of psychological measurement. Clinical diagnosis of mental disorders, 97-146. doi:10.1007/978-1-4684-2490-4_4

Phan, P. H., Wong, P. K., & Wang, C. K. (2002). Antecedents to entrepreneurship among university students in Singapore: Beliefs, attitudes and background. *Journal of Enterprising Culture*, *10*(2), 151–174. doi:10.1142/S0218495802000189

Pretheeba, P. (2014). Predicting entrepreneurial intention among business and engineering students in Sri Lanka. *Ruhuna Journal of Management and Finance*, *1*(1), 25–36.

Rao, V. (2017). *Can Student Entrepreneurship be the answer to India's Jobless-growth problem?* Retrieved Date 05 September 2018 from https://yourstory.com/2017/07/student-entrepreneurship-sv-co

Robinson, P. B., Stimpson, D. V., Huefner, J. C., & Hunt, H. K. (1991). An attitude approach to the prediction of entrepreneurship. *Entrepreneurship Theory and Practice*, *15*(4), 13–32. doi:10.1177/104225879101500405

Rocha, E. L. C., & Freitas, A. A. F. (2014). Evaluation of entrepreneurship teaching among university students through the entrepreneurial profile. *Contemporary Administration Magazine*, *18*(4), 465–486.

Schmidt, S., & Bohnenberger, M. C. (2009). Entrepreneurial profile and organizational performance. *Contemporary Administration Magazine*, *13*(3), 450–467.

Segal, G., Borgia, D., & Schoenfeld, J. (2005). The motivation to become an entrepreneur. *International Journal of Entrepreneurial Behaviour & Research*, *11*(1), 42–57. doi:10.1108/13552550510580834

Souitaris, V., Zerbinati, S., & Al-Laham, A. (2007). Do entrepreneurship programmes raise entrepreneurial intention of science and engineering students? The effect of learning, inspiration and resources. *Journal of Business Venturing*, *22*(4), 566–591. doi:10.1016/j.jbusvent.2006.05.002

Srivastava, S., & Misra, R. (2017). Exploring antecedents of entrepreneurial intentions of young women in India. *Journal of Entrepreneurship in Emerging Economies*, *9*(2), 181–206. doi:10.1108/JEEE-04-2016-0012

Standish-Kuon, T., & Rice, M. P. (2002). Introducing engineering and science students to entrepreneurship: Models and influential factors at six American universities. *Journal of Engineering Education*, *91*(1), 33–39. doi:10.1002/j.2168-9830.2002.tb00670.x

Tegtmeier. (2012). Empirical implications for promoting students entrepreneurial intentions. *Journal of Enterprising Culture, 20*(2), 151–169.

Tiwari, P., Bhat, A. K., & Tikoria, J. (2017). Predictors of social entrepreneurial intention: An empirical study. *South Asian Journal of Business Studies*, *6*(1), 53–79. doi:10.1108/SAJBS-04-2016-0032

Van Gelderen, M., Brand, M., Van Praag, M., Bodewes, W., Poutsma, E., & Van Gils, A. (2008). Explaining entrepreneurial intentions by means of the theory of planned behaviour. *Career Development International*, *13*(6), 538–559. doi:10.1108/13620430810901688

Wang, C. K., & Wong, P. K. (2004). Entrepreneurial interest of university students in Singapore. *Technovation*, *24*(2), 163–172. doi:10.1016/S0166-4972(02)00016-0

Yang. (2013). The theory of planned behavior and prediction of entrepreneurial intention among Chinese undergraduates. *Social Behavior and Personality, 41*(3), 367–376.

Zhao, H., Hills, G. E., & Seibert, S. (2005). The mediating role of self-efficacy in the development of entrepreneurial intentions. *The Journal of Applied Psychology*, *90*(6), 1265–1272. doi:10.1037/0021-9010.90.6.1265 PMID:16316279

Zhao, H., Seibert, S. E., & Hills, G. E. (2005). The mediating role of self-efficacy in the development of entrepreneurial intentions. *The Journal of Applied Psychology*, *90*(6), 1265–1272. doi:10.1037/0021-9010.90.6.1265 PMID:16316279

Section 2
The International Case Studies

Chapter 3
Driving Economic Development:
Unveiling the Transformative Power of Women Entrepreneurs in Algeria

Naima Bentouir
University of Ain Temouchent, Algeria

Mohammed El Amine Abdelli
https://orcid.org/0000-0002-5784-4306
University of Brest, France

Akinyo Feyisayo Ola
University of Bristol, UK

ABSTRACT

This chapter aims to provide insights into the importance of empowering women in entrepreneurship and its potential impact on economic growth. In this study, the authors analyze the influence of women's entrepreneurship on economic growth with a particular focus on Algeria's environment. The research highlights the significant role played by Algerian women in contributing to the country's economic development. To conduct this empirical investigation, they employed five variables: GDP, businesswomen ownership, women in the industrial sector, force labor women, and women's unemployment. The findings shed light on the crucial need to empower women in entrepreneurship and its potential benefits to economic growth 1990 to 2019 using annual data. According to the Johansen test, they found a long-run association between the GDP and the rest of the variables based on the vector error correction model and the co-integration test. The outputs of the VECM model confirmed the first results with a significant and negative coefficient, which means a long-run relationship between the variables.

DOI: 10.4018/978-1-6684-7127-2.ch003

I. INTRODUCTION

Securing financing is crucial to sustaining a successful enterprise in today's business landscape. Shockingly, despite owning and operating more than 30% of registered companies worldwide, women encounter significant obstacles in obtaining financial support for their formal small and medium-sized enterprises (SMEs). Disturbingly, nearly 70% of these women-owned SMEs in developing nations report being refused by financial institutions or needing help accessing services that align with their needs. This disparity has resulted in an estimated annual funding shortfall of approximately $300 billion for women-led formal SMEs. Additionally, the lack of valuable networks, high-value market contacts, and knowledge impedes female entrepreneurialism. The growth of the economy and job market is significantly aided by female entrepreneurs, especially for those in the lowest 40% of the population. However, women face several obstacles when it comes to financing, owning, and expanding their businesses. These challenges include limited access to technology and capital, a lack of networking and knowledge resources, and legal and regulatory limitations. In more profitable industries like software, electronics, or construction, women-owned enterprises are not as joint as those with weaker profitability and growth prospects, such as retail and services. Women often struggle to pursue their business goals due to a shortage of professional connections, role models, and mentorship opportunities, putting them at a disadvantage compared to men. The businesses of women entrepreneurs in World Bank Group client countries may suffer in the long run. However, there is hope in the form of the Women Entrepreneurs Finance Initiative (We-Fi), which offers over $1 billion in funding to help them achieve their full potential. This funding will provide more access to capital, technical assistance, and investment in programs and projects that empower women and women-led small and medium enterprises (SMEs). To achieve its goal of raising at least $800 million through commercial financing and international financial institutions, We-Fi plans to collaborate with funds, other market participants, and financial intermediaries, using models similar to the International Finance Corporation's (IFC) Women Entrepreneurs Opportunity Facility/Banking on Women program. Furthermore, the We-Fi facility aims to eliminate financial access barriers and provide additional services such as mentorship, network access, capacity building, and opportunities to engage with local and foreign markets. The ultimate goal of We-Fi is to improve the business environment for women-led or women-owned SMEs in developing nations.

We-Fi is a groundbreaking initiative that supports women-led businesses in their early stages of development. It aims to facilitate access to equity and insurance services and build on the achievements of previous and ongoing projects from various partners, including the World Bank Group. The program also seeks to assist public sector initiatives that complement its efforts by improving the business environment and expanding the markets available to female entrepreneurs. We-Fi addresses the gap left by the lack of a substantial fund or facility that focuses on the public and private sectors' all-encompassing combination to address the challenges faced by female entrepreneurs. It provides specific tools to foster innovation and creative solutions to overcome the obstacles that prevent female entrepreneurs from achieving success. Additionally, it aims to raise awareness of the issue and encourage governmental and private sector action. We-Fi is a Financial Intermediary Fund (Erdost Torun, Afife Duygu Ayhan Akdeniz, Demireli, & Grima) based on the World Bank's vast expertise in setting up and overseeing these Funds, guaranteeing best practices for efficacy and governance, Serving as the facility's Trustee and Secretariat, the Bank leverages its financial infrastructure and extensive experience providing similar services for other FIFs. There are several multilateral development banks qualified to suggest public and private sector initiatives that the Facility should support as implementing partners, including the World Bank and the IFC. The Facility's original contributors will form a Governing Committee to determine the distribution of these initiatives.

According to UNESCO research, for the digital revolution to be smart, it must be inclusive. Algeria has the highest ratio of female engineers globally, with 48.5% of all engineering graduates being female, surpassing countries like France (26.1%), Canada (19.7%), and Japan (14%). Despite this, the number of female business owners is low, and this is due to two distinct sets of limitations. The first set is composed of deeply rooted social standards, such as inflexible gender roles and a shortage of assistance from family. The second set includes financial barriers, including a lack of capital and institutional support to obtain cash through bank loans or investments.

II. THEORETICAL FRAMEWORK

1. World Bank Strategies

The World Bank Group has a wealth of expertise working on issues related to gender equality and women's economic empowerment in several nations, including:

- Gender Equality and Development Report, World Development, 2012

The 2012 World Development Report on Gender Equality and Development notes progress for women, but identifies disparities in various sectors and offers policy recommendations.

- Empowering Women and Girls for Shared Prosperity via Voice and Agency

This research provides potential and launching points for long-term change, including cross-sectoral interventions including conditional cash transfers, life skills training, mentorship, and education on sexual and reproductive health.

- Industry, Women, and Law

Women, Business and the Law, a publication by the World Bank Group, gathers information on the rules and legislation that restrict women from starting their own enterprises or working.

- Investing in Women

Giving women and men the same opportunities benefit local economies, families, communities, and corporations new evidence for the business case.

- Evaluation of EDGE Certification in Gender Equality

The main international criterion for gender equality in the workplace is called Economic Dividends for Gender Equality (EDGE). The World Bank Group headquarters in Washington, DC, is the first location of an international financial organisation to receive this accreditation at the EDGE Assess level (World Bank, 2023).

2. Women Entrepreneurship Statistics

Small and medium-sized businesses (SMEs) run by women include a minority of formally recognized SMEs in developing nations and confront several challenges in their pursuit of growth. Women are exposed to additional limitations and less favourable terms when obtaining credit. Reducing prohibitions will increase competition and open up more opportunities for women entrepreneurs (Figure 1).

Development Relevance: The expertise and analysis provided by Women, Business and the Law provides a solid financial case for legislation that upholds women's rights. Better performance in the areas monitored by the Women, Business, and Law Index is correlated with more women in the workforce, greater earnings, and better development outcomes. Access to the law and equal opportunity are justifiable social objectives that also make sense economically. Provided that women and men engage equally in society, every economy will have an opportunity to realize its full potential. Women, Business, and the Law's ultimate goal is to influence governments to amend laws that prohibit women from holding business ownership and employment positions in light of the importance of women's empowerment for the economy (Figures 2-3).

III. LITERATURE REVIEW

Entrepreneurs are the driving force behind innovation and economic growth (Abdelli, Ul-Durar, & Wasef Hattab, 2023). Shastri, Shastri, & Pareek (2019) purpose to investigate the driving forces behind and significant difficulties faced by female entrepreneurs operating small companies in Rajasthan's Jaipur city. The study's key finding states that the desire for self-expression, innovation, independence, and a desire to benefit society are the primary pull factors that drive female entrepreneurs to launch their businesses. According to institutional theory, informal institutions are the main source of problems for female entrepreneurs (Cho, Li, & Chaudhuri, 2020). This special issue aims to look into the reasons behind, obstacles to, and opportunities faced by women entrepreneurs in eight Asian nations (China, India, Indonesia, Japan, Korea, Malaysia, Thailand, and Vietnam). After conducting theoretical research, it was determined that while women entrepreneurs encounter obstacles and hurdles, the chances they provide for business growth can serve as a role model for aspirant female entrepreneurs in Asia and other regions (Panda, 2018). This essay strives to list and rate the obstacles that women business owners in developing nations must overcome. It provides a framework to distinguish between the limitations experienced by male and female business owners. The findings show that barriers to entry for women entrepreneurs in developing nations include gender discrimination, work-family issues, challenges in raising capital, a lack of infrastructure, unstable BEP environments (business, economic, and political), a lack of education and training, and personality differences. According to the study, insecure BEP settings need to be addressed as a high priority in addition to financial restrictions (Rosca, Agarwal, & Brem, 2020). This essay strives to list and rate the obstacles that women business owners in developing nations must overcome. It provides a framework to distinguish between the limitations experienced by male and female business owners. The findings show that barriers to entry for women entrepreneurs in developing nations include gender discrimination, work-family issues, challenges in raising capital, a lack of infrastructure, unstable BEP environments (business, economic, and political), a lack of education and training, and personality differences. According to the study, insecure BEP settings need to be addressed as a high priority in addition to financial restrictions (Afshan, Shahid, & Tunio, 2021). The research paper highlights the brand-new knowledge the female entrepreneurs learned through their participation in COVID-19. Fresh learning was included in the change from manual commercial dealings and financial transactions to virtual dealing and online transactions. The report also offers insights into the difficulties faced by female entrepreneurs, the approaches employed, and the takeaways from the pandemic corona virus. What was learned from experience demonstrated the importance of business operations and technical know-how during a crisis (Dahiya, Panghal, Sindhu, & Siwach, 2021). In this study, the most strategic issues with the greatest potential to affect other issues were "poor government assistance" and "low awareness" among the stakeholders. Contrarily, "poor financial choices" and "fewer buyers" appeared as the most significant obstacles for Indian women entrepreneurs in the organic food industry (Mustafa, Khursheed, Fatima, & Rao, 2021). The findings, which specifically consider household income, business sales, lifestyle, and mental health, offer insightful information on how the COVID-19 problem affected women entrepreneurs. Women-owned firms closing down demonstrated the need to reevaluate innovation and digitalization for business viability. Additionally, the findings showed that the COVID-19 pandemic's effects on women's physical, mental, and economic well-being underscore the necessity of taking gender inequality concerns into account when creating COVID-19 response plans in developing nations (Jaim, 2021). This research highlights the varied gendered experiences of women in private and public domains as they continued their business activities during the pandemic period based on interviews with women business owners in Bangladesh. As a result of the COVID-19 situation, it also exposes patriarchal behaviours about women quitting their businesses or shutting them down (Stefan et al., 2021). The study's major findings offer practical suggestions for creating a workplace that is gender-balanced. The paper's last section covers women's preferences for sustainable business models, the perceived value of gender stereotypes in the creation of sustainable business models, and the applicability of the new digital economy trend to Romanian women entrepreneurs (Ogundana, Simba, Dana, & Liguori, 2021). After analysis, a number of components were discovered to explain their business-development actions. It illustrates how the development of women-owned firms depends on three key factors: money (access and use), the market (customer intelligence), and management (nonformal education and experience). Motherhood (duties at home) and micro- and macroenvironments (socioeconomic and cultural conditions) affected the growth of businesses, made it more difficult for women entrepreneurs to get and use capital, markets, and management, and changed the way they developed their companies (Stefan et al., 2021). Following examination, various constructs that explain their business-development actions were found. It illustrates how the development of women-owned firms depends on three key factors: money (access and use), the market (customer intelligence), and management (nonformal education and experience). Motherhood (duties at home) and micro- and macroenvironments (socioeconomic and cultural conditions) affected the growth of businesses, made it more difficult for women entrepreneurs to get and use capital, markets, and management, and changed the way they developed their companies (Dane, Akyuz, & Opusunju, 2021). Results showed that COVID-19 had a negative and negligible impact on women entrepreneurs' creativity and entrepreneurship development in Adamawa State, Nigeria. The study suggested that the government of Adamawa State, Nigeria, should work to support female entrepreneurs since they are impacted by COVID-19 and the application of its policies, which include social distancing and lock-downs, as a result of an increase in COVID-19-related deaths, tests, and confirmed cases (Hossain et al., 2021). Finding financial motivation and independence were shown to be essential components in the establishment of firms owned by women entrepreneurs. According to the "Entrepreneurial Economic Success Index" (EESI), service-sector entrepreneurs had significantly higher entrepreneurial success than entrepreneurs in other sectors, with 15% of women entrepreneurs being extremely successful, 65% successful, and 20% failed (Al-Qahtani, Fekih Zguir, Al-Fagih, & Koç, 2022). Without the input of women, who comprise a sizable portion of the country's educated and skilled population, such diverse and sustainable development cannot be realized. Yet, a number of socioeconomic factors either prevent or undervalue women's ability to fully contribute to society and the economy, even though the state has been clearly supporting women in encouraging their active economic participation as part of Qatar National Vision 2030 (Ingalagi, Nawaz, Rahiman, Hariharasudan, & Hundekar, 2021). The main conclusion of the research is that every aspect significantly affects the organization's success. Researchers and practitioners' reactions to the research findings are examined, and recommendations have also been offered (Isa, Muhammad, Ahmad, & Noor, 2021). The findings demonstrate how Chinese and Malay business owners use ICT in their daily operations, including AutoCAD, HRM software, accounting systems, purchase order systems, production systems, and warehouse management systems (Thaher, Radieah, & Wan Norhaniza, 2021). The findings indicated that, regarding financial services, the most crucial requirements for women entrepreneurs are adequate financing and the availability of necessary financial facilities, such as extending the grace period and lowering interest rates. In contrast, non-financial services should include holding specialized courses, gaining access to counseling services, offering incentives and psychological support, supporting marketing efforts, and monitoring and evaluating progress (Mehta, Qamrozzaman, & Serfraz, 2022). Financial accessibility has a favorable and statistically significant impact on the growth of women's entrepreneurship, according to structural equation modeling. A positive correlation between knowledge level and the growth of women's entrepreneurship was also observed. Women's entrepreneurship has been favorably and indirectly associated with transformational leadership, which mediates leadership approaches. SMEs, which stands for small- and medium-sized enterprises, are likely to be the most susceptible to economic hardships (Khalil, Abdelli, & Mogaji, 2022).

Small and medium enterprises (SMEs) are the backbone of the economy, accounting for a significant portion of employment and production. However, they tend to focus on low-value products and services instead of high-value ones (Arabeche Z et al., 2022). In Algeria, various incubators have been established across the country to support the development of small and medium-sized enterprises (SMEs) (Zina Arabeche & Abdelli, 2021).

The importance of women in entrepreneurship has been recognized more and more recently in the pursuit of sustainable development and economic progress. Women entrepreneurs have made essential contributions to the economic development of their communities and countries by demonstrating extraordinary tenacity, inventiveness, and commitment in various areas. Agri-preneurship, which includes producing, processing, and distributing agricultural goods, is one significant field where women's entrepreneurship is crucial. This literature review examines the dynamic relationship between women in agriculture, highlighting how their involvement not only increases the availability and accessibility of wholesome food but also strengthens local economies and, consequently, promotes global economic growth. We uncover the varied contributions that women entrepreneurs make economic development by examining the complex relationships between their involvement in agri-preneurship and the broader economic environment. This analysis provides priceless insights into the advantages of supporting women's entrepreneurship for sustainable growth (Dedehouanou & Araar, 2020). In Niger, where gender disparities in resource accessibility are decreased, examine the impact of home entrepreneurship on ruaral development. They discover a link between owning female-run non-agricultural businesses and food availability for female-headed households. The findings highlight the need to address gender disparities in entrepreneurship's access to resources to improve Agri-preneurship (Adeyanju et al, 2021). This study looked at how youth agri-preneurship performance in Nigeria was affected by agricultural training programs. According to the results, the program's participation was strongly influenced by age, years of formal education, marital status, place of residence, kind of employment, and perception of training. After controlling for endogeneity, the empirical analysis also demonstrated that participation in the program improved performance, as measured by average income from agri-preneurship activities.

By analysing the characteristics of the production, consumption, and entrepreneurship domains as well as the accomplishments of community food business development (PUPM) in the Province of East Nusa Tenggara (NTT), this research seeks to construct a regional development model. The results of the analysis show that the PUPM's performance in NTT, which is determined by the characteristics of the production, consumption, and entrepreneurial domains, has only been reached to a sufficient degree (Nona et al, 2019). Fitz-Koch et al. (2018) perform a thorough analysis of the literature on agricultural entrepreneurship. Researchers can explore entrepreneurship theory and practice in a dynamic environment thanks to recent rapid vertical integration and rationalization within the agricultural industry. The writers identify the agricultural sector's three most important contextual dimensions. Identity, family, and institutions are three areas with the potential to advance existing theoretical and empirical assessments of entrepreneurship research and offer attractive avenues for future study. Sargani et al. (2020) check if the ambition to build sustainable businesses is impacted by the importance placed on the triple bottom line. The results demonstrated that indicators of a positive, sustainable attitude, support for subjective norms, control behaviours, proper opportunity recognition, and encouragement of the triple bottom line significantly influenced the intention to promote sustainability in business (Petrariu et al, 2021). This study sought to investigate the relationship in more detail by statistically evaluating the financial and economic indicators provided by active enterprises at the county level, based on data from the Romanian Ministry of Public Finance. The consequences of the policies in the WEFW sectors are outlined in research findings. Furthermore, the efficiency of entrepreneurial endeavours was assessed from the perspective of financial outcomes (Sinyolo & Mudhara, 2018). This study examines how entrepreneurial skills affect rural farming households' access to the development in KwaZulu-Natal, South Africa (SA). According to the estimated findings, entrepreneurship improved agriculture (Sinyolo, 2020). This study evaluated the effects of smallholder farmers in KwaZulu-Natal, South Africa adopting better maize varieties on household. The results showed that yearly food expenditure per capita levels increase by approximately R4000 for every additional 1 ha of land planted in better maize varieties. Female farmers were likelier to adopt enhanced maize varieties, spend more to maintain household in agriculture, and profit more from adoption than their male counterparts (Martinho, 2020). This study aims to investigate the entrepreneurial aspects of European Union agriculture to create a more sustainable industry. Farm management without an economic component could undermine the sustainability of the enterprise in the long term. The analysis reveals that the reality in the various European Union member states is distinct, with the common agricultural policies' tools, for instance, potentially playing a key role in encouraging greater farming entrepreneurship more sustainably (Yoshida et al, 2019). In order to determine the economic and social sustainability of these farms, this research will identify sophisticated, diverse farms that demonstrate entrepreneurship, skilled farm management, and social networks. Only 10% of the sample could be classified as advanced diversified farms, according to the data, and the majority of other diversified farms lacked entrepreneurial traits. Additionally, regression analysis demonstrated that increased variety enhances the social performance and financial sustainability of farms (Sargani et al., 2020). This essay utilizes South Korea as an example to discuss sustainable entrepreneurship-related challenges. Results highlight the significance of a flexible and gradual transition to a market efficiency model while actively utilizing nonmarket techniques and maintaining the selective protection of the domestic market from commodities imports (Kan et al., 2018). This study aims to assess how well the Young Farmer Project Support in Turkey supports entrepreneurship. Young Farmer Project Support, which has the goal of enticing young people to work in agriculture in rural regions, is, therefore, a boon. However, these aids must be directed toward establishing an economically viable enterprise (Hudcová et al, 2018). This article explores social farming, a cutting-edge social entrepreneurship in the agriculture industry that sustains rural communities. This essay provides some background on the rural social integration systems practice, which is a retro-innovative approach. It investigates the function of the social farm in rural development using semi-structured and in-depth interviews, and it primarily addresses the topic of whether social farming complies fully with the social entrepreneurship stream (Sher et al, 2019). This study explores the China-Pakistan Economic Corridor's impact on agricultural entrepreneurship and farmer performance (CPEC). The findings show that market orientation, entrepreneurial orientation, innovation orientation, and opportunity recognition all benefit agriculture entrepreneurship, which in turn helps ensure rural and regional development by allowing the timely distribution of food commodities. According to additional research, entrepreneurship adoption enhances farmers' marketing, operational, and financial success (Rozhkova & Olentsova, 2020). The article provides information on the situation of small businesses in the agricultural sector in the Krasnoyarsk area. The region's agricultural sector's small business operational issues are considered. Support programs for small and medium-sized agriculture businesses are described in the Krasnoyarsk region (Rasel et al, 2022). This study breaks down locational factors into "first-nature" and "second-nature" geography. It contends that due to technological and financial externalities, the concentration of entrepreneurial activities in second-nature geography helps entrepreneurs find opportunities for growth and incentivizes them to integrate their businesses with nearby supporting activities (Savastano et al, 2022). The results, which were obtained by carefully reviewing and analysing the body of research on green entrepreneurship and agriculture, point to a conceptual framework that highlights the internal and external elements that, when strategically matched, promote the establishment of green agricultural firms (Hussain et al, 2022). Using the entrepreneurial event model and the theoretical framework of determinants of entrepreneurial intentions, this chapter aims to further research on factors influencing entrepreneurial desires in the agriculture sector. The results show that an entrepreneurial attitude is favourably connected with perceived desirability, perceived viability, personal background, and triggering events. Furthermore, an entrepreneurial attitude has a large and beneficial impact on entrepreneurial aspirations in the agriculture sector.

IV. DATA AND METHODOLOGY

• **The econometric model**

1. VECM Model

The vector Error correction model is one of the multivariate time series analyses. It is a system of equation approach (Md Reza, Fan, Wang, Bhuiyan, & K. M. Mehedi, 2019, p. 4) based on the vector auto-regression model (Thasnimol & Rajathy, 2021, p. 19) (VAR, was populated by Sims 1980), under the following equation:

$Y_t = \beta_0 \sum_{i=1}^{p} A_i Y_{t-1} + BX_t + \upsilon$ (Kazanas, 2017, p. 4)

It is determined according to the characteristics of the data. These models do not need the theoretical information of the relationship between the variables; we need only the results of the stationary test, which means if the variables are not stationary at the level, they should be converted as stationary at the first level. If this condition exists, the co-integration test can be established before using the VECM model.

VECM model is considered a restricted VAR in the case of the co-integrating of time series. The equation of the VECM model is given as follow(Leonard, Humayun, Haiyue, & Yunjie, 2020, p. 139):

$$\Delta Y_t = \beta_0 \sum_{i=1}^{p} \Gamma_i Y_{t-1} + \Pi y_{t-1} + BX_t + \upsilon_t$$

2. Co-Integration Test

Johansen and Granger (1987) presented the concept of co-integration (Engsted & Johansen, 1997, p. 1) test, which enables the execution of the co-integration test for time series and is necessary differencing operations minimum number to make time-series stationary. If a set of variables are co-integrated, then there is a long-run relationship between the variables, though there is a dynamic short-run relationship. The co-integration equation is written as follows:

$Y_t = \beta_0 + BZ_t + e_t$ (Hylleberg, Engle, Granger, & Yoo, 1990, p. 20)

The Empirical Study Model

The following equation represents our model for the estimation.

$$GDP = \alpha_0 + \beta_1 BUSW + \beta_2 FLW + \beta_3 INDW + \beta_4 UNEMP + e_t$$

Our empirical study was based on macro/micro-economic data in Algeria, covering 1990 to 2019 using annual data. The investigation sample collected from the World Bank database includes five variables: GDP, Female labor in the industrial sector, Business done by women, female unemployment, and female labor force. This investigation aims to test the impact of the independent variables on the dependent variable (GDP) by examining the long-run association between the variables using the Vector Error Correction Model (VECM). Table 1 describes the variables.

Table 1. Data descriptive

Variable	Definition
Dependent Variable	
GDP	Gross domestic production per capita
Independent Variables	
BUSW	Businesses done by women
FLW	female labor force
ANDREW	Female labor in the industrial sector
UNMP	female unemployment

Source: Authors

V. RESULTS AND DISCUSSION

Table 2 shows the stationary test using the summary test function; according to the outputs, the variables are not stationary at the level indicated by the P-value, which is more than 5%. The second part of the table highlights that all the variables do not have a unit root, which means they are stationary at the first difference. We accept the alternative hypothesis and reject the null hypothesis because the P-value supports our findings with less than 5%. The time series can be said to be co-integrated at (I1). Building on the stationary test results, we can run the VECM model, but before that, we have to run the co-integration test using (Johansen-Jose Luis) test. This test can help us to determine the long-run association between the dependent and independent variables.

Table 2. The summary of the stationary test using AIC criteria

At Level						
		GDP	**BUSW**	**FLW**	**ANDREW**	**UNMP**
With Constant	t-Statistic	-2.2944	-0.8081	-3.1807	-1.5058	-1.5793
	Prob.	0.1806	0.8018	0.0344	0.5160	0.4801
		n0	n0	**	n0	n0
With Constant & Trend	t-Statistic	-1.8972	-2.1217	-2.3257	-1.4086	-2.6294
	Prob.	0.6292	0.5128	0.4050	0.8360	0.2710
		n0	n0	n0	n0	n0
Without Constant & Trend	t-Statistic	-1.8603	0.7876	1.0886	-2.0205	-0.0397
	Prob.	0.0608	0.8777	0.9238	0.0433	0.6612
		*	n0	n0	**	n0
At First Difference						
		d(GDP)	**d(BUSW)**	**d(FLW)**	**d(INDW)**	**d(UNMP)**
With Constant	t-Statistic	-8.4390	-5.2589	-2.8829	-2.6949	-4.6203
	Prob.	0.0000	0.0002	0.0001	0.0075	0.0010
		***	***	***	***	***
With Constant & Trend	t-Statistic	-8.7840	-5.1852	-3.2299	-2.6833	-4.5231
	Prob.	0.0000	0.0013	0.0099	0.0009	0.0063
		***	***	***	***	***
Without Constant & Trend	t-Statistic	-8.5822	-5.1962	-2.5699	-1.9636	-4.7222
	Prob.	0.0000	0.0000	0.0122	0.0489	0.0000
		***	***	**	**	***

(***) significance at 1%, (**) significance at 5%, (*) significance at 10%, (no), no stationary.
Source: Authors

We must first make the lag selection step to estimate the Co-integration test. The following table will give the appropriate lag for the variables.

The table above (03) shows the VAR Lag Order Selection under the AIC criteria; according to these criteria, the variables are significant at three lag order selections.

The co-integration test hypotheses:

H_0: There is no long-run relationship.

H_1: There is a long-run relationship.

The Johansen-Juseluis

Based on the test results, we can confirm that there are five cointegrating equations at a significance level of 5%. This indicates that the variables are co-movements

Table 3. VAR lag order selection criteria

Lag	LogL	LR	FPE	AIC	SC	HQ
0	-293.4052	NA	2737.694	22.10409	22.34406	22.17544
1	-160.8071	206.2636*	0.982337	14.13386	15.57368*	14.56199
2	-136.9240	28.30587	1.320649	14.21660	16.85626	15.00151
3	-94.97446	34.18114	0.713398*	**12.96107***	16.80059	14.10276*

Source: Authors

Table 4. The co-integration test

Hypothesized		Trace	0.05	
No. of CE(s)	Eigenvalue	Statistic	Critical Value	Prob.**
None *	0.999812	371.9216	69.81889	0.0001
At most 1 *	0.968949	148.8451	47.85613	0.0000
At most 2 *	0.704017	58.57024	29.79707	0.0000
At most 3 *	0.485687	26.91645	15.49471	0.0006
At most 4 *	0.309491	9.628466	3.841466	0.0019

Trace test indicates 5 cointegrating eqn(s) at the 0.05 level
* denotes rejection of the hypothesis at the 0.05 level
**MacKinnon-Haug-Michelis (1999) p-values.
Source: Authors

in the long run, as the P-value is less than 5%. With these findings, we are able to utilize the VECM model. (Table 4)

In Table 05, we can observe the Vector Error Correction Model (VECM) outputs. The coefficient (C1) of VECM is negative and has a significant value of -0.44 (p=0.0013), which is less than 5%. These results confirm the existence of a long-term relationship between the variables. Therefore, the equilibrium will take 5% as the annual correction.

Table 6 shows the results of the Breush-Godfrey test, indicating no serial correlation between residuals. Based on the Chi-Square probability of less than 5%, we can conclude that our model is adequate.

After analyzing the long-term relationship between the variables, we also examined if the variables are related in the short-term. Based on the Chi-square probability, which has a significance level of more than 5%, we can conclude that there is no short-term relationship between the variables (Table 7).

Table 5. VECM model

	Coefficient	Std. Error	t-Statistic	Prob.
C(1)	**-0.448547**	0.252732	-1.774793	**0.0013**
C(2)	-0.275794	0.201214	-1.370652	0.0356
C(3)	-0.421363	0.776618	-0.542562	0.5974
C(4)	-0.998059	0.647568	-1.541242	0.1492
C(5)	-0.004581	0.318648	-0.014376	0.9888
C(6)	0.008762	0.261570	0.033496	0.0238
C(7)	-0.092887	0.163356	-0.568613	0.5801
C(8)	0.018258	0.165563	0.110276	0.9140
C(9)	0.336318	1.097182	0.306529	0.0645
C(10)	1.720127	1.298958	1.324236	0.2101
C(11)	1.059082	1.377964	0.768584	0.0701
C(12)	0.622455	1.493017	0.416911	0.0041
C(13)	0.360307	0.247079	1.458265	0.1704
C(14)	0.038369	0.233701	0.164181	0.8723
C(15)	0.271258	0.783298	0.346302	0.7351
R-squared	0.723276			
Adj R-squared	0.400431			
F-statistic	2.240321			
Prob(F-stat)	0.004426			

Source: Authors.

Table 6. Serial correlation test between residual

Breusch-Godfrey Serial Correlation LM Test
F-statistic 0.075676 Prob. F(2,23) 0.9273
Obs*R-squared 0.196124 Prob. Chi-Square(2) **0.9066**

Source: Authors.

VI. DISCUSSION

This investigation has found a long-term relationship between GDP and the independent variables BUSW, FLW, INDW, and UNEMP. We began our empirical study by testing for stationary variables co-integrating at the first level, and the summary stationary test showed that the p-value was less than 5%. The second step involved the Johansen-Juisis test, which indicated almost five cointegrated equations.

Table 7. Wald test

Equation: Untitled			
Test Statistic	Value	Df	Probability
t-statistic	-0.175433	12	0.8637
F-statistic	0.030777	(1, 12)	0.8637
Chi-square	0.030777	1	**0.8607**
Null Hypothesis: C(06)+C(07)+C(08)=0			
Equation: Untitled			
Test Statistic	Value	Df	Probability
t-statistic	1.433278	12	0.1773
F-statistic	2.054285	(1, 12)	0.1773
Chi-square	2.054285	1	**0.1518**
Null Hypothesis: C(09)+C(10)+C(11)=0			
Equation: Untitled			
Test Statistic	Value	Df	Probability
t-statistic	0.663044	12	0.5198
F-statistic	0.439627	(1, 12)	0.5198
Chi-square	0.439627	1	**0.5073**
Null Hypothesis: C(12)+C(13)+C(14)=0			

H0: There is no short-run relationship.
H1: There is a short-run relationship.
Source: Authors

This can be explained by the significant contribution of Algerian women's labor force to the development of economic growth, represented by GDP per capita.

After the cointegration test, the Vector Error Correction Model (VECM) was established to determine the error correction coefficient, which was negative (-0.44) and significant (0.0013). This means that the annual correction for GDP in Algeria will be 5%. Consequently, there is a long causal relationship between BUSW, FLW, INDW, UNEMP, and GDP.

We conducted a Wald test to determine if there was a short dynamic relationship. The test results indicated the absence of a short-term relationship. This means that the independent variables cannot cause GDP in the short term.

These findings can be explained by integrating women's forced labor into the economic cycle in Algeria. It can give a significant boost to economic growth in various sectors, such as industrial, own businesses, and others. One of the independent variables, unemployment, showed a long-term relationship, which led us to conclude that women's unemployment can have a negative impact on economic growth.

In conclusion, Algerians have proved themselves by creating their businesses and opening up many opportunities for new jobs. The causal relationship between GDP and dependent variables may undergo several changes in the future. Finally, Algerian women have increased their skills in the labor force and have made significant contributions to local development.

VII. CONCLUSION

In today's developing countries, especially in Africa, women are increasingly participating in labor markets, although female labor force participation rates vary significantly between poorer and wealthier countries. In our study, we focused on Algeria to shed light on the employment environment for women in the country. Our objective was to investigate the existence of a long-term relationship between economic growth and independent variables such as BUSW, FLW, INDW, and UNEMP. Our main findings suggest that these variables have a significant impact on the GDP over a long period, but we found no short-term association between them. These results indicate that integrating female labor into economic development can effectively promote women's employment in Algeria. Another key finding in our empirical study is the considerable influence of women entrepreneurs in the agricultural sector, also known as agripreneurs, who are included in the business women variable. These women have demonstrated their ability not only to cultivate crops but also to foster economic growth. By actively participating in agripreneurship, women have not only improved food security, but also played a significant role in the broader economic development of our nation. Our study highlights the importance of investing in women's entrepreneurship, which can enhance female labor force skills and contribute to economic growth.

REFERENCES

Abdelli, M., Ul-Durar, S., & Wasef Hattab, H. (2023). Entrepreneurship Ecosystems and Their Opportunities and Challenges. IGI Global. doi:10.4018/978-1-6684-7140-1

Adeyanju, D., Mburu, J., & Mignouna, D. (2021). Youth agricultural entrepreneurship: Assessing the impact of agricultural training programmes on performance. *Sustainability (Basel), 13*(4), 1697. doi:10.3390u13041697

Afshan, G., Shahid, S., & Tunio, M. N. (2021). Learning experiences of women entrepreneurs amidst COVID-19. *International Journal of Gender and Entrepreneurship.*

Al-Qahtani, M., Fekih Zguir, M., Al-Fagih, L., & Koç, M. (2022). Women Entrepreneurship for Sustainability: Investigations on Status, Challenges, Drivers, and Potentials in Qatar. *Sustainability (Basel), 14*(7), 4091. doi:10.3390u14074091

Arabeche & Abdelli. (2021). The New Trends Technology of Entrepreneurship in the Incubators A Case Study of Cyberpark Sidi Abdallah. In *Big Data for Entrepreneurship and Sustainable Development.* Taylor and Francis.

Arabeche, Z., Soudani, A., Brahmi, M., Aldieri, L., Vinci, C. P., & Abdelli, M. E. A. (2022, April 25). Entrepreneurial Orientation, Organizational Culture and Business Performance in SMEs: Evidence from Emerging Economy. *Sustainability (Basel), 14*(9), 5160. Advance online publication. doi:10.3390u14095160

Cho, Y., Li, J., & Chaudhuri, S. (2020). Women entrepreneurs in Asia: Eight country studies. *Advances in Developing Human Resources*, *22*(2), 115–123. doi:10.1177/1523422320907042

Dahiya, S., Panghal, A., Sindhu, S., & Siwach, P. (2021). Organic food women entrepreneurs-TISM approach for challenges. *Journal of Enterprising Communities: People and Places in the Global Economy.*

Dane, S., Akyuz, M., & Opusunju, M. I. (2021). COVID-19 and entrepreneurship development among Nigerian women. *Journal of Research in Medical and Dental Science*, *9*, 312–318.

Dedehouanou, S. F. A., & Araar, A. (2020). Gender, entrepreneurship and food security in Niger. *Review of Development Economics*, *24*(3), 815–830. doi:10.1111/rode.12657

Engsted, T., & Johansen, S. (1997). *Granger's representation theorem and multi-cointegration*. Academic Press.

Fitz-Koch, S., Nordqvist, M., Carter, S., & Hunter, E. (2018). Entrepreneurship in the agricultural sector: A literature review and future research opportunities. *Entrepreneurship Theory and Practice*, *42*(1), 129–166. doi:10.1177/1042258717732958

Hossain, S. M., Akbar, A., Tehseen, S., Poulova, P., Haider, S. A., Sheraz, F., & Yasmin, F. (2021). Evaluation of entrepreneurs success: A special reference to women entrepreneurs in Bangladesh. *Academy of Entrepreneurship Journal*, *27*, 1–13.

Hudcová, E., Chovanec, T., & Moudrý, J. (2018). Social entrepreneurship in agriculture, a sustainable practice for social and economic cohesion in rural areas: The case of the Czech Republic. *European Countryside*, *10*(3), 377–397. doi:10.2478/euco-2018-0022

Hussain, S. A., Ahmad, G., Khan, A., Hassan, A., & Shamim, M. (2022). Cognitive antecedents of the agricultural entrepreneurship intentions of Indian university students. In *Driving factors for venture creation and success in agricultural entrepreneurship* (pp. 121–140). IGI Global. doi:10.4018/978-1-6684-2349-3.ch006

Hylleberg, S., Engle, R. F., Granger, C. W., & Yoo, B. S. (1990). Seasonal integration and cointegration. *Journal of Econometrics*, *44*(1-2), 215–238. doi:10.1016/0304-4076(90)90080-D

Ingalagi, S. S., Nawaz, N., Rahiman, H. U., Hariharasudan, A., & Hundekar, V. (2021). Unveiling the crucial factors of women entrepreneurship in the 21st century. *Social Sciences (Basel, Switzerland)*, *10*(5), 153. doi:10.3390ocsci10050153

Isa, F. M., Muhammad, N. M. N., Ahmad, A., & Noor, S. (2021). Effect of ICT on women entrepreneur business performance: Case of Malaysia. *Journal of Economics and Business*, *4*(1). Advance online publication. doi:10.31014/aior.1992.04.01.326

Jaim, J. (2021). Exist or exit? Women business-owners in Bangladesh during COVID-19. *Gender, Work and Organization*, *28*(S1), 209–226. doi:10.1111/gwao.12546

Kan, A., Kan, M., Dogan, H. G., Tosun, F., Ucum, I., & Solmaz, C. (2018). *Evaluatıon Of Young Farmers Project Support Program İn Terms Of Agrı-Entrepreneurshıp İn Turkey*. Academic Press.

Kazanas, T. (2017). A Vector Error Correction Forecasting Model of the Greek Economy. *Hellenic Fiscal Council*, (2), 2–6.

Khalil, A., Abdelli, M. E. A., & Mogaji, E. (2022). Do Digital Technologies Influence the Relationship between the COVID-19 Crisis and SMEs' Resilience in Developing Countries? *Journal of Open Innovation*, *8*(2), 100. doi:10.3390/joitmc8020100

Leonard, N., Humayun, K., Haiyue, Z., & Yunjie, T. (2020). A Vector Error Correction Model (VECM) Approach in explaining the relationship between Fixed Investment and Economic Growth in Rural China. *Pacific International Journal, 3*(3), 138-145.

Martinho, V. J. P. D. (2020). Agricultural entrepreneurship in the European Union: Contributions for a sustainable development. *Applied Sciences (Basel, Switzerland), 10*(6), 2080. doi:10.3390/app10062080

Md Reza, S., Fan, H., Wang, B., Bhuiyan, M. A., & Mehedi, K. M., A. (. (2019). Trade (exports) as an opportunity for Bangladesh: A VECM analysis. *The International Trade Journal*, *33*(1), 95–110. doi:10.1080/08853908.2018.1511489

Mehta, A. M., Qamrozzaman, M., & Serfraz, A. (2022). The Effects of Finance and Knowledge on Entrepreneurship Development: An Empirical Study from Bangladesh. The Journal of Asian Finance. *Economics and Business*, *9*(2), 409–418.

Mustafa, F., Khursheed, A., Fatima, M., & Rao, M. (2021). Exploring the impact of COVID-19 pandemic on women entrepreneurs in Pakistan. *International Journal of Gender and Entrepreneurship*, *13*(2), 187–203. doi:10.1108/IJGE-09-2020-0149

Nona, R. V., Ambarawati, I. G. A. A., Darmawan, D. P., & Budiasa, I. W. (2019). Realizing Regional Food Security Through Community Food Business Development in East Nusa Tenggara Province, Indonesia. *International Journal of Agriculture System*, *6*(2), 146–155. doi:10.20956/ijas.v6i2.1593

Ogundana, O. M., Simba, A., Dana, L.-P., & Liguori, E. (2021). Women entrepreneurship in developing economies: A gender-based growth model. *Journal of Small Business Management, 59*(sup1), S42-S72.

Panda, S. (2018). Constraints faced by women entrepreneurs in developing countries: Review and ranking. *Gender in Management*, *33*(4), 315–331. doi:10.1108/GM-01-2017-0003

Petrariu, R., Constantin, M., Dinu, M., Pătărlăgeanu, S. R., & Deaconu, M. E. (2021). Water, energy, food, waste nexus: Between synergy and trade-offs in Romania based on entrepreneurship and economic performance. *Energies*, *14*(16), 5172. doi:10.3390/en14165172

Rasel, S., Heijman, W. J., & Reinhard, S. (2022). Economic geography and entrepreneurial diversification in the agricultural sector. *Regional Studies, Regional Science*, *9*(1), 347–370. doi:10.1080/21681376.2022.2074307

Rosca, E., Agarwal, N., & Brem, A. (2020). Women entrepreneurs as agents of change: A comparative analysis of social entrepreneurship processes in emerging markets. *Technological Forecasting and Social Change*, *157*, 120067. doi:10.1016/j.techfore.2020.120067

Rozhkova, A., & Olentsova, J. (2020). *Regional support of small business in the agriculture sphere of the krasnoyarsk region.* Paper presented at the "New Silk Road: Business Cooperation and Prospective of Economic Development" (NSRBCPED 2019). 10.2991/aebmr.k.200324.151

Sargani, G. R., Zhou, D., Raza, M. H., & Wei, Y. (2020). Sustainable entrepreneurship in the agriculture sector: The nexus of the triple bottom line measurement approach. *Sustainability (Basel)*, *12*(8), 3275. doi:10.3390u12083275

Savastano, M., Samo, A. H., Channa, N. A., & Amendola, C. (2022). Toward a Conceptual Framework to Foster Green Entrepreneurship Growth in the Agriculture Industry. *Sustainability (Basel)*, *14*(7), 4089. doi:10.3390u14074089

Shastri, S., Shastri, S., & Pareek, A. (2019). Motivations and challenges of women entrepreneurs: Experiences of small businesses in Jaipur city of Rajasthan. *The International Journal of Sociology and Social Policy*, *39*(5/6), 338–355. doi:10.1108/IJSSP-09-2018-0146

Sher, A., Mazhar, S., Abbas, A., Iqbal, M. A., & Li, X. (2019). Linking entrepreneurial skills and opportunity recognition with improved food distribution in the context of the CPEC: A case of Pakistan. *Sustainability (Basel)*, *11*(7), 1838. doi:10.3390u11071838

Sinyolo, S. (2020). Technology adoption and household food security among rural households in South Africa: The role of improved maize varieties. *Technology in Society*, *60*, 101214. doi:10.1016/j.techsoc.2019.101214

Sinyolo, S., & Mudhara, M. (2018). The impact of entrepreneurial competencies on household food security among smallholder farmers in KwaZulu Natal, South Africa. *Ecology of Food and Nutrition*, *57*(2), 71–93. doi:10.1080/03670244.2017.1416361 PMID:29271664

Stefan, D., Vasile, V., Oltean, A., Comes, C.-A., Stefan, A.-B., Ciucan-Rusu, L., Bunduchi, E., Popa, M.-A., & Timus, M. (2021). Women entrepreneurship and sustainable business development: Key findings from a SWOT–AHP analysis. *Sustainability (Basel)*, *13*(9), 5298. doi:10.3390u13095298

Thaher, L. M., Radieah, N. M., & Wan Norhaniza, W. H. (2021). The effect of microfinance services on women entrepreneurship: A case study in Jordan. The Journal of Asian Finance. *Economics and Business*, *8*(5), 807–815.

Thasnimol, C. M., & Rajathy, R. (2021). Vector Error Correction Model for Distribution Dynamic State Estimation. Springer Science and Business Media Deutschland GmbH. doi:10.1007/978-981-15-8815-0_2

Torun, Akdeniz, Demireli, & Grima. (2022). Long-Term US Economic Growth and the Carbon Dioxide Emissions Nexus: A Wavelet-Based Approach. *Sustainability, 14*. doi:10.3390/su141710566

World Bank. (2023). *Firms with female participation in ownership (% of firms).* Author.

Yoshida, S., Yagi, H., Kiminami, A., & Garrod, G. (2019). Farm diversification and sustainability of multifunctional peri-urban agriculture: Entrepreneurial attributes of advanced diversification in Japan. *Sustainability (Basel)*, *11*(10), 2887. doi:10.3390u11102887

Chapter 4
Unlocking Algeria's Economic Potential:
The Entrepreneurship's Effect on Growth

Amira Driss
University of Ain Temouchent, Algeria

Naima Bentouir
University of Ain Temouchent, Algeria

ABSTRACT

The distinction between entrepreneurship and rent-seeking is acknowledged, highlighting the significant role that entrepreneurship education plays in fostering employment opportunities, productivity, economic growth, innovation, and competitiveness. This approach ultimately enhances a country's standing in the global market. This study aims to evaluate the effect of entrepreneurship on Algeria's economic development. Using annual data from 2006 to 2020, the Autoregressive Distributed Lag (ARDL) co-integration methodology is used to accomplish this. The analysis's main conclusions show that the variables of interest have a consistent, long-term relationship. Furthermore, the findings show that tertiary education (as a percentage of gross enrollment), new business density, and school enrolment all positively influence GDP growth over the short and long terms. These results offer strong proof of the beneficial impact of entrepreneurship on economic growth.

DOI: 10.4018/978-1-6684-7127-2.ch004

I. INTRODUCTION

Entrepreneurs are the engine of economic expansion and innovation (Abdelli, Ul-Durar, & Wasef Hattab, 2023). Generally speaking, the economy has experienced significant change, particularly in recent decades. Research on the factors contributing to economic growth has expanded, as has the emphasis on indicators of the economy's sustainability. As a result, entrepreneurship and its impact on economic growth rates have come under closer scrutiny. Since Schumpeter's initial works, the notion of a strong and positive correlation between entrepreneurship and economic growth has undoubtedly spread around three key concepts:

First idea: Innovations are the primary source of long-term growth.

Entrepreneurial investments (in R&D, training, computer purchases, etc.) yield second-idea innovations. Economic incentives produced by institutions and policies about the economy also influence entrepreneurs. Stated differently, growth built on innovation is a social process involving growth policies and institutions.

The third concept is creative destruction, whereby new inventions supplant outdated technology; hence, the term "political economy of growth" (Aghion, 2018, p. 696) when a result, when more people become entrepreneurs, economic growth will rise because of their abilities and, more specifically, their tendency to innovate (Dejardin, 2012, p. 2).

In emerging nations especially, the majority of economists are attempting to provide answers to the following questions: How can economic growth be improved, and what are the growth conductors (I. D. Maja, Krsticbojan, & Radenovic, 2022, p. 66). Almost all emerging nations struggle with two main problems: the first is how to achieve and the second is how to maintain economic growth. Maintaining a rapid pace of growth is more challenging in developing nations (Arshad & Munir, 2017, p. 183). This caused many countries to reevaluate how they implement their economic policies. Algeria, in particular, with its sizable youth labor force and low-income level, was severely affected and began to shift its policies to support entrepreneurship as an exciting means of growth.

Regarding entrepreneurship as one of the primary drivers of economic growth, the Algerian economy has shifted its attention from natural resources to the skills and abilities of individuals in entrepreneurship. This has been achieved by differentiating between entrepreneurship and rent-seeking, and by realizing the important role that entrepreneurship education plays in creating job opportunities, productivity, economic growth, innovation, and competitiveness as well as in enhancing the competitiveness of nations in the international market. Therefore, the study's focus is on how entrepreneurship has affected economic growth in Algeria's economy between 2006 and 2021.

II. LITERATURE REVIEW

The majority of empirical study has been done to explain how entrepreneurship in Algeria contributes to economic progress; many academics believe that entrepreneurship effectively plays a role in emerging nations' economies, as follows (Klapper, Amit, Guillén, & Quesada, 2009): According to The World Bank Group Entrepreneurship, this database contains cross-country, time-series data on the total and newly registered businesses in 101 countries for the maximum period of 2000 to 2008, which is used in this paper to provide new evidence on entrepreneurship and firm formation across countries. The quality of the legal and regulatory framework, governance, and measures of economic and financial development and growth have substantial correlations with entrepreneurial activity in this study. The data demonstrates how crucial electronic registration processes are to promoting more business registration. These findings can inform wise policy decisions and provide fresh tools for evaluating the effects of changes. SMEs, which stands for small- and medium-sized enterprises, are likely to be the most susceptible to economic hardships (Khalil, Abdelli, & Mogaji, 2022). However, they tend to focus on low-value products and services instead of high-value ones (Arabeche Z, Soudani A, Brahmi M, Vinci CP, & MEA., 2022). In Algeria, various incubators have been established across the country to support the development of small and medium-sized enterprises (SMEs) (Zina Arabeche & Abdelli, 2021).

Bunyasrie (2010)'s goal is to provide a critical analysis of theoretical and empirical studies on the relationship between entrepreneurship and economic growth, as well as any policy implications. Compared to high-income and transitional countries, research shows that entrepreneurship has no appreciable effect on economic growth in low-income countries. Consequently, the divergent results may be explained by the absence of growth-oriented entrepreneurs in low-income nations and the fact that most new businesses in these nations are born out of necessity, as opposed to high-income nations where entrepreneurship is believed to be opportunity-driven (Arabeche Z et al., 2022).

Overall, the study suggested that the government should play a crucial role in supporting new experiences in the economy by offering investment guarantees to entrepreneurs, assisting in establishing connections and networks, fostering social innovation, suggesting incentives for businesses and research institutions, and promoting private employment and labour (Zaki & Rashid, 2016). In this work, the effects of entrepreneurship on economic growth in seven developing nations (Egypt, Hungary, India, Mexico, Indonesia, Turkey, and Romania) between 2004 and 2014 are examined using regression analysis. The level of baseline GDP, entrepreneurship, and labour productivity are the only elements that significantly affect economic growth in emerging countries, according to the findings of testing and verifying OLS assumptions. On the other hand, there has been no discernible impact of physical capital, postsecondary education, or research & development spending on economic growth. As anticipated, there is a positive correlation between the country's economic growth and both the GDP level and the growth in labor productivity. The relationship between entrepreneurship and economic growth was found to be significantly inverse, which highlights the significance of other factors like institutional framework and investment in "new economy" sectors in influencing this relationship (Lepojević, Đukić, & Mladenović, 2016). This paper compares the effects of various forms of entrepreneurship on GDP growth rates in developed and developing nations. It also looks at the variations in the effects of entrepreneurship on economic performance over a three-year period in a sample of 22 countries, with developed nations being Belgium and France. Finland, Denmark Island of France Italy, Japan, the Netherlands, Norway, and Slovenia Britain, USA, Spain, and rising nations like Serbia România Turkey; Bosnia and Herzegovina Colombia Standing on seven important macroeconomic factors are the following: GDP Growth Rate, Gross Capital Formation, Foreign Direct Investment, Labour Force, Opportunity Entrepreneurial Activity, High-expectation Entrepreneurship, and Necessity Entrepreneurial Activity (Dominican Republic, Venezuela, South African Republic). Research indicates that industrialised countries see a greater contribution from entrepreneurship towards economic development when compared to emerging nations. which support the dominance of HEA and OEA entrepreneurship, which is more significant for GDP growth than NEA, which is more common in developing nations (Khyareh & Amini, 2021). This study uses data from the Global Entrepreneurship Monitor (GEM) to apply a three-stage least squares (3SLS) regression to examine the effects of six governance indicators on the growth of entrepreneurship in 64 countries between 2010 and 2018: GDP, labor productivity, capital in a country, trade openness, inflation rate, and final government consumption. The findings demonstrated that economic growth is significantly influenced by entrepreneurship and governance factors. Depending on the nation's current state of development. In particular, the results note that entrepreneurship can accelerate economic growth in countries driven by innovation as opposed to countries driven by efficiency and other variables. However, (ODE) only has a positive correlation with innovation-driven economic growth. In contrast, the economic growth of countries driven by factors and efficiency is adversely connected with (NDE). Furthermore, the survey results demonstrate that in the three categories of nations analyzed, entrepreneurial activity is positively correlated with governance quality metrics (Ivanovic Đukic & Tamara, 2022). This study examines the effects of different forms of entrepreneurship on growth in emerging markets using data from the Global Entrepreneurship Monitor (GEM) to identify the profitable types of entrepreneurship. For the years 2011–2018, the panel data analysis of 20 emerging nations (Argentina, Brazil, Chile, Colombia, Estonia, Greece, Hungary,

India, and Indonesia) revealed regression results that showed entrepreneurship had a negligible positive impact on economic growth due to various flaws in the entrepreneurial ecosystem. The results also show that innovative entrepreneurship has a statistically significant beneficial influence on economic growth, in contrast to necessity-driven entrepreneurship, which has a negative impact. to demonstrate that, in emerging markets, unproductive and harmful forms of entrepreneurship include necessity-driven entrepreneurship and informal entrepreneurship (I.-Đ. Maja, Tamara, & Talić, 2021). This paper examined the effects of four types of innovative entrepreneurship on GDP growth in emerging markets: new products entrepreneurship, new technology development entrepreneurship, high growth expectation entrepreneurship, and average growth expectation entrepreneurship. The goal was to identify the type of entrepreneurship that contributes most to economic growth and to propose actions that macroeconomic policy makers could take to achieve sustainable economic growth. Regression analysis was done to find out how different types of creative entrepreneurship affected economic growth in thirteen emerging markets. panel data covering Argentina, Brazil, Chile, China, Croatia, Estonia, Hungary, Latvia, Poland, Russia, Slovakia, Slovenia, and Uruguay from 2011 to 2018. Despite the high growth expectations associated with entrepreneurship in emerging nations, empirical study has shown that this sector contributes little yet statistically significantly to economic growth. Furthermore, the findings show that innovative entrepreneurship offering new items has a greater impact on economic growth than creative entrepreneurship offering new technologies (Bozkurt, 2020). This study's main goal was to investigate the connections between employment, entrepreneurship, and economic growth using data from a panel of 27 countries. From 2006 to 2016, a Panel (VECM) model was in use. The results indicate a one-way, short-term causal link between entrepreneurship and employment and growth. On the other hand, a lengthy study has found a unidirectional causal relationship between economic growth and employment, with the former being significantly influenced by entrepreneurship (Urbano & Aparicio, 2016). The impact of entrepreneurship capital types (operationalized through necessity TEA, opportunity TEA, and the most well-known GEM measure, overall TEA rates) on economic growth is investigated in this research. utilizing an unbalanced panel of data based on an expanded Cobb-Douglas production function for the years 2002–2012. The primary conclusions are as follows: First, there is proof that overall TEA and economic growth are positively correlated. Second, opportunity TEA and economic growth have a positive link, but with a smaller influence than overall TEA and a larger influence than necessity TEA (which is not statistically significant). These findings imply that entrepreneurship capital kinds particularly total and opportunity TEA may play a significant role in fostering economic expansion. Furthermore, it's critical that decision-makers rethink the tactics used in each nation to promote entrepreneurship. Entrepreneurial initiatives that are driven by opportunity analysis and exploration are critical for long-term growth. If not, entrepreneurial activity spurred by need could address immediate issues but have no bearing on long-term economic expansion.

III. MODEL SPECIFICATION AND METHOD

A. Data Description

Three main stages have been identified in the economic growth theory research process. The role of labour and material capital substitution was emphasised in the second stage, whereas the first stage focused on the value of physical capital. The focus of the third stage moved to how human capital contributes to economic growth. Investments in human capital can come from a variety of sources, including education (Abdelhadi & Eddine, 2021, p. 555).

Following an extensive analysis of empirical research, an estimate was developed about the contribution of entrepreneurship to Algeria's economic growth (Nachega & Fontaine, 2006; Shahzad & Munir, 2015; Zaki & Rashid, 2016). Based on yearly data spanning the years 2006–2020, we employed an Autoregressive Distributed Lag (ARDL) co-integration methodology, which included six important macroeconomic variables:

GDP growth rate in year t in country i;

GDPPPP in t-1 year the model incorporates a one-time period lag to control for the historical impact of GDP, which could be difficult to account for in other ways and potentially lead to present changes in the dependent variable. To put it another way, lagged GDP has been introduced to remove serial correlation because it has been estimated that the GDP's present values are a function of its historical values;

New Business Density as a proxy for entrepreneurship in year t;

Gross Kapital Formation measured as a % of GDP in year, representing physical capital, where (Long & H.Summers, 1991) proves that machinery and equipment investment has a strong association with growth by increasing the economy's capital stock, Which embodies the most advanced technological knowledge;

Growth in Labor Productivity

Tertiary school enrollment in year t represents human capital, where Becke (1993) and Jella and Bouzahzah (2012) the text emphasizes the positive impact of the quality of education on encouraging the accumulation of human capital, which in turn makes individuals more productive and innovative. This proves the vital link between education and economic growth. In developing countries, human capital is important in effectively adopting new technologies from abroad. The variables and analysis period were obtained from the World Bank and the Organization of Islamic Cooperation (OIC).

B. Model Selection

The "Autoregressive Distributed Lag (ARDL)" bound test is a new cointegration method that has gained considerable traction in recent research for determining long-term associations between variables. Its origins date back to 1996 when Pesaran and Shin initially introduced it, followed by further refinements from Pesaran and Pesaran (1997), Pesaran and Smith (1998), and Pesaran et al. (2001). The ARDL approach combines "Auto Regressive Distributed Lag" models to achieve its modeling technique. Stepwise delay models, also known as distributed lag DL models, which use Xt and its historical values as explanatory variables, and AR autoregressive models, which use historical values of the variable to be explained as explanatory factors (Benyakoub & Es-salmani, 2021, p. 4). The model comprises three key features:

- 1. Unlike most standard co-integration tests, which require a large sample size for more efficient findings, the ARDL test can be used with small sample sizes. It is comparatively more effective when dealing with tiny and finite sample data sizes (Hakima, Adem, & Abbes, 2020, p. 45).
- 2. It may be useful in situations where the running variables' integration order is unclear, such as when they are I(0), I(1), or I(0) / I(1), which is unacceptable in conventional methods. But none of the explanatory factors can be I(2) or higher, and the dependent variable must be of I(1) in levels (Fatukasi, Olorunleke, Olajide, & Alimi, 2015).
- 3. Using the ARDL technique, various variables may have varying ideal lag times (Pahlavan, Wilson, & Worthington, 2005, p. 8). Moreover, we can acquire objective estimations of the long-run model by using the ARDL technique (Belloumi, 2013, p. 10).

For optimal long-term parameter results, a sufficient number of time lags is required in the ARDL model. This model effectively distinguishes between short-term and long-term effects, and assesses the soundness of both the dependent and independent variables. Additionally, it enables us to determine the impact and magnitude of each independent variable on the dependent variable. The outlined methodology below summarizes the steps used.

Series of stationary order for ARDL model estimation, followed by bound, diagnostic, and parameter stability tests.

IV. EMPIRICAL RESULTS

1. Order of Stationary of Series

Several studies in the field of econometrics have been conducted to analyze economic data and to study the relationship between different economic variables (Stock & Watson, 1988; C & Plosse, 1982; J, 1991; Yule, 1926). Time series of macroeconomic variables can be unstable, as demonstrated during Yule in 1926, which gives rise to the spurious regression problem. This is seen by the deceptive outcomes that are produced even in the absence of a true relationship between the variables when R2 values are high. Therefore, it is essential to ensure the stability of variables before drawing any conclusions. In this study, we have utilized the Augmented Dickey Fuller (ADF) test, which is a widely used unit root test, to evaluate the stability of the time series. The null hypothesis assumes the existence of a unit root, which implies instability in the time series variable. The probability value is examined to test this hypothesis, with a threshold of 0.05. If the calculated ADF statistic surpasses the critical value, the null hypothesis is refuted, indicating the absence of a unit root and the stability of the time series variables.

Table 1. Stationary test using ADF

Variables	Lag	ADF						Decision
		Intercept		Trend and Intercept		None		
		Level	1st deff	level	1st deff	level	1st deff	
GDP growth	3	0.9760	0.1516	1.0000	0.2800	0.3904	0.0243**	*I(1)*
LogGDPPPP	3	0.1850	0.2188	0.4331	0.4676	0.9914	0.0653*	*I(1)*
Log NB	3	0.6382	0.0235	0.7619	0.0621*	0.7871	0.0024**	*I(1)*
GCF	3	0.1375	0.0706	0.6893	0.3411	0.8252	0.0057**	*I(1)*
LPgowth	3	0.0016***	0.0001***	0.0104**	0.0211**	0.0002***	0.0000***	*I(1)*
Edu-Ter	3	0.4815	0.3826	0.3208	0.1520	0.9185	0.2948	*I(1)*

Source: Authors

The phrase "significant at levels 1%, 5%, 10%, successively" means that the results of a statistical analysis are considered significant if they reach a certain level of probability. Specifically, if the probability of the results occurring by chance is less than 1%, they are considered significant at the 1% level. Similarly, if the probability is less than 5%, the results are significant at the 5% level, and if it is less than 10%, the results are significant at the 10% level.

As shown in Table 1, it is noticeable that all economic factors, aside from labor productivity growth, do not exhibit stationarity at a level below the critical value. This implies that the hypothesis of a unit root's presence can be accepted for these factors. But, upon taking the initial difference, all factors have achieved stability at a 5% abstract level. In simpler terms, all factors have an integration order of I(1), except for labor productivity growth, which is integrated at level and order I(0).

As per, (Mamta, 2004), the ADF test is not capable of distinguishing the statistics of time series effectively. Therefore, the Philips-Perron test will be conducted, which is known for providing accurate estimates in the case of series with serial correlation and non-constant variance.

Table 2 shows that all economic variables are not stable at the initial level, with a probability greater than 0.05, with the exception of labour productivity growth. As a result, there is data in favour of accepting the null hypothesis that a unit root exists. At the 5% threshold of significance, all variables stabilised following the initial difference. This implies that all variables, with the exception of labour productivity growth, which is constant at the starting level and has an order of integration of I(0), have an order of integration of I(1). The null hypothesis that the variables are not integrated can be rejected after comparing the data and accounting for the integration of the variables at I (0) and I (1) as well as the non-integration of the variables at the second degree. Therefore, we will use an autoregressive lag time lag (ARDL) model.

Table 2. Stationary test using Philips Perron

Variables	PP						Decision
	Intercept		Trend and Intercept		None		
	Level	1st deff	level	1st deff	level	1st deff	
GDP growth	0.9971	0.1516	0.9998	0.1640	0.3904	0.0223**	*I(1)*
LogGDPPPP	0.2193	0.2329	0.6743	0.4869	0.9816	0.0800*	*I(1)*
Log NB	0.6513	0.0218**	0.7619	0.0317	0.8009	0.0023***	*I(1)*
GCF	0.1375	0.0797*	0.6799	0.1261	0.8252	0.0059***	*I(1)*
LPgowth	0.0017***	0.0001***	0.0110**	0.0001***	0.0002***	0.0001***	*I(1)*
Edu-Ter	0.9488	0.5176	0.7263	0.9411	0.9974	0.2948	*I(1)*

***, **,* 1%, 5%, 10%.

Source: Authors

ARDL Model Estimation

The appropriate order of lags for variables must be determined prior to using the ARDL bounds testing method for cointegration (Fatukasi, Olorunleke, Olajide, & Alimi, 2015). To determine the optimal ARDL model, we extract the lag graph with the smallest AIC value, according to Akaike information criteria. In this case, ARDL (4,0,0,0,0,0) is the best (Figure 1).

Table 3. Unrestricted ARDL model

Variable	Coefficient	Prob.*
GDP_GROWTH__ANNUAL___(-1)	-1.992033	0.4815
GDP_GROWTH__ANNUAL___(-2)	-3.767400	0.5574
GDP_GROWTH__ANNUAL___(-3)	-0.283641	0.8992
GDP_GROWTH__ANNUAL___(-4)	2.369312	0.0676
LABOR_PRODUCTIVITY_GROWT	-0.582936	0.4695
NEW_BUSINESS_DENSITY__NE	1.8388	0.0483
SCHOOL_ENROLLMENT__TERTI	-1.048754	0.3820
GCF_GDP	0.412597	0.0520
GDPPPP	-1.61E-10	0.5088
C	80.92449	0.4958
0.049029 **Prob(F-statistic)** **Adjusted R-squared** 0.502431 **Durbin-Watson stat** 2.749893		

Source: Authors.

The outcomes of the unrestricted ARDL model are examined in Table 3. With an adjusted R-squared of 0.50, the independent variables (LogGDPPPP, NB, GCF, LPgowth, and Edu-Ter) account for 50% of the variation in GDP. Furthermore, the Fisher's probability value was less than 0.05, at 0.049029. This implies that it is possible to reject the null hypothesis, which states that all regressors have zero coefficients in all circumstances.

Bound Test

The Bounds Approach is a powerful tool used to determine whether a dependent variable and a group of explanatory variables have a long-term equilibrium relationship. This method involves conducting tests that use conventional F- and t-statistics to assess the statistical significance of the lagged levels of variables within a first-difference regression model.

This study presents two sets of asymptotic critical values. The first set assumes that all the regressors are integrated of order 1 (I(1)), while the second set assumes that all the regressors are integrated of order 0 (I(0)). These critical values encompass all possible classifications of the regressors into I(0), I(1), or mutually cointegrated states. As a result, several bounds testing approaches have been proposed.

The substantial uncertainty surrounding the varied integration sequence makes this application very pertinent (Pesaran, Shin, & Smith, 1999, p. 1).

Using the (4,0,0,0,0,0) model specification, a bound test is performed to ascertain whether cointegration is present. Evaluating the f-statistics against the upper bound critical values I(1) and the lower bound critical values I(0), as derived from Pesaran and Pesaran's (1997) research, is the limits test for cointegration. At a significance level of 5%, the resultant f-statistic surpasses the upper bound critical value of 3.79, as shown in Table 4. The dependent variable is export volume. This suggests that there is insufficient evidence to support the null hypothesis, which states that cointegration is absent. Consequently, it can be said that the variables have a cointegration connection (Seema & Nayaran, 2004, p. 106). Therefore, the variables LogGDPPPP, NB, GCF, LPgrowth, and Edu-Ter have a long-term relationship with GDP.

Table 4. ARDL bounds test

k	Value	Test Statistic
5	99.01548	**F-Statistic**
	Critical Value Bounds	
I(1) Bounds	**I(0) Bounds**	**Significance**
3.35	2.26	10%
3.79	2.62	5%
4.18	2.96	2.5%
4.68	3.41	1%

Source: Authors.

2. Diagnostic Tests

Before estimating the long-run and short-run parameters, diagnostic tests must be carried out to guarantee correct conclusions. These tests, which include the heteroscedasticity test, the no serial correlation test, and the Jarque-Bera test for residual normality, assess the power of the ARDL model. The outcomes of these

Table 5. Diagnostic tests

Test F	Statistics (p-Values)	Results
Jarque Berra Test Normality	0.669147 0.715643	Normal distribution
Heteroscedasticity: **Breusch-Pagan-Godfrey Test**	2.589463 0.4503	No Heteroscedasticity
Serial Correlation: **Breusch-Godfrey LM Test**	4.001604 0.0787	No serial correlation

Source: Authors.

tests are displayed in Table 5. Furthermore, Figure 02 attests to the lack of serial association.

3. Parameters Stability Test

It is important to conduct a thorough investigation on the stability of the model, even when no correlation is observed among the residuals. This is because having a co-integration relationship between variables does not necessarily ensure that the calculated coefficients are stable.

The analysis of Figure 3 reveals that the CUSUM line, depicted as a continuous line, stays within the bounds of the confidence limits, represented by the two dashed lines. This finding indicates that the model demonstrates temporal stability with a statistically significant level of 5%. As a result, we can deduce that the estimated parameters remain consistent throughout the study's duration, which supports moving forward to the next stage.

Long-Run and Short-Run Dynamics

In the field of macroeconomics, long-term consequences hold more significance than short-term implications. Therefore, this study primarily focuses on interpreting the long-term relationship between the variables. The study aims to provide a comprehensive analysis of the subject matter, examining the implications it holds for businesses and academia. The language employed in the study is formal and error-free, with a clear and concise presentation of the information. The study is informed by the use of appropriate vocabulary and grammar, which conveys professionalism and expertise, making it suitable for a business or academic setting. (Taallah & Chine, 2020, p. 7). The bound test identifies a long-run relationship between GDP and LogGDPPPP, NB, GCF, LPgrowth, and Edu-Ter. The estimated long-run parameters are shown in Table 6.

Table 6. Long run dynamic

Cointeq = GDP_G- (-0.0000*GDPPPP + 23.9291*NB -0.1247*LPG -0.2244*Edu__TER + 0.0883*GCF + 17.3146)	
Variables	**Coefficient**
LogGDPPPP	-0.000000 **0.3445**
Log NB	23.929062 **0.0736**
LPG	-0.124725 **0.5562**
Edu-Ter LPgowth	-0.224392 **0. 7761**
GCF	0.088279 **0.0362**

Source: Authors.

The variables New Business Density (NB) and Gross Capital Formation (GKF) have a positive and statistically significant impact on economic growth at a significance level of 10%. This implies that they make a meaningful contribution to the economy. A long-term convergence relationship between the two variables and economic growth justifies this finding. A 1% increase in New Business Density and Gross Capital Formation results in a significant long-term association of 23.93% and 0.09%, respectively. However, the relationship between growth in labor productivity and tertiary school enrollment and economic growth is not statistically significant. This can be attributed to the marginal impact of a 1% increase in these factors. In particular, the rise in growth in labor productivity and tertiary school enrollment is associated with a reduction of 0.56% and 0.77%, respectively. These findings suggest that the current economic system in Algeria may be inefficient, and the education sector should be prioritized for expansion to facilitate decision-making processes.The short-run model's results indicate an error correcting mechanism is present, as shown in Table 6. The negative sign and statistical significance at the 5% level of the coefficient for the error correction term, CointEq (-1), suggest its existence. Additionally, the CointEq coefficient of -4.67 indicates that deviations from the long-term growth rate in GDP are adjusted by 4.67%, equivalent to a speed of adjustment of 46.7%. However, both the net balance (NB) and government consumption expenditure (GCF) have a positive but statistically insignificant impact on short-term economic growth. In the short term, LPG (liquefied petroleum gas) and EDU-TER (education-tertiary) have a negative impact on economic growth, with the latter showing no meaningful influence.

Table 7. Short-run dynamic

Variables	Coefficient
D (LogGDPPPP)	-0.000000 **0.5088**
D(Log NB)	111.838752 **0.4838**
D(LPG)	-0.582936 **0.4695**
D(Edu-Ter LPgowth)	-1.048754 **0.3820**
D(GCF)	0.412597 **0.5200**
CointEq(-1)	-4.673762 **0.0486**

Source: Authors.

V. CONCLUSION

The purpose of this research is to determine whether or not entrepreneurship supports Algeria's economic expansion between 2006 and 2020. According to the ARDL model, Gross Capital Formation (GCF) and New Business Density (NBD) both positively and statistically significantly affect economic growth, demonstrating their contribution to growth. A 1% rise in new business intensity results in a growth rate increase of 23.93%, and a 1% increase in total capital formation leads to a growth rate increase of 0.09%. These data demonstrate a long-term convergence relationship between the two variables and economic growth. Although the Algerian economy has shown improvement in a few quantitative measures, challenges remain. It has been determined that the nation's educational policies impede advancement. For instance, a 1% rise in college enrollment and labour productivity growth can each add 0.56 and 0.77 percent to economic stagnation, respectively. Therefore, more investigation is required into the elements, such as total factor productivity, that support entrepreneurship and economic growth in Algeria. Recently, decision-makers in Algeria have shown even more interest in helping people advance their knowledge and expertise in the fields of development and entrepreneurship. Rather than depending entirely on natural resources, they intend to accomplish this by making use of their sizable youth labour force. In order to implement this strategy, it is necessary to differentiate between entrepreneurship and rent-seeking and acknowledge the important role that entrepreneurship education plays in generating employment possibilities. Increased productivity, economic growth, innovation, competitiveness, and the nation's ability to compete on the international stage are the objectives of these initiatives.

REFERENCES

Abdelhadi, M., & Eddine, K. A. (2021). The Impact of Human Capital on Economic Growth in Algeria During the Period 1970-2018: Application of ARDL Approach to Cointegration. *Strategy and Development Review*, *11*(3), 554–571. doi:10.34276/1822-011-003-030

Abdelli, M., Ul-Durar, S., & Wasef Hattab, H. (2023). Entrepreneurship Ecosystems and Their Opportunities and Challenges. IGI Global. doi:10.4018/978-1-6684-7140-1

Aghion, P. (2018). Innovation and Growth from a Schumpeterian Perspective. Dalloz. *Revue d'Économie Politique*, *128*(5), 693–711. doi:10.3917/redp.285.0693

Arabeche & Abdelli. (2021). The New Trends Technology of Entrepreneurship in the Incubators A Case Study of Cyberpark Sidi Abdallah. In *Big Data for Entrepreneurship and Sustainable Development.* Taylor and Francis.

Arabeche, Z., Soudani, A., Brahmi, M., Aldieri, L., Vinci, C. P., & Abdelli, M. E. A. (2022, April 25). Entrepreneurial Orientation, Organizational Culture and Business Performance in SMEs: Evidence from Emerging Economy. *Sustainability (Basel)*, *14*(9), 5160. Advance online publication. doi:10.3390u14095160

Arshad, S., & Munir, K. (2017). Factor Accumulation and Economic Growth in Pakistan: Incorporating Human Capital. *International Journal of Social Economics*, *45*, 180–199.

Becke, G. S. (1993). Human Capital-A Theoretical and Empirical Analysis with Special Reference to Education (3rd ed.). The University of Chicago Press.

Belloumi, M. (2013). The relationship between Trade, FDI and Economic growth in Tunisia: An application of autoregressive distributed lag model. *Economic Systems*, 269–287.

Benyakoub, B., & Es-salmani, M. (2021). The ARDL bounds cointegration test for the verification of the. *Revue Internationale du Chercheur*, *2*(4), 1–24.

Bozkurt, E. (2020). Is The Entrepreneurship Still Popular as A Growth Dynamic? *Journal of Academic Value Studies*, *6*(2), 225–230. doi:10.29228/javs.42914

Bunyasrie, V. (2010). THE Role of Entrepreneurship on Economic Growth. *Executive Journal*, 149-156.

C, N., & Plosse, C. (1982). Trends and Random Walks in Macroeconomic Time Series: Some Evidence and Implications. *Journal of Money Economics*, 10.

Dejardin, M. (2012). entrepreneurship and economic growth: An obvious conjunction? *CORE*.

Fatukasi, B., Olorunleke, G. K., Olajide, G. F., & Alimi, R. S. (2015). Bounds Testing Approaches to the Analysis of Macroeconomic Relationships In Nigeria. *European Journal of Business and Management*, *7*(8), 26–34.

Hakima, L., Adem, H., & Abbes, B. E. (2020). Investment in education and economic growth: ARDL Model. *Economic Sciences, Management and Commercial Sciences Review, 13*(2), 39-50.

Ivanovic Đukic, M. B., & Tamara, R. (2022). Entrepreneurship and economic growth in emerging markets: An empirical analysis. *Acta Oeconomica*, *72*(1), 65–84. doi:10.1556/032.2022.00004

J, M. J. (1991). *Critical Values for Co integration Test in Long-Run Relationships: Reading in Co integration*. Oxford University Press.

Jella, M., & Bouzahzah, M. (2012). Governance education and economic growth. *Munich Personal RePEc Archive*, 1-19.

Khalil, A., Abdelli, M. E. A., & Mogaji, E. (2022). Do Digital Technologies Influence the Relationship between the COVID-19 Crisis and SMEs' Resilience in Developing Countries? *Journal of Open Innovation*, *8*(2), 100. doi:10.3390/joitmc8020100

Khalil, A., Abdelli, M. E. A., & Mogaji, E. (2022). *Do Digital Technologies Influence the Relationship between the COVID-19 Crisis and SMEs' Resilience in Developing Countries?* Academic Press.

Khyareh, M. M., & Amini, H. (2021). Governance Quality, Entrepreneurship and Economic Growth. *Journal of Competitiveness*, *13*(2), 41–64. doi:10.7441/joc.2021.02.03

Klapper, L., Amit, R., Guillén, M. F., & Quesada, J. M. (2009). *Entrepreneurship and Firm Formation Across Countries*. Research Gate.

Lepojević, V., Đukić, M. I., & Mladenović, J. (2016). Entrepreneurship and economic development: A comparative analysis of developed and developing countries. *Economics and Organization*, *13*(1), 17–29.

Long, J. D., & Summers, H. (1991). Equipment Investment and Economic Growth. *The Quarterly Journal of Economics*, *106*(2), 445–502. doi:10.2307/2937944

Maja, I. D. (2022). Entrepreneurship and economic growth in emerging markets: An empirical analysis. *Acta Oeconomica*, *72*(1), 65–84. doi:10.1556/032.2022.00004

Maja, I.-Đ., Tamara, R., & Talić, M. (2021). Innovative entrepreneurship and economic growth in emerging markets. *ЕКОНОМИКА*, *67*(4), 55–64.

Mamta, C. (2004). *Currency Crisis and Stock Prices in East Asian Countries:an Applicatin of Cointegratin Granger Causality*. School of Economics and Finance.

Nachega, J.-C., & Fontaine, T. (2006). Economic Growth and Total Factor Productivity in Niger. *International Monetary Fund Working Papers*, 1-28.

Pahlavan, M., Wilson, E., & Worthington, A. C. (2005). Trade-GDP Nexus in Ir ade-GDP Nexus in Iran: An Application of the Autoregressive Distributed e Distributed Lag (ARDL) Model. *Social and Behavioral Sciences Commons*, 1-23.

Pesaran, M. H., Shin, Y., & Smith, R. J. (1999). Bounds Testing Approaches to the Analysis of Long-run Relationships. Edinburgh School of Economics.

Seema, N., & Nayaran, P. K. (2004). Determinants of Demand for FIJI's Exports an Ampirical Investigation. *The Developing Economies*, 95–112.

Shahzad, A., & Munir, K. (2015). *Factor Accumulation and Economic Growth in Pakistan: Incorporating Human Capital.* Munich Personal RePEc Archive.

Stock, J. H., & Watson, M. W. (1988). Testing for Common Trends. *Journal of American Statistical Association, 83*.

Taallah, L., & Chine, L. (2020). Total Factor Productivity and Sources of Economic Growth in Algeria (1970-2018) by Uusing ARDL Approach. *Revue des Réformes Economiques et Intégration En Economie Mondiale*, *14*(03), 1–11.

Urbano, D., & Aparicio, S. (2016). *Entrepreneurship capital types and economic growth: International evidence.* Science Direct.

Yule, G. (1926). Why Do We Some Times Get Nonsense-Correlations Between Time-Series? A Study in Sampling and the Nature of Time-Series. *Journal of the Royal Statistical Society*, 89.

Zaki, I. M., & Rashid, N. H. (2016). Entrepreneurship Impact on Economic Growth in Emerging Countries. *The Business and Management Review*, *7*(2), 31–39.

Chapter 5
The Legal Framework Start-Ups in Algeria:
Applications and Solutions

Soumia Benchouat
Djilali Liabes University, Algeria

Riadh Kadri
University Center Maghnia, Algeria

Mohammed El Amine Abdelli
University of Brest, France

Naima Bentouir
Ain Temouchent University, Algeria

Lorenzo Mateo Bujosa Vadell
University of Salamanca, Spain

ABSTRACT

The main goal of this academic investigation is to improve theoretical and practical understanding of the startup industry. This includes a thorough analysis of the essential elements and drivers that support the development of a healthy ecosystem. A thorough examination of numerous models' representative of startup ecosystems, including the 3M model, improved from the previous 5M framework, is at the heart of this endeavour. This model is the focus of the analysis because of its extreme importance. The inquiry also looks at how it might be used in Algeria, where the model's components are sharply projected onto the local topography. An extremely thorough examination follows, with a special emphasis on Executive Decree No. 20/254, a piece of legislation outlining the boundaries of startups and their legal requirements. This thorough evaluation helps us understand the complex interactions between conceptual frameworks, legal definitions, and practical implementation.

DOI: 10.4018/978-1-6684-7127-2.ch005

INTRODUCTION

The business world today is undergoing rapid change. Its viewpoints are more frequently linked to new scientific understanding, applications, and quick worldwide technological transfers. Transferring the outcomes of research and development into industrial life is made possible by various inventive businesses (Peterková, Czerná et al. 2022). Schumpeter (1912) theorized about entrepreneurs' role in the well-known process of "creative destruction" or innovation more than a century ago (Motoyama and Knowlton 2017).

The concept of startups is based on the embodiment of innovative ideas on the ground and considering innovation as the pillar of entrepreneurship. It is known that entrepreneurship contributes to economic growth and development (Berger & Kuckertz, 2016), which are considered the goal of different countries, and on this basis are adopted and supported centres to activate the field of entrepreneurship and contribute to the formation of an entrepreneurial community by various governments (Hechavarria & Ingram, 2014). In other word startup is a company that is just starting to run its activities (Bhatt, Saurabh et al. 2022). The entrepreneurial community can be defined as the individuals estimated for the entrepreneurial field aware that it is the driving force of growth and economic development. (Audretsch, 2009).

According to research, entrepreneurs spur innovation, accelerate economic structural changes, introduce new competition, and contribute to productivity, job creation, and national competitiveness (Rehman, Arif et al. 2022). As a result, entrepreneurship is essential for socioeconomic development and prosperity since it immediately affects employment by generating new positions and encouraging innovation. It is widely acknowledged that innovation is essential to economic expansion. Start-up businesses, which are human institutions designed to create a new product or service under conditions of extreme uncertainty, have been explicitly linked to it. In this regard, the majority of developed countries institutionally support the growth of start-ups by streamlining the regulatory framework governing their establishment and operation, fostering an environment that is conducive to investment, and fostering direct interaction with the educational community and other segments of the community (Ziakis, Vlachopoulou et al. 2022).

What the world can support inevitably limits the urge to reach ever-higher levels of economic development (Danquah, Mensah et al. 2023). One of the biggest threats to every society on the globe, not just the environment as a whole, is the violation of planetary boundaries, which are the natural limits of so-called earth system processes. However, possibilities often arise from global issues, particularly for businesspeople who can give solutions by generating value that lessens the effects of those issues. The idea that there is more room for entrepreneurial activity the bigger the problem, according to the academic discourse on entrepreneurship. This is due to the fact that when market processes are ineffective, adverse ecological consequences might present opportunity for sustainable enterprises (Kuckertz, Berger et al. 2019).

The ecosystem of startups is the basis that ensures their emergence and success, and in this regard, we find Silicon Valley, which is an example of a thriving ecosystem of startups, but it is known that imitating them elsewhere is challenging to produce the same results, and this is due to the characteristics related to each region of cultures, customs, and traditions.

The research paper provides an academic contribution related to the concept of startups and the nature of the term that is widely spread, and we also address the ecosystem that supports and makes these institutions appear on the ground last. We move on to discuss the situation of startups in Algeria, whether from a legal point of view or in terms of the existing ecosystem, as well as addressing the challenges faced by startups in Algeria.

First: Startups and their business environment

1. DEFINITION OF STARTUPS

The term startups appeared, and interpretations differed in its meanings, and its emergence dates back to after World War II with the emergence of venture capital companies, where it began to be used and traded (Vodwa et al., 2021, p. 117). Referring to the meaning of the term, differed in its definition by many researchers, but its meaning can be interpreted according to the French dictionary that the term means projects or institutions active in the field of technology and newly established., The English dictionary is the beginning of the beginning, in the sense of a new project, any newly established, and high and intended to refer to high growth. The term has also evolved and is commonly used in balance with the development of global life at the social or economic level (Dictionary, 2021; Larousse, 2021).

In an explanation of the term start-ups over time, we find the variation in the definitions provided by different researchers and compatibility in some points, of which we find that the term expresses the early years of the beginning of the institution's activity (Bruyat, 1993, p. 295), as the name is given to a startup in the project's first three to five years (Sammut, 1996, p. 12). It is also defined as the subsequent stage of the legal establishment of the institution, and it is also defined as the newly established institution where it was recently created; one of its advantages is the presence of innovation, whether in its field of activity or the way it manages or markets its products, and it is an institution characterized by the rapid growth of its sales and capital (SAMMUT 1998, Hurel 2000) Quoting (Cauvin & Bescos, 2002, p. 3). The startup is also defined as characterized by innovation and technology and is known for its rapid development and growth in the appropriate environment as it is a small and medium enterprise (Cauvin & Bescos, 2002, p. 3). They are innovative enterprises that exist in their sales and marketing activities, and operate in an uncertain potential market, resulting in risk-taking trade (Marty, 2002, p. 7), which starts from scratch (Kolvereid & Isaksen, 2006). Quoting Montani et al. (2020), in addition, these organizations operate in markets where there is extreme uncertainty as a result of introducing new products to the market, and operate according to a reproducible and scalable business model; therefore, startups face the risk of repeated failure as they work according to the principle of continuous learning from their customers to adapt their decisions to the required needs and improve the innovative product or service (Blank and Dorf 2012; Ries 2012; Blank, 2013, p. 5). Thus, a market-driven market-fighting organization works to ensure growth (Salamzadeh & Kawamorita Kesim, 2015, p. 1). It relies on modern technologies and the amount of knowledge-intensive in carrying out its main activity and is characterized by high and rapid growth with the availability of innovation (Passaro et al., 2017, p. 3).

The concept of the emerging institution can be defined as an institution based on innovation with a new product or service that creates its markets and meets unmet needs; as it works in a state of extreme uncertainty, it relies in its work on flexibility in its organization and has an innovative business model that can be repeated, as this allows it to develop and proliferate, it is often exposed to repeated failures before its success. It is considered a temporary stage that separates the beginning of the institution and the embodiment of the idea, and the emerging institution emerges to grow and achieve development.

2. START-UPS UNDER ALGERIAN LAW

The law of any country is considered the reference for building social and economic foundations, and the term emerging institutions has evolved with the development of life in the whole world; this is what necessitated countries to find legal texts that define this new type of institutions, and Algeria, like other countries, developed Executive Decree No. 20/254 of September 15, 2020, which legally governs Algerian emerging enterprises and controls their concept, as they are defined according to the decree by requiring a set of conditions, represented in:

- The start-up is based in Algeria and subject to Algerian law. Its lifespan is eight years, divided into two four-year phases during which the competent authority evaluates the start-up.
- Its turnover should not exceed 4 billion Algerian dinars, and the number of workers should not exceed 250.

- Innovation and growth are two conditions, as innovation requires its presence in the product or service provided by the startup, while growth, is related to the future of the startup, where its aspirations must have high growth potential.
- To own a capital that must be at least 50% owned by another startup, investment funds, or natural persons.

The Algerian legislature specified the total conditions under which the mark of a startup is granted. The definition of startups worldwide is respected, as it stipulates the innovative idea in producing goods and services while ensuring the growth potential of the startup activity, which is what most of the definitions agreed upon from the studies that studied startups. However, it notes some contradictions, as the turnover was roofed at 4 billion dinars. Referring to the condition of high growth potential, the specified business number may be relatively small; that is, the emerging institution may exceed its stage of growth, but the Algerian legislator has a look from another door that may be taking into account that the emerging institution is only a stage and graduates to become a small, medium or large enterprise, as well as about the number of workers that does not exceed 250 workers, which is observed in the launch of the startup. However, the possibility of exceeding this number remains at the growth stage of the emerging enterprise; here, it is noted that the analogy with small and medium enterprises has been approximated in terms of turnover. The number of workers, but the emerging enterprise dealing with the innovative idea of its product differs in the stages it passes compared to traditional institutions.

3. STARTUP BUSINESS ENVIRONMENT

3.1 Definition of the Business Environment for Startups

Business environments vary from one country to another, each according to its surroundings. However, it is agreed that the business environment is characterized by complexity resulting from the number of components and the relationships between these components that constitute the entire ecosystem. It is about supporting entrepreneurial work, especially by linking the scientific parts of knowledge and technology that lead to the emergence of successful and sustainable businesses that contribute to creating high-level jobs to ensure quality of life (Krajcik & Formanek, 2015, p. 14).

The business environment has evolved about emerging enterprises with the development of these types of institutions that need a unique environment that contributes to their emergence and development, which depends on adopting an effective way to promote regional innovations and provide new ideas that, in turn, contribute to the development of the business environment while providing new jobs and GDP growth (Krajcik & Formanek, 2015, p. 14).

An ecosystem for startups has been provided and well implemented in a few places, especially Silicon Valley, where London and Berlin are the few models that can be emulated (Berger & Kuckertz, 2016, p. 2). The transition of enterprises to providing ecosystem conditions is considered a significant paradigm shift (Kenney & Von Burg, 1999).

3.2 Structural Components of the Startup Ecosystem

Perspectives on the components of the startup ecosystem vary according to the backgrounds and theories of researchers and analysts. Efficiency mass theory (Gunnard Eliasson & Eliasson, 1996). The components of the startup ecosystem can be grouped by economic operators in 1. Competent and active customers, 2. Innovators who integrate technologies in new ways, 3. Contractors Who recognize profitable innovations, 4. Competent venture capitalists who recognize and finance Contractors, 5. Exit from markets that facilitate change of ownership and move to new projects, 6. Industrialists who move successful innovations into production on an industrial scale (Gunnar Eliasson, 2001, p. 226).

The business environment also consists of start-ups, various political agencies incubators and accelerators, and venture capital provider (Kenney & Von Burg, 1999) as we find a framework 3M, which urges that in order to build a new project, there must be a market (Market) and money (Money) and management (Management) (Bates et al., 2007), which has been expanded to include the medium environment (Meat) and college (Macro and go to the framework 5M (Brush et al., 2009). Note that the medium environment is related to regional support and public policies, while the macro environment is related to cultural and social aspects (Berger & Kuckertz, 2016, p. 2).

However finding a local startup ecosystem that brings together all economic actors is very rare (Breznitz & Taylor, 2014). The startup ecosystem is not just a set of constituent elements but a procedural process that allows building successful startups (Peters, 2009).

The startup ecosystem results from the participation of the various entities involved, taking into account the importance of the social environment and economic culture, where it is essential to focus on social networks with the emergence of the technological superiority of the entrepreneurial ecosystem (Breznitz & Taylor, 2014).

From the above, the ecosystem can be considered a complex dynamic system where elements interact with it. Definitions and models vary to determine a thriving ecosystem. However, it is considered successful Every ecosystem pushes emerging institutions to emerge and emerge. It can also be seen as a social system in which new, innovative, and creative ideas appear that are transformed into fundamental institutions and companies that provide job opportunities and contribute to social development after its development, in which the various links between the prominent emerging institution and the external environment contribute, Thus, the interrelationship between the startup and the elements of the ecosystem emerges, as both contribute to the development and development of the other.

Second: the reality and challenges of algerian startups in light of the business environment.

1. STARTUPS IN ALGERIA

Through its policies, Algeria encourages the creation of public institutions, and Figure (01) shows the number of institutions that were established in the first semester of 2021, where the number reached 2,164,037 institutions, combining 215,332 institutions with legal personality and 1,984,805 individual institutions with a natural personality, which is a significant number of institutions, reflecting Algeria's interest in encouraging the establishment of public institutions, which is observed in the growth and increase in the total business intensity rate from 2.55 institutions per 1,000 adult citizens in 2010 to 3.77 institutions per 1000 people. (World Bank).

Clearly, Algeria cares about its business climate and encourages the establishment of institutions, and this is what previous statistics show With the development of reality and the emergence of emerging institutions in the field, Algeria welcomed these types of institutions on its land and facilitated work for holders of ideas to establish their emerging institutions without restriction to step after this and put the law above to control the concept of emerging enterprises in the land of Algeria. Algeria ranked 2021 fifth in Africa regarding technological startups after Nigeria, Egypt, South Africa, and Kenya; it raised US$30 million, as shown in Figure 2:

What is noted about startups is that Algeria shined in the field of transport, as it is considered the first in Africa in the field, thanks to the startup Yassir, which obtained in previous years the highest financing value reached in 2022, 150 million US dollars, which exceeds what was collected by startups in the field of transport in other countries such as South Africa and Nigeria, which is supported by Figure 3.

Figure 4 shows that Yassir, which was established in 2016 and is active in the field of people transport, is the first in terms of funds raised compared to other startups in Algeria in 2022, amounting to 218 million US dollars, followed by the startup General Emballage, which is active in the field of packaging, where the amount raised in 2022 was about 55 million, which represents about a quarter of what was raised from the Yassir Foundation.

2. THE CHALLENGES OF ALGERIAN STARTUPS IN LIGHT OF THE BUSINESS ENVIRONMENT

The startup has many challenges, and they vary according to their types (Shepherd et al., 2000, p. 395). Startups in Algeria face several challenges due to their nature and the ecosystem of Algerian business because they rely on innovative ideas in their products that make their viability and continuity difficult and the probability of failure high due to the high risks associated with innovation, the challenges facing this type of institution can be summarized in (Othman and Arabi, 2020):

- Funding: One of the biggest challenges facing startups is finding funding to invest in the innovative idea at the beginning of the road, as the innovative idea imposes an unknown market, which makes predicting the market and customer behavior weak, which leads to a lack of interested investors due to the high degree of risk, as they avoid investing their money in projects that they do not know the extent of their success. However, it remains a challenge that can be overcome through modern means of financing the launch of startups, such as crowdfunding platforms available at the level of the Arab or international world, which is done by presenting the idea and explaining it on the platform to be seen by interested investors belonging to the platform and investing in it, and then after the success of the idea and its development, the project begins to grow, which requires significant funds, if not huge, which requires huge investments to achieve rapid and significant growth, as it is considered one of the characteristics of emerging institutions.
- The size and conditions of the market: As emerging institutions generally keep pace with developments and due to the small size of the market for these emerging institutions, in addition to the prevailing business conditions of the weakness of the Internet to some extent, the lack of multiple methods of electronic payment and so on, this makes it somewhat difficult to market and distribute the institution's products to reach the largest segment of customers, and it remains a challenge for emerging institutions where many contractors have found a way to penetrate the market and market their products by finding other alternatives.
- Lack of experience among the owners of emerging institutions: The creation of a startup needs diverse experience and a great scientific and technical level, where the lack of experience makes the project holder means others who may

invest their experience in the emerging institution, the emerging institution needs a special deal in the management of the unknown that it faces in light of the marketing of innovative products and penetrating relatively new markets or completely for this often and due to the lack of experience and the need for it, we find this type of institution intended support mechanisms such as incubators and accelerators.

- Team: Most successful startups in the world started with a team that pushes them to succeed, and the challenge facing startups at this point is to find a supportive team with the necessary competencies, especially in that the beginning of the idea and the launch of the institution is with minimal resources, so the owner of the idea goes to the circle of acquaintances and relatives, and the challenge remains in finding the appropriate team members to advance and develop the idea.

3. STARTUPS IN ALGERIA BETWEEN THE LEGAL FRAMEWORK AND THE REGULATION OF THE BUSINESS ENVIRONMENT

As mentioned above, it is difficult to identify the elements of a thriving startup ecosystem. However, with the diligence of researchers, several elements that make up this ecosystem have been identified, including the 5M model, which includes the 3M model mentioned earlier; we will project these components on the startup environment in Algeria in the legal framework regulating them:

3.1 Microenvironment Analysis

- Funding: It is considered one of the biggest and most important challenges in the whole world, where the lack of access to appropriate funding in a timely manner means the cessation of work on the idea, and the disruption of the establishment of the institution in terms of transforming the idea into a commercial reality or in terms of expanding the institution to achieve the required growth; The Algerian state is trying to alleviate this challenge by seeking to implement a set of auxiliary decisions, including granting facilities and setting a flexible legal framework for venture capital institutions under Law 06 – 11 of June 24, 2006 relating to venture capital companies, which are companies that provide the required capital to startups where they bear the risks associated with innovative ideas, as we find Executive Decree 16-205 of July 25, 2016 on the modalities for establishing, managing and practicing the activity of the Investment Funds Management Company, which regulates the functioning of venture capital, venture or venture capital companies due to the risk associated with investing funds in startups at the start-up stage, Transformation or growth and expansion; Also, incubators, which came with Executive Decree 20-254, provide a variety of services, including financing services, as they collect sources of funding to help startups when searching for funds for investment, as well as the Startup Support Fund was established under Article 131 of the Finance Law for the year 2020, where it finances the burdens of the project and bears the risks associated with startups, and it is remarkable to finance Institutions that have received the label of "start-up" after meeting certain conditions by a special committee that has been created, all this is in the desire of the state to accompany projects based on innovation and specialization in accompanying start-ups within the framework of supporting entrepreneurship in Algeria.

- Market: The startup contractor in the Algerian market suffers with regard to the availability of means to facilitate integration into the market and the ease of delivery of the product to the consumer, as this type of institution often relies on technology and its work revolves around relying on it, and as it is known, Algeria is still striving to find appropriate solutions to facilitate electronic transactions and is striving to develop the ecosystem with what is in line with the needs of emerging enterprises, and we note the recent national efforts to modify the flow of the Internet as well as the upgrade of related services, as well as in order to establish An effective startup ecosystem has been Launching and activating a platform for this type of organization since October 2020, where activists and actors in the ecosystem and data building are brought together their own which will be a rich resource for future startups and in the development of the business network and ecosystem for business in Algeria in general (Meziane and Ammarouche 2020).
- Management: The Algerian ecosystem is full of organizations that overcome the difficulties faced in the management and leadership of start-ups, such as the National Agency for the Support and Development of Entrepreneurship (ANADE), the National Agency for the Management of Microcredit (ANGEM), the National Unemployment Insurance Fund (CNAC), where they are considered agencies that train the individual who has entrepreneurial orientations in the management and management of projects in general, as well as allocating courses and mediating with institutes and training centers to train the individual with specialization according to the idea of his project, as well as incubators that Organized by Executive Decree 20-254, which incubates the contractor and his idea and provides a range of services, including management consulting that is concerned with teaching and teaching the individual the skills of leading his project and how to

transform his idea into a commercial project and run his institution in the future and sweep the market where incubators are defined by Algerian law as each structure of the public or private sector or both together in partnership between them specialized in incubating emerging institutions and innovative projects, and Article 25 of the same decree specified that the role for which it arises Incubators that are considered economic institutions are represented in supporting innovative projects.

Whereas it was recognized that High-quality education is a critical factor for the success of any innovative environment (Johansson et al., 2015). Algeria is trying to upgrade the level of its education in various fields with the integration of entrepreneurship in various disciplines and levels and to alleviate the challenges of contractors in managing their projects and their success on the ground. incubators Business is the tool that increases the chances of success and growth of startups by providing support and accompaniment factors (Bouchaer, 2018).

3.2 Analysis of the Medium Environment

The medium environment includes regional support and policies by Berger & Kuckertz (2016, p. 2). As for regional support, taking into account the size of Algeria and its population, each region has its culture first and the diligence of its members who are present in public administrations that serve emerging institutions and innovation in general, and thus it is noticeable that regional bodies or groups have been formed that support emerging enterprises, which differ from one state to another, for example, universities play a role in promoting entrepreneurial thought and supporting innovation in the surroundings in which they are located, especially with the bodies created in this sector, represented in the role of entrepreneurship and incubators of emerging institutions, and here it differs Influence from one region to another in the Algerian state, for example, the University of M'sila, despite the small size of the state compared to other states, but it has proven successful in the field of innovations and inventions, and this indicates only the efforts of individuals in charge of innovation support bodies, which reflects regional support and encouragement for innovative projects and emerging institutions in the state of Messila, as we find agencies DID Across the various wilayas of the country, it supports young people regionally to innovate ideas and commercialize them, and embraces, guides and encourages holders of ideas through its various courses held in partnership with the various agencies in the region, including vocational training institutes, universities and others. It indicates Algeria's interest in the field and its goal of building an ecosystem that supports this type of institution. Algeria's public policies regarding start-ups are supportive and encourage innovation and the creation of this type of institution.

3.3 Analysis of the Overall Environment

- The macro environment of the startup ecosystem concerns the cultural and social aspect (Berger & Kuckertz, 2016, p. 2). Analysts have argued that the cause of the Atlanta recession was due to Lack of a coherent social structure Despite the advanced technology that was available (Breznitz & Taylor, 2014). Hence, the importance of the cultural and social environment supporting emerging enterprises appears, i.e. in the sense of the business environment, which is full of a popular entrepreneurial culture on the one hand and encourages innovation and bears the risk in experimenting with new products, the stimulating society of the entrepreneur helps in developing his capabilities and increasing his confidence in his innovations, which pushes him to try his product and market it even after failure with his first attempts, Algeria is trying to strengthen society with entrepreneurial culture by instilling it in different generations while consolidating the culture of self-employment and accepting it among Algerian society as a phenomenon with results Positive, and this is what we see in various publications and seminars by audiovisual and audiovisual communication, whether by public or private channels, in addition to supporting young people with entrepreneurial orientations through social networking sites, as well as holding competitions for innovative ideas and emerging institutions, and personally honoring the President of the Republic for the participating individuals, all of which are efforts by the state to draw a positive image among members of Algerian society, establish a general entrepreneurial culture and accept products with creative and innovative ideas.

CONCLUSION AND IMPLICATIONS

Startups can be defined as an institution based on innovation with a new product or service that creates its own markets and meets unmet needs where it operates in a state of extreme uncertainty, Algeria and towards the countries of the world developed Executive Decree 20-254 to regulate the field of startups and related on the one hand, as it defined a definition of startups, innovative project and incubators, elements whose concept was required to be defined in the business ecosystem in Algeria to raise the circumstances in its definition, and therefore was the cornerstone of the launch In building a supportive and thriving ecosystem, the conditions that must be met for the institution to be a startup in Algeria have also been determined, where what exists globally has been respected according to global studies that have been concerned with defining the concept of emerging institutions, represented in the institution's activity based on the innovative idea with great growth potentials, of course, while respecting the geographical location of the Algerian state, but the only criticism is the roofing of the turnover by 4 billion Algerian dinars and the number of workers by 250 workers, which is known for emerging enterprises in their growth stage. Startups are active in the middle of a country-specific ecosystem. There is no general agreement on its components and elements, and every ecosystem that contributed to the emergence of successful startups is considered successful.

References differ in listing the components of the startup ecosystem, including the 5M model, which means: market, money, management, micro, and macro, where the medium environment concerns regional support and public policies, while the macro environment is related to cultural and social aspects, by analyzing the elements of the environment that make up this model with what is included in the startup ecosystem in Algeria. The efforts of the Algerian state remain ongoing and diligent in strengthening the ecosystem with what the situation in the country requires to successfully support entrepreneurs and idea holders to embody their innovative projects in general and encourage the creation of startups in general, which is evident by allocating a particular delegate ministry only for startups and the knowledge economy.

You can take advantage of the ecosystem model in Switzerland, which is an excellent example compatible with what has been developed in Algeria, where the CTI Center has been dedicated to the Committee on Technology and Innovation, a Swiss federal agency responsible for encouraging and promoting scientific innovation activities and also supports the transfer of knowledge and technology, as well as trying to lead innovators towards the creation of new start-ups, as well It improves the economic climate and ecosystem of young entrepreneurs.

This committee carries out its work of support by providing a range of advisory services, networks, and also financing in order to support the growth of the local economy more effectively, and the support focuses on projects with innovative ideas that show market potential and that will remain untapped without CTI support; therefore, innovative projects that meet the actual demand in the market are supported to serve local economic growth and local citizens—the ability to achieve economic success or added value to society.

REFERENCES

Audretsch, D. B. (2009). The entrepreneurial society. *The Journal of Technology Transfer, 34*(3), 245–254. doi:10.100710961-008-9101-3

Bank, W. (2018). *Tech Startup Ecosystem in West Bank and Gaza: Findings and Recommendations*. World Bank. doi:10.1596/31075

Bates, T., Jackson, W. E. III, & Johnson, J. H. Jr. (2007). Advancing research on minority entrepreneurship. *The Annals of the American Academy of Political and Social Science, 613*(1), 10–17. doi:10.1177/0002716207303405

Berger, E. S. C., & Kuckertz, A. (2016). Female entrepreneurship in startup ecosystems worldwide. *Journal of Business Research, 69*(11), 5163–5168. doi:10.1016/j.jbusres.2016.04.098

Blank, S. (2013). Why the lean start-up changes everything. *Harvard Business Review, 91*(5), 63–72.

Bouchaer, S. (2018). The role of business incubators in supporting and developing startups: A case study of Algeria. *Journal of Economic Bashaer, 4*(2), 417–431.

Breznitz, D., & Taylor, M. (2014). The communal roots of entrepreneurial–technological growth–social fragmentation and stagnation: Reflection on Atlanta's technology cluster. *Entrepreneurship and Regional Development, 26*(3–4), 375–396. doi:10.1080/08985626.2014.918183

Brush, C. G., De Bruin, A., & Welter, F. (2009). A gender-aware framework for women's entrepreneurship. *International Journal of Gender and Entrepreneurship, 1*(1), 8–24. doi:10.1108/17566260910942318

Bruyat, C. (1993). *Business creation: epistemological contributions and modeling*. Pierre Mendès-France-Grenoble II University.

Cauvin, E., & Bescos, L. (2002). *Performance evaluation: A comparison between the practices of start-ups and traditional French and American companies. Information Technology and Management: Challenges and Impacts in Accounting, Control and Auditing*.

Eliasson, G. (2001). Industrial policy, competence blocs and the role of science in economic development. In *Capitalism and Democracy in the 21st Century* (pp. 223–247). Springer. doi:10.1007/978-3-662-11287-8_12

Eliasson, G., & Eliasson, A. (1996). The biotechnological competence bloc. *Revue d'Economie Industrielle, 78*(1), 7–26. doi:10.3406/rei.1996.1641

Hechavarria, D. M., & Ingram, A. (2014). A review of the entrepreneurial ecosystem and the entrepreneurial society in the United States: An exploration with the global entrepreneurship monitor dataset. *Journal of Business and Entrepreneurship*, *26*(1), 1–35.

Johansson, B., Lööf, H., & Savin, M. (2015). European r&d efficiency. *Economics of Innovation and New Technology*, *24*(1–2), 140–158. doi:10.1080/10438599.2014.897857

Kenney, M., & Von Burg, U. (1999). Technology, entrepreneurship and path dependence: Industrial clustering in Silicon Valley and Route 128. *Industrial and Corporate Change*, *8*(1), 67–103. doi:10.1093/icc/8.1.67

Kolvereid, L., & Isaksen, E. (2006). New business start-up and subsequent entry into self-employment. *Journal of Business Venturing*, *21*(6), 866–885. doi:10.1016/j.jbusvent.2005.06.008

Krajcik, V., & Formanek, I. (2015). Regional startup ecosystem. *European Business & Management*, *1*(2), 14–18.

Marty, O. (2002). The life of Start-up (s′) Investing in innovative companies. *Manage and Understand. Annals of Mines*, *67*, 4–15.

Montani, D., Gervasio, D., & Pulcini, A. (2020). Startup Company Valuation: The State of Art and Future Trends. *International Business Research*, *13*(9), 1–31. doi:10.5539/ibr.v13n9p31

Passaro, R., Quinto, I., & Thomas, A. (2017). Start-up competitions as learning environment to foster the entrepreneurial process. *International Journal of Entrepreneurial Behaviour & Research*, *23*(3), 426–445. doi:10.1108/IJEBR-01-2016-0007

Peters, B. (2009). *Early Exits: Exit strategies for entrepreneurs and angel investors (but maybe not venture capitalists)*. Basil Peters.

Salamzadeh, A., & Kawamorita Kesim, H. (2015). Startup companies: Life cycle and challenges. *4th International Conference on Employment, Education and Entrepreneurship (EEE)*.

Sammut, S. (1996). The small business start-up process. Complexity of the management system and emergence of start-up scenarios. *Proceedings of the VI Conference of the International Association of Strategic Management*.

Shepherd, D. A., Douglas, E. J., & Shanley, M. (2000). New venture survival: Ignorance, external shocks, and risk reduction strategies. *Journal of Business Venturing*, *15*(5–6), 393–410. doi:10.1016/S0883-9026(98)00032-9

Vodwa, M., Mimouni, B., & Beniba, M. (2021). The role of business incubators in supporting and developing startups in Algeria. *Journal of Economic Growth and Entrepreneurship*, *6*(4), 116–125.

Chapter 6
The Effect of Entrepreneurship on the Achievement of Business Performance:
Approach Through the Psychological Traits of the Entrepreneurs – Case Study

Arabeche Zina
https://orcid.org/0000-0003-3893-3378
Ahmed Zabana University of Relizane, Algeria

Mohammed El Amine Abdelli
https://orcid.org/0000-0002-5784-4306
University of Brest, France

Shajara Ul-Durar
University of Sunderland, UK

ABSTRACT

Entrepreneurship is vital to economic growth, innovation, competitiveness, and poverty reduction. This chapter examines the degree of entrepreneurial orientation (EO) of 101 Algerian manufacturing SMEs and the consequences of EO dimensions such as innovation, proactivity, and risk-taking on business performance. Data were collected throughout a survey with a specifically designed questionnaire, and quantitative techniques were applied for their analysis. The results showed that Algerian SMEs have an average low entrepreneurial orientation. The authors concluded that there are some statically significant relationships between two dimensions of entrepreneurial orientation (proactivity and risk-taking) and SME performance. Thus, the Algerian entrepreneur is characterized by two specific

DOI: 10.4018/978-1-6684-7127-2.ch006

psychological traits: the need for achievement and entrepreneurial self-efficacy. These results could help entrepreneurs plan their activities towards developing the entrepreneurial spirit of Algerian SMEs.

1. INTRODUCTION

The phenomenon of entrepreneurship is in vogue. All the world's countries have become aware of its importance in reducing unemployment, accelerating production rates, promoting productivity and creating economic and social value. For many authors, entrepreneurship is limited to business creation Shane (2008). In contrast, this activity goes beyond creation alone to include creating new tasks, activities, and processes by existing companies or, more broadly, exploiting new market opportunities (Jarillo & Stevenson, 1990; Shane & Venkataraman, 2000). Thus, this notion is the core of organizational entrepreneurship (Corporate Entrepreneurship). Corporate entrepreneurship is defined as entrepreneurship in an existing business. The literature has used a variety of names for this concept, for example, corporate venturing (Biggadike, 1979), entrepreneurship (Zahra, 1991), intrapreneur (Pinchot, 1985), internal corporate entrepreneurship (Burgelman, 1985), internal entrepreneurship (Schollhammer; Vesper, 1984), strategic renewal (Guth, Ginsberg, 1990; Stopford & Baden-Fuller, 1994), strategic change, strategic revival, transformation venturing (Hornsby, Kuratko and Zahra, 2002), which is the subject of a reference to the Entrepreneurial Orientation of existing companies (Fayolle & Cherchem,2010).

The notion of Entrepreneurial Orientation (EO) is relatively recent; it has been in constant use over the past few years. It is conceived as a multidimensional construct that can be broken down into three main variables: proactivity, innovation and risk-taking (Covin & Slevin, 1989) and this concept has been developed and widely used to measure an organization's entrepreneurial intensity.

Entrepreneurship is widely valued since the entrepreneur "creates wealth, jobs..., is a real gift that society must hasten to recognize, value and set an example" (Fortin, 2004). So, the entrepreneur is of decisive importance to the success of his/her business, and it seems necessary to discuss the literature related to this crucial character of business. Literature on this topic has two main approaches. One part of it, known as "deterministic", focuses on the entrepreneur's traits, while the other, known as "behavioural", describes the entrepreneurial process as a result of his/her activity. In this paper, we concentrate on the elements of the first perspective because many researchers present the relationship or interaction between the personality of the entrepreneur and the Entrepreneurial Orientation. Behaviourists present the "deterministic" approach as a psychological vision that focuses on the individual's personality traits and motivations (Voda & Florea, 2019; Sahin et al., 2019; Munir et al., 2018; Karabulut,2016; Zainol & Ayadurai, 2011; Nga Hwee,2010).

Many studies (Hoque et al., 2019; Kuckertz & Christopher, 2019; Soares & Perin, 2019; Rose & Mamabolo, 2019; Hoque et al., 2018; Rauch et al.,2009; Lumpkin & Dess, 1996; Covin & Wales, 2012) have concentrated on the relationship between a firm's Entrepreneurial Orientation and its performance. The effects of the dimensions of EO can be comprehended in terms of sustainability, survival and growth.

In this work, we coincide with Shane and Venkataraman (2000) In that companies with a more excellent entrepreneurial orientation are more inclined to identify and exploit business opportunities abroad, given the situation of the domestic market. More entrepreneurial firms will also tend to take advantage of these opportunities more efficiently to improve their competitive position (Soares & Perin, 2019; Peterson & McGee, 2019; Wales et al.,2019; Li et al.,2008).

We were influenced by some of the previous research on this topic, cited as follows:

A study by Zina et al. (2022) found that SMEs can perform through a robust entrepreneurial orientation based on innovation, proactively, and risk-taking within a corporate culture mainly focused on bureaucratic and ad-hocratic culture. A study by Soares and Perin (2019) found a direct and positive influence of Entrepreneurial Orientation on business performance, and this impact is more substantial for multi-item performance indicators. A study by Hoque (2018) also highlighted the significance of EO in predicting SME performance and how organizational culture gets involved in understanding the relationship between EO and Bangladeshi SME performance. Another research by Karabulut (2016) showed that internal locus of control, need for achievement, risk tolerance, and entrepreneurial alertness positively impacted the entrepreneurial intention of Turkish graduate students.

A study by Voda and Florea (2019) indicate that locus of control, need for achievement, and entrepreneurial education have tended to be critical elements for developing projects by young students, whether independently or under the control variables action. The Poon and al (2006) results showed that internal locus of control was positively associated with firm performance, and in this correlation, EO did not play a moderating effect. In addition, self-efficacy did not directly influence organizational performance; even so, it affected firm performance significantly through its impact on entrepreneurial orientation. Also, self-attributed achievement motives were not strongly connected to entrepreneurial orientation or business performance. A study by Okhomina (2010) results confirm significant positive relations between psychological characteristics and EO. Results also indicate that the environment moderates the interactions between psychological traits and EO. The most important characteristic of this study compared to previous studies is: It proposes three variables, EO, psychological traits and business performance in Algerian companies; the relationship between these three variables has received considerable scholarly attention, but very few investigations studies have been led among Algerian SMEs.

Main question: To what extent can the Entrepreneurial Orientation of entrepreneurs promote the achievement of performance in Algerian SMEs?

The literature review allowed us to formulate the following hypotheses:

H1- The personality of the manager positively affects the entrepreneurial orientation.
H1-a The Need for the achievement of the manager positively affects the EO.
H1-b The internal locus of control of the manager positively affects the EO.
H1-c The entrepreneurial self-efficacy of the manager positively affects
H2-An entrepreneurial solid orientation is positively correlated with business performance.

The fundamental objective of this study is to determine the relationship between entrepreneurial orientation and the manager profile, firstly and, secondly, their influence on the firm's performance. To this end, this paper will be presented in three parts.

First, we present the theoretical framework for analyzing the relationship between the manager's profile, the EO and the performance of SMEs. Then, we present the methodology implemented and the profiles of the sample. Finally, we end with the leading results. We conclude with this study's main theoretical, methodological and managerial implications. Danjou (2002) states: "The entrepreneur is distinguished from other citizens by specific character traits, which can be identified and used as indicators of an individual's entrepreneurial potential". Many results confirm the significant positive relationships between psychological traits and Entrepreneurial Orientation (Okhomina,2010).

2. THEORETICAL REVIEW AND HYPOTHESES

2.1 Entrepreneurial Orientation

The term entrepreneurial orientation (EO) originates from an article by Miller (1983) in which this author explains the path to entrepreneurship by type of organization. To measure entrepreneurial intensity, Miller created a scale by including three dimensions. In fact, an entrepreneurial company, according to Miller (1983), is a company that engages in innovation (i.e. innovativeness), takes the risk (i.e. risk taking), pursues opportunities and acts proactively (i.e. proactiveness), so it must be autonomous and demonstrate a certain competitive aggressiveness (Lumpkin & Dess, 1996). Put, entrepreneurial orientation is a combination of innovation, risk-taking, and proactivity (Wiklundand Shepherd, 2003). Zahra (1996) called for a high entrepreneurial orientation to lead to improved overall business performance. Covin and Slevin (1989) further emphasized the importance of these dimensions: "The EO of a company is demonstrated by the extent to which senior management is willing to assume business risks (risk-taking dimension), to promote change and innovation in order to gain a competitive advantage for the company (innovation dimension) and to compete fiercely with other companies (proactivity dimension)".

Conversely, Hoque et al. (2018e) mentioned that entrepreneurial orientation demonstrates a company's capacity for innovation, creation and proactivity to satisfy eventual client needs through new goods or services, exploiting resources and facing risk before competitors. In our work, we also consider the EO as a construct that contains several (three) dimensions. As such, Covin and Slevin's (1989) definition seems more apparent to us: EO is a set of behaviours that emerge

Figure 1. Distinction between entrepreneurial orientation and entrepreneurship (Lumpkin & Dess, 1996)
Entrepreneurship (New entry)

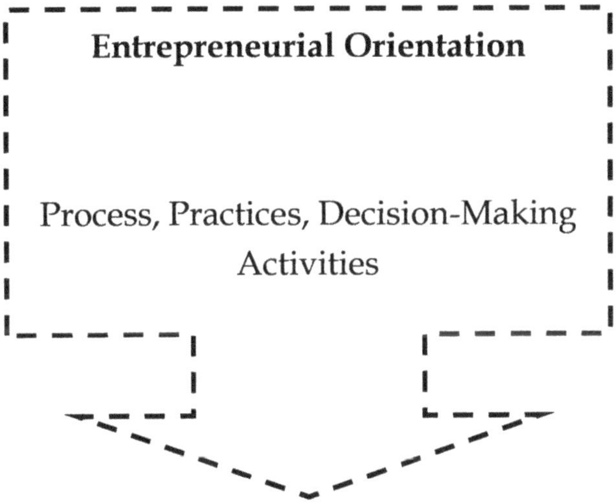

Entrepreneurship (New entry)

within a company to the extent to which the manager is inclined to assume business risks, foster innovation and change in order to gain a competitive advantage and compete aggressively with other firms. In 1996, another academic trend emerged dealing with the construction of the EO based on the redefinition of Lumpkin and Dess (1996): "EO refers to decision-making processes, practices and activities that lead to a new entry". Entrepreneurship is the result of the company's commitment to the EO perspective. Lumpkin and Dess (1996) announce: "That is, new entry explains what entrepreneurship consists of, and entrepreneurial orientation describes how new entry is undertaken".

2.2 Personality of the Manager and Entrepreneurial Orientation

Behaviourists describe the "deterministic" approach as a psychological vision that aims to highlight the individual's personality traits and motivations. Danjou (2002) states: "The entrepreneur is distinguished from other citizens by specific character traits, which can be identified and used as indicators of an individual's entrepreneurial potential". Several results confirm the significant positive relationships between psychological traits and entrepreneurial orientation (Voda & Florea, 2019; Sahin et al., 2018; Munir et al., 2018; Karabulut,2016; Zainol & Ayadurai, 2011; Nga,2010; Okhomina,2010).

Miller (1983) showed that the entrepreneur's personality contributed to entrepreneurial dynamics in simple organizations. Thus, Lumpkin and Dess (1996) describe the characteristics of the leader among the factors that may interact between entrepreneurial orientation and organizational performance. This perspective considers the entrepreneur as the unit of analysis to establish a standard profile that responds to specific personal characteristics identified through psychological and socio-demographic characteristics, motivations, personality traits, skills, and networks. Previous studies have also widely discussed that psychological characteristics justify entrepreneurial tendency and activity (Feereira et al., 2018; Munir et al.,2018). Also, Fayolle and Cherchem (2010) have shown a relationship between certain psychological traits of the entrepreneur and specific company characteristics, such as performance, strategy, and entrepreneurial intent in the psycho-managerial dimension (Nambubbi, 2016). Indeed, people with these psychological traits have the potential to act in an entrepreneurial way, according to Sahin and al (2019); Munir and al (2018); Bello and al (2018); Zainol and Ayadurai (2011), Basso (2009).

In our research, we focus on well-established literature; we have retained the terms "need for achievement", "internal locus of control", and "entrepreneurial self-efficacy" to discern to what extent the personality of the manager influences the entrepreneurial dynamics of his / her company.

a. ***Need for Achievement*:** Of all the personal characteristics related to the entrepreneur, the "Need for achievement" or "the need for accomplishment" is the oldest and best known.

The need for accomplishment attribute encases a person's tendency towards significant achievements, accomplishing moderate objectives and looking for self-improvement. The need for accomplishment should lead people to look for difficulties that match their character and upgrade their confidence in the probability of their prosperity, which may prompt an expansion of the general society's growth (Voda & Florea, 2019). According to Randerson et al. (2011), the interaction between the "Need for achievement" and the development of the strategy or organizational structure has been empirically established (Miller & Toulouse, 1986); the entrepreneur driven by this characteristic will be more proactive and willing to take risks, more likely to exploit entrepreneurial opportunities, than an entrepreneur with a low need for achievement. According to Poon, Ainuddin and Junit (2006, p67): "we expect entrepreneurs high on achievement motivate to be more likely to take a forward-looking and competitive perspective (related to the innovativeness and proactiveness dimensions of entrepreneurial orientation relative to those low on this trait". This allows us to identify the first sub-hypothesis:

H1.a The need for achievement of the manager positively affects the EO.

b. ***Locus of control*:** Locus of control is the level of control of an individual over his/her life. Internal locus of control shows that an individual accepts that his/her choices can control his/her life. In contrast, the external locus of control manifests that an individual's life is influenced by outside variables, for example, prosperity, luck, destiny, and other persons beyond his/her choices. Individuals with an internal locus of control are expected to decide their career ways, have entrepreneurial intentions and begin their businesses (Karabulut,2016). According to Munir et al. (2018), internal locus of control is the conviction that occasions result from an individual's aptitudes, characteristics, practices or activities. Internal locus of control is defined as the person's convictions regarding what controls his/her life. So, a high internal locus of control, according to Schjoedt and Shaver (2012), has been connected with the entrepreneurial figure and entrepreneurial prosperity, and this allows us to determine the second sub-hypothesis:

H1.b: The internal locus of control of the manager positively affects the EO.

c. ***Entrepreneurial Self-Efficacy***: In the entrepreneurship field, the entrepreneurial self-efficacy concept, according to McGee (2009): "measures a person's belief in their ability to successfully launch an entrepreneurial venture" and requires prevailing in errands like development, marketing, finance and innovation that are identified with the establishment of another venture (Sahin et al., 2019). The practicality of entrepreneurial activities is a significant precursor to entrepreneurial goals; thus, higher degrees of entrepreneurial self-efficacy increase the expectation of choosing entrepreneurship as a profession (Hsu et al., 2017). This allows us to identify the third sub-hypothesis:

H1.c: The entrepreneurial self-efficacy of the manager positively affects the EO.

2.3 Entrepreneurial Orientation and Business Performance

Zhou and Gao (2019) depict how companies are the driving wellspring of the modern economy which animates the progression of innovative organizations and upgrades the performance of new business enterprises. Various researchers (Napitupulu et al., 2018; Zafar & Mustafa, 2017; Dwyer et al., 2019; Niebel,2018) have demonstrated how SMEs are an inalienable part of innovation and development in a dynamic economy; Thus, SMEs have a significant capacity in job creation. The word performance for any type and size of the company remains a concept that is vague, nuanced and nonconsensual about its meaning and measures (Iuliana & Maria, 2016). For small and medium-sized companies, a practical performance analysis must, in addition to this ambiguity, consider the personal influence that the entrepreneur has on his or her business (St-Pierre,2005). Wong (2014) noticed that EO leads to the achievement of new goods by encouraging businesses to distinguish and proactively take advantage of new market chances. As indicated by Shepherd and Wiklund (2003), Entrepreneurial Orientation can speed up the actions of a company and thus allow them to be in front of the competition more frequently; entrepreneurial orientation is considered as a higher request form, and each aspect of Entrepreneurial orientation construct (innovation, proactivity, risk-taking) can have a different correlation to the performance factors (Zeebaree & Siron, 2017). Hence, EO is a significant resource impacting SMEs' performance.

Performance is a concept which is having different undertone in the scholarly literature. Usually, small and medium enterprises' performance signifies the firm's considerable results in terms of proficiency of investment, effectiveness of policies, accomplishing consumer satisfaction, expanding market share, development and returns and which are delivered by taking a perplexing series of activities that integrate abilities and knowledge (Hoque et al.; 2017).

Obiwuru and al, (2011) expressed that small and medium-sized firms' performance articulates how good a firm is doing. Additionally, Hoque and Awang (2019) described SME performance is regarded to be the result of valuable management actions, and it very well may be evaluated by exploiting various norms, which contain efficiency, viability, productivity, and development.

As a matter of fact, Small and medium-sized enterprises' performance is the working capacity to achieve the desires of a company's partners (Smith & Reece, 1999). Hence, performance is the intensity of a company to yield satisfactory activities (Davood & Morteza, 2012). In this manner, a firm can perceive its situation regarding solid just as powerless focuses through surveying SME performance. Therefore, Small and medium-sized enterprises' performance appraisal aims to improve the result by pursuing new chances internally and externally, enhancing overall capabilities, and increasing justifiable development at the appointed time. Lumpkin and Dess (1996) indicated that an OE of a company is a crucial element for organizational performance. So, The correlation between OE and performance has been tested many times according to Wiklund (1999) and Zahra (1991); even empirically, Zahra (2000) has also shown that there is a positive effect between organizational entrepreneurship and firm performance at least on a few dimensions of performance. Covin and Slevin (1991)say: "The growing interest in the study of entrepreneurship is a response not only to the belief that entrepreneurial activity will result in positive macroeconomic outcomes but to the belief that such activity can lead to improved performance in established organizations."

On the other side, Miller (1983) was sceptical about the relationship between EO and performance, suggesting that increased entrepreneurial activity may pose a risk to the company's financial performance on the company over time. Hence the second hypothesis:

H2. A strong entrepreneurial orientation is positively correlated with company performance.

Figure 2. Search model
Research conceptual model

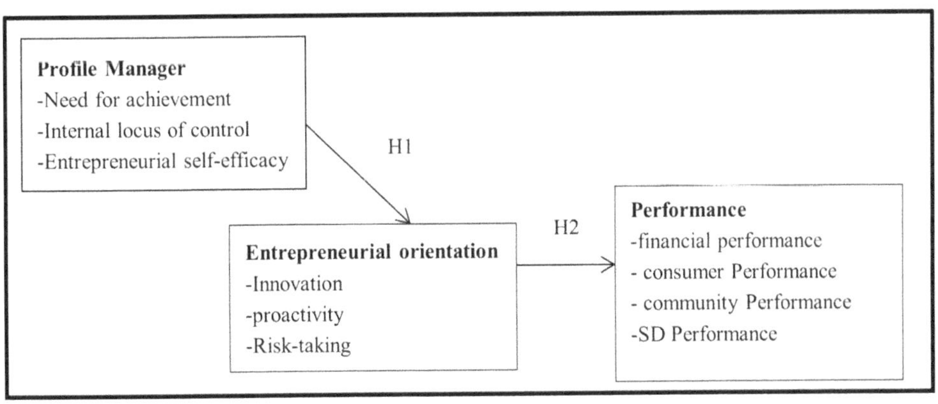

Cherchem and Fayolle's (2010) conceptual model seems the most synthetic and most transparent because it connects all the variables of our research work. Indeed, this model was established through a literature review; these authors (op-cit) highlight the importance of the entrepreneur's vision (his entrepreneurial orientation) and his values on the company's performance.

3. METHODS AND MATERIALS

3.1 Research Identification Process

We used the method of non-probability. In this case, the sample is based on a reasoned choice based on several criteria (Mayrfoer, 2006, p. 45). According to Lewis and Thornhill (2009), the survey method is a deductive strategy popular in business research. We visited 180 Algerian firms and focused on entrepreneurs. One hundred-one questionnaires were selected for analysis, representing a response rate of 56.11%. So, to test our hypotheses, we examined them in the manufacturing sector in northern Algeria. Indeed, this choice is made with the help of the orientation of the regional chamber of commerce of Oran, the chamber of commerce and industry of Algiers, and the chamber of commerce and industry of Mostaganem; thus, the site of the Ministry of SME Industry and Investment Promotion[1]. We used the SPSS (19) to explain the behaviour of our variables. To answer our problem and test our research hypotheses, we continued the univariate analysis (flat or simple sorting) and the bivariate analysis. We have selected the area of research that best meets the subject. In addition, our research aim is to define Algerian SMEs' behaviour in terms of entrepreneurial orientation and performance.

3.2 Questionnaire

The questionnaire is composed of 39 questions divided into four parts:

The first part, entitled "General information about the firm", consists of 08 questions on the company, its age, size, domination, identification, sector of activity, executive age, gender and level of training.

The second part, entitled "The Entrepreneurial Orientation of the Entrepreneur", includes 09 statements divided into three groups:

- The first part contains 03 statements concerning innovation,
- The second part contains 03 statements concerning proactivity,
- The third part contains 03 statements concerning risk-taking.

We used a Likert scale of five points to measure intentions and attitudes. We adopted the question of the graduated proposal in which we presented a scale from weak to strong and from weak to medium to firm.

The third part, entitled "Corporate Performance", is composed of 08 questions divided into four groups:

- Financial performance component: With 03 questions
- Customer performance component: With 03 questions
- Community Performance Component: 01questions
- Sustainable development performance component: with 01questions

The fourth part, entitled "Profile of the Entrepreneur", comprises 14 questions.

- Need for achievement: It contains 04proposals
- Internal locus of control: It contains 04 proposals
- Entrepreneurial Self Efficacy: It contains 06proposals

3.4 Measures

Indicators developed by Covin and Slevin (1989) were used to measure Entrepreneurial Orientation. This notion includes nine items in three dimensions: innovation, proactivity and risk-taking; each of the dimensions contains three items measured on the 5-point Likert scale: "01" = totally disagree to "5" = totally agree.

Cronbach's alphas exceed acceptable standards (innovation = 0.709, proactivity = 0.778 and risk-taking = 0.897). As was said before, the literature indicates that there needs to be a consensus on the performance measurement concept.

In our case, we measure it through 04 indicators: financial performance, customer performance, community performance and sustainable development performance, according to the proposal of Nkanyou et al. (2011) based on the work of Dess and Robinson (1984) objective and subjective measures were used both in the evaluation of this concept.

The financial performance comprises three items (revenue growth, employee growth and profit margin), and Cronbach's alpha is 0.785. Customer performance also includes three items (quality of customer service, variety of customer service, and customer satisfaction); as with the previous measure, it is one-dimensional, and Cronbach's alpha is 0.815. Finally, community performance has only one indicator and sustainable development performance (respect for the environment and sustainable development and Cronbach's alpha are 0,756 and 0,791, respectively.

For the "Psychological Traits of the Manager " variable, we based on the paper of McGraw and al (2001), Rotter (in Phares,1976), and DeNoble et al. (2007) to measure the variables: the need for achievement, the internal locus of control, and entrepreneurial self-efficacy, respectively.

4. RESULTS AND DISCUSSION:

4.1 Descriptive Statistics on the Demographic Characteristics of SMEs From the Survey

From the 2000s, the creation of enterprises in Algeria accelerated significantly; at the end of the first half of 2019, SMEs in Algeria constituted a large part of the economic fabric with 1171945 companies. Most SMEs are mainly active in services,

Table 1. Descriptive analysis

	Demographic Characteristics	Algerian SME	
		Frequency	Percentage (%)
M/W	Man	81	80%
	Woman	20	20%
Age of the respondent	30 - 40 years	20	20%
	41 - 50 years old	67	66%
	> 50 years old	14	14%
Level of education	Bachelor's degree	11	11%
	Professional training	58	57%
	University Studies	32	32%
Age of the company	1 - 5 years	4	4%
	6- 10 years	15	15%
	11 - 20 years	28	28%
	21 - 30 years	26	26%
	31 - 40 years	18	17%
	41 - 50 years old	10	10%
	>50 years	0	0
Number of employees	10 - 50	16	16%
	51- 100	35	35%
	101 - 200	41	40%
	201-300	09	9%
	>300 employees	0	0

Source: Conducted by researchers

handicrafts and the BTPH, while only 8,71% are industrial SMEs (Newsletter et al. n°35, Ministry of Industry and Mines, Algeria). The vast majority of SMEs had between 51 and 200 employees (or 76 companies in our sample), which reflects the moderately important role they play in the employment of Algerians; a similar result was reached by the Ministry of Industry and Mines (2019). Furthermore, the World Bank's annual ranking on business climate (Doing Business)[2] places Algeria in an unfavourable situation (152nd out of 190 countries for 2020), we think that the government has made considerable progress in entrepreneurship and business creation, considering the Algerian economy's particulars.

We realize that Algeria's number of female entrepreneurs remains relatively low (20%). We met a woman leader with a pseudonym used by a relative of the other sex to obtain from the commercial register. Among the difficulties faced by women, according to this entrepreneur: first, the slowness and cumbersomeness of administrative operations; second, the difficulties of recruiting competent staff; difficulties in accessing the market and finally, the culture of Algerian society, which has a tendency towards masculinity, which is on line with the results of an investigation led by Ghiat (2018), Setting (2017), Ouadah and al, (2015), Hattab (2012), Arabeche,(2011) who concluded that in Algeria is still exceptionally commanded by men, a manly environment. The frequency table shows that most Algerian entrepreneurs surveyed are relatively old: 66% are between 41 and 50, while only 20% are between 30 and 40. To this end, in OECD countries, the typical entrepreneur is between 30 and 35 years old and has extensive professional experience acquired in a medium or large company (OECD, 1998, p. 197).

The frequency table shows that 57% of Algerian entrepreneurs surveyed have pursued vocational training. They agree that their university education did not set them up for dynamic professional life since education is still the traditional method in Algeria; Only 32% of entrepreneurs have completed a university education and set up their businesses, which is in line with the results of an investigation led by Izzrech and al (2013) who concluded that there are a few shortcomings in the necessary abilities, like productivity, innovativeness, communication technology, critical thinking and distance learning.

According to GEM (2013), Algeria has the lowest percentage of adults who believe they have the knowledge and skills to start a business. Similar outcomes are reached by Setti (2017) articulated that: being educated in Algeria reduces entrepreneurial orientation, while the young who are educated in Iran are bound to create a company in the following three years when contrasted with Turkey.

4.2 Descriptive Analysis of the Entrepreneurial Orientation of Algerian Entrepreneurs From the Survey

a. Innovation

Table 2. Univariate analysis of innovation

EO (Innovation)	Algerian Entrepreneurs From the Sample
Innov1[3]	30%
Innov2[4]	38%
Innov3[5]	50%

Source: Conducted by researchers

70% of managers focus on something other than research and development (R&D) and technological change and innovation. Thus, 61.5% of entrepreneurs need to introduce new product processes. In addition, 50% of the SMEs surveyed still need to change their products or services radically. According to the Algerian entrepreneurs surveyed, the lack of financial resources, expertise, skills, and lack of mastery of new technology requires not thinking about innovation. According to them, banks do not provide significant credit to SMEs, so there needs to be more market space that ensures a risk capital offer.

b. Proactivity

Table 3. Univariate analysis of proactivity

EO (Proactivity)	Algerian Entrepreneurs From the Sample
Proact1[6]	73,3%
Proact2[7]	36,7%
Proact3[8]	67,2%

Source: Conducted by researchers

73.3% of managers assume that their companies undertake actions to which competitors respond. However, 37% of the entrepreneurs questioned admit that their firms are often the first to introduce new products, techniques and production methods. Also, according to 67.20% of the interviewees, their firms are in a very competitive position to reduce competition. In short, Algerian managers are moderately proactive as they seek new opportunities by anticipating future demand and product development regarding customer needs.

c. Risk-Taking

Table 4. Univariate analysis of risk-taking

EO (Risk Taking)	Algerian Entrepreneurs From the Sample
Risqu1[9]	30%
Risqu2 [10]	50%
Risqu3 [11]	87%

Source: Conducted by researchers

68% of Algerian survey participants do not support high-risk projects, but only 30% tend to take risks. Again, according to 87% of the managers surveyed, risk-taking shows the firm's willingness to mobilize resources to invest in new domains.

According to the univariate analysis, we have distinguished that Algerian entrepreneurs have an average low Entrepreneurial Orientation.

4.3 Descriptive Analysis of the Company's Performance

According to the descriptive performance table, entrepreneurs attach more importance to financial performance (79%), in other words, to increasing turnover and market share. This seems clear to us because everyone involved is, first and foremost, seeking profit for the survival and sustainability of the firm. Furthermore, regarding customer performance, managers prioritize customer satisfaction because customer satisfaction and loyalty lead the company to generate profits and step forward according to them.

Table 5. Simple performance sorting

	Not Important	Not Very Important	Neutral	Important	Very Important
Per. Finan	/	/	/	21%	79%
Per. client	/	/	/	35%	65,34%
Per. comm		20%	/	50%	30%
Per. SD	11%	39%	/	37%	13%

Source: Conducted by researchers

For some of the leaders surveyed (20%), community performance is not a significant indicator, while the rest say that teamwork performance and collective achievement seem essential for the firm's operations.

Sustainable development has a less meaningful indicator, we met managers (50%) who are not even familiar with the concept of sustainable development, so they answered that this performance is not a priority at the moment. For the other respondents, the performance of SD helps them to give their businesses a good image of also encourages them to export their goods to the outside world.

So, it is understandable that every manager would like to give a good image of himself and his company.

4.4 Interpretation of the Univariate Analysis of the Profile of the Algerian Entrepreneurs From the Survey

From the empirical results, we have noted that a moderately high need for achievement characterizes the personality of the Algerian entrepreneur. This is explained by the fact that 74% of Algerian managers think they have many good qualities. Thus, the main objective of 80% of these responsible is to perform better than most competitors. However, half of Algerian managers say they are capable of doing things as well as their competitors.

According to the empirical investigation in the Algerian context, we noted that Algerian managers have a moderately strong internal locus of control. 64% of entrepreneurs agree that their performances come from their personal actions. Also, 87% of Algerian entrepreneurs cite that luck cannot be essential in their lives. Thus 65% of managers can attain their objectives when they make policies and plans.

Table 6. Univariate analysis of entrepreneur profile

Entrepreneur Profile	Algerian Entrepreneurs
Need 1	74%
Need 2	50%
Need 3	80%
Intercl 1	64%
Intercl 2	87%
Intercl 3	65%
Selfeff1	57%
Selfeff2	64%
Selfeff3	67%

Source: Conducted by researchers

57% of Algerian managers say they can create new ideas. Thus, 64% can see new market opportunities for new products. 67% of respondents agree with developing a work environment encouraging employees to try something new. Thus, the Algerian entrepreneur has an average high level of entrepreneurial self-efficacy.

4.5 Hypothesis Testing

The data analysis method used in our work is quantitative. Indeed, the linear correlation method will allow us to analyze the correlation between two variables measured with metric scales (scale from 1 to 5). Also, this method will allow us to interpret the meaning of the correlation. The correlation is positive if the Pearson coefficient "r" is positive. Thus, the correlation is only validated if its significance does not exceed the level of risk of error.

We crossed the variables according to the relationship of the hypotheses formulated in order to test them.

H1.a Need for the achievement of the manager positively affects the EO.

Table 7. Bivariate analysis (Need for achievement and entrepreneurial orientation)

Hyp	Crossing of Variables	Sig	Correlation	Result
H1.1	Need for achievement * Entrepreneurial Orientation	0,021	0,423	Partially Confirmed

Source: Conducted by the researchers

From the simple sorting, we found that a medium-high need for achievement characterizes Algerian entrepreneurs. The linear correlation we have performed between the variables of need for achievement and entrepreneurial orientation can allow us to know if people with this psychological trait have the potential to act in an entrepreneurial way. In other words, to discern the extent to which the manager's personality influences the entrepreneurial dynamics of his company.

Following the interpretation of the correlation table, we have noticed that there are six out of nine statically significant tests. This leads us to say that our sub-hypothesis H1.1 is partially confirmed. Therefore, there is a relationship between the Algerian leader's need for achievement and entrepreneurial orientation.

H1-b The internal locus of control of the manager positively affects the EO.

Following the interpretation of the correlation table, we did not find any significant links between internal locus of control and entrepreneurial orientation. So, our sub-hypothesis H1. 2 is not confirmed. The internal locus of control does not influence entrepreneurial dynamics in the Algerian context.

Table 8. Bivariate analysis (internal locus of control and OE)

Hyp	Crossing of Variables	Sig	Correlation	Result
H1.2	internal locus of control * Entrepreneurial Orientation	0,101	0,290	Not confirmed

Source: Conducted by the researchers

H1.c The entrepreneurial self-efficacy of the manager positively affects the EO

From the univariate analysis, we found that Algerian entrepreneurs have a moderately high level of self-efficacy. The linear correlation method that we have carried out between the variables of self-efficacy and the dimensions of entrepreneurial orientation can allow us to know if this psychological trait influences the entrepreneurial orientation of Algerian entrepreneurs.

Table 9. Bivariate analysis (entrepreneurial self-efficacy and EO)

Hyp	Crossing of Variables	Sig	Correlation	Result
H1.3	entrepreneurial self-efficacy * Entrepreneurial Orientation	0,019	0,690	partially confirmed

Source: Conducted by the researchers

Following the interpretation of the correlation table, we have noticed that there are five out of nine statically significant tests. This leads us to say that our sub-hypothesis H1.3 is partially confirmed. Thus, self-efficacy is positively correlated with entrepreneurial orientation. Algerian entrepreneurs believe in their ability to take up challenges, act on their environment, introduce new ideas to innovate, be proactive, and assume risks.

Our hypothesis is rather confirmed, the personality of the Algerian leader is characterized by two psychological traits: the need for achievement and self-efficacy. For the "internal locus of control" feature, we did not find enough significant tests between the variables. There is a positive relationship between the personality of the leader (Need for achievement - entrepreneurial self-efficacy) and the EO in the Algerian context. Indeed, Algerian entrepreneurs possess these two psychological traits, so they do not have the potential to act in an entrepreneurial way.

H2. A strong entrepreneurial orientation is positively correlated with company performance

To see if there are correlations between Entrepreneurial Orientation and each of the dimensions of business performance, we performed correlation tests using the SPSS statistical software presented in the following table:

Table 10. Correlation matrix

Variables	Mean	Standard Deviation	1	2	3	4	5	6
OE-innov	2,55	1,08						
OE-proa	2,02	1,09	,679**					
OE-Risk	3,85	1,08	,344**	,556**				
PER-F	4,04	,76	,109	,003	,006			
PER-clt	3,57	,76	,334	,156	,176	,098**		
PER- DDD	3,90	,76	,109	,156	,004	,434	,556**	
P-Com	3,77	,89	,912*	,008*	,097	,098**	,234	0,067

*=p 0.05, **=p0.01

PER-F=Financial performance, PER-clt= Customer performance, PER-DD = Sustainable development performance, P-Com= Community performance.

From the table above, it can be seen that there are some statically significant relationships between some dimensions of the independent variable (EO) and some performance dimensions (dependent variable).

There are no statistically significant relationships between innovation and the different dimensions of performance. This allows us to say that Algerian leaders need to give more importance to innovation to improve their performance. The Algerian economic environment is increasingly globalized and competitive, and in such a context, it seems essential for Algerian companies to boost their R&D and innovation efforts. This effort allows it to improve its competitiveness, develop new markets, achieve social responsibility or survive.

Indeed, Algerian entrepreneurs do not innovate enough; according to them, the main reasons for this delay in innovation can be summarized in the following points: difficult access to funding, Low importance given to the R&D department, insufficient collaboration between university research laboratories and different types of companies; low internationalization.

There is a statically significant relationship between proactive activity and financial performance (sig=003) and community performance (sig=,008), which allows us to say that the adoption of proactive behaviour by Algerian leaders requires a vision, managerial skills and an enabling environment to support growth for the company. This hypothesis is not confirmed. Algerian entrepreneurs need highly proactive behaviour, which does not allow them to achieve performance with all these dimensions.

Risk-taking is positively correlated with sustainable development performance and financial performance. So, the Algerian entrepreneur is characterized by this ability to take risks and control uncertainty to maintain financial performance.

Despite the meanings of some of the relationships between the third EO variable and the performance variables, more is needed to say that this sub-hypothesis is confirmed because several tests are not statistically significant. Generally, the Algerian entrepreneur is cautious, suspicious and wise. This mistrust leads him/her to imitate the actions of others even though they may prove ineffective. It means that he needs to be more daring but able to grasp a good decision, thanks to the future contingency.

The Algerian leader acts in uncertainty, facing contingent events, such as unforeseen initiatives by the public authorities and/or decisions by entrepreneurs. One of the entrepreneurs said: "I know that I can win more soon if I am careful". The objective of the Algerian entrepreneur is to make the company he manages to survive; in fact, this constraint of survival obliges him to imagine the future and foresee it.

Our second hypothesis is instead invalidated. We deduce that the Algerian entrepreneur needs an innovative spirit that facilitates the achievement of performance. We note that Algerian SMEs are moderately proactive, which does not make it possible to achieve the various performance dimensions.

4.6 Regression Models

A multiple regression analysis was conducted to assess the influence of each dimension of the EO on the achievement of performance at the level of Algerian manufacturing SMEs.

Taking 'Financial Per.' as the dependent variable, the regression analysis shows that the global model is significant (sig=0.000). However, we note that proactivity and risk-taking have a significant and positive influence (R=0,701, R2= 0,565, R2 adjusted =0,541) on Performance / Per. Financial. In other words, the more

Table 11. ANOVA

Model	Sum of Squares	Df	Mean Square	F	Sig.
Regression **Residual** **Total**	7,710 6,590 14,300	3 26 29	3,237 ,330	9,796	,000[a]

a. Predictors: (constant) "My firm, for the most part, has a solid proclivity for high-risk projects." "In dealing with competitors, my company normally starts activities which competitors then point react to."

b. Dependant Variable: "Financial Performance"

Table 12. Model summary

Model	R	R Square	Adjusted R Square	Std. Error of the Estimate	Change Statistics					Durbin-Watson
					R Square Change	F Change	Df1	Df2	Sig. F Change	
1	,701[a]	,565	,541	,789110	,754	7.475	2	35	,000	1,652

c. Predictors: (constant) "My firm, for the most part, has a solid proclivity for high-risk projects." "In dealing with competitors, my company normally starts activities which competitors then point react to."

d. Dependant Variable: "Financial Performance"

proactive and risk-taking entrepreneurs are, the more financially successful their companies will be.

For "Customer Performance", the regression model shows that the model is globally significant (sig= 0.020). We note that only one dimension of Entrepreneurial Orientation significantly and positively influences the " Customer Performance" indicator. Let the risk-taking (sig<0.005 and Beta>0). The global model explains an average part of 'Customer Performance", i.e. 38.3% (R=0.785, R2=0.574, Adjusted R2= 0.383). The more risk-taking attitudes the manager adopts, the luckier his company will be in satisfying its customers regarding product quality.

We also found that there is a significant positive relationship (sig<0 and Beta>to 0, (R=0.685, R2=0.589, Adjusted R2= 0.483) between the only psychological trait that characterizes the Algerian entrepreneur "the Need for achievement" and proactivity, one of the dimensions of entrepreneurial orientation. However, we did not find statically significant relationships between the other psychological traits and EO.

The Entrepreneurial Orientation of Algerian entrepreneurs can be assessed through proactivity and risk-taking. The latter gives to the achievement of financial and customer performance. Innovation capacity was not identified as a significant factor influencing performance in the multiple regression analysis. This shows that this dimension is absent in Algerian SMEs.

Table 13. Model summary

Model	R	R Square	Adjusted R Square	Std. Error of the Estimate	Change Statistics					Durbin-Watson
					R Square Change	F Change	Df1	Df2	Sig. F Change	
1	,785[a]	,574	,383	,88440	,854	9.475	2	35	,020	1,652

Figure 3. Proposed model after regression: Case of Algeria
Source: Conducted by researchers

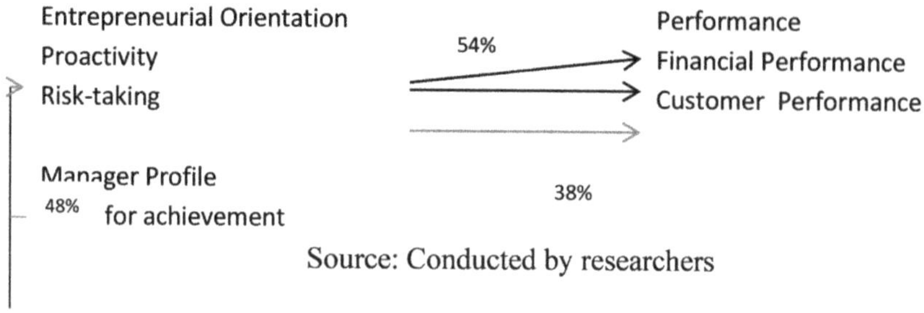

Source: Conducted by researchers

Algerian entrepreneurs still need to pay more attention to environmental protection and waste recycling requirements because we did not find significant links between the dimensions of entrepreneurial orientation and sustainable development performance.

5. CONCLUSION

In the Algerian economy, we have noted the existence of a specific entrepreneurial environment, linked mainly to the socio-economic and socio-cultural dimensions (informal economy and unemployment), cumbersome administrative procedures the lack of financing, skills and/or training, expertise and as well as the uncertainty that has characterized the Algerian market for decades (Zina and Ettayib, 2011).

In developed countries, SMEs are the critical employment and growth engine source. Their role in the economic fabric of Algeria, though, remains relatively timid and weak. The main guidelines of this research are:

Entrepreneurship must be encouraged, and the rapid growth of innovative SMEs must be facilitated as an effective means of reducing poverty, creating new jobs, and increasing productivity through the income they distribute, thereby improving the living standards of citizens.

Facilitating access to capital, development, technology and international markets for Algerian SMSs; Ultimately, the essential thing is to profoundly change the mentalities of Algerians in general and economic and political decision-makers in particular with regard to the need for entrepreneurship. A courageous and relevant goal is to teach entrepreneurship in secondary school classes. Indeed, this objective is a fundamental condition for the desired change in mentality. It will be feasible and possible only with a robust political will, fuelled by a keen awareness of the problems that hinder, or even block, the necessary adaptation of the structures and rules that govern Algeria's functioning to the requirements of a complex and profoundly changing environment.

The results of this research open an exciting avenue for future studies in an emerging field of research: the role of contextual culture and entrepreneurial culture in achieving performance.

REFERENCES

Acha, N. (2013). Accompagnement de l'Orientation entrepreneuriale par un management entrepreneurial: Une approche par les ressources. *XXII International Strategic Management Conference(AIMS).*

Acquier, A., & Aggeri, F. (2008). Une généalogie de la penséemanagérialesur la RSE. *Revue française de gestion, 180.*

Austin. (2006). Social and Commercial Entrepreneurship: Same, Different, or Both? *Entrepreneurship Theory and Practice, 30*(1).

Bergeron, H. (2002). *La gestionstratégique et les mesures de la performance non financière des PME.* 6th Congrès international francophone sur la PME, Montréal, Canada.

Biggadike, R. (1979). The Risky Business of Diversification. *Harvard Business Review, 57*(3), 103–111.

Boyd, N. G., & Vozikis, G. S. (1994). The Influence Of Self-Efficacy On The Development Of Entrepreneurial Intentions And Actions. *Entrepreneurship Theory and Practice, 18*(4), 63–77. doi:10.1177/104225879401800404

Burgelman, R. A. (1983). A model of the interaction of strategic behavior, corporate context, and the concept of strategy. *Strategic Management Journal.*

Cassar, G. (2007). Money, money, money? A longitudinal investigation of entrepreneur career reasons growth preferences and achieved growth. *Entrepreneurship and Regional Development, 19*(1), 89–107. doi:10.1080/08985620601002246

Covin, J. G., & Wales, W. J. (2012). The measurement of entrepreneurial orientation. *Entrepreneurship Theory and Practice, 36*(4), 677–702. doi:10.1111/j.1540-6520.2010.00432.x

DeNoble, A., Ehrlich, S., & Singh, G. (2007). Toward the development of a family business self-efficacy scale: A resource-based perspective. *Family Business Review, 20*(2), 127–140. doi:10.1111/j.1741-6248.2007.00091.x

Dess, G. G., & Robinson, R. B. Jr. (1984). Measuring organizational performance in the absence of objective measures: The case of the privately-held firm and conglomerate business unit. *Strategic Management Journal, 5*(3), 265–273. doi:10.1002mj.4250050306

Fayolle, A., & Cherchem, N. (2010). Culture d'entreprise, profil du dirigeant et orientation entrepreneuriale des PME: Un modèlethéorique. 10 èmecongrès international Francophone surl'entrepreneuriat et la PME, Bordeaux, France.

Forbes, D. P. (2005). The Effects of Strategic Decision Making on Entrepreneurial Self- Efficacy. *Entrepreneurship Theory and Practice, 29*(5), 599–626. doi:10.1111/j.1540-6520.2005.00100.x

Fortin, P.A. (2004). *La culture entrepreneuriale, un antidote à la pauvreté*. Collection Entreprendre.

Ginsberg, A., & Guth, W. (1990). Corporate Entrepreneurship (Guest Editors' Introduction). *Strategic Management Journal, 11*, 5–15.

Gray, C. (2002). Entrepreneurship, resistance to change and growth in small firms. *Journal of Small Business and Enterprise Development, 9*(1), 61–72. doi:10.1108/14626000210419491

Jarvis, R., Curan, J., Kitching, J., & Et Lightfoot, G. (2000). The use of quantitative and qualitative criteria in the measurement of performance in small firms. *Journal of Small Business and Enterprise Development, 7*(2), 123–134. doi:10.1108/EUM0000000006834

Kaplan, R., & Norton, D. (1996). Linking the Balanced Scorecard to Stategy. *California Management Review, 39*(1), 53–79. doi:10.2307/41165876

Kuratko Donald, F., & Audretsch David, B. (2009). Strategic Entrepreneurship: Exploring Different Perspectives of an Emerging Concept. *Entrepreneurship Theory and Practice, 33*(1), 1–17. doi:10.1111/j.1540-6520.2008.00278.x

Lucien, B. (2014). Entrepreneurship is not a whim, it is a necessity. *The Business Journal, 29*. https://www.lesaffaires.com/strategie-d-entreprise/entreprendre/

Lumpkin & Dess. (1996). Clarifying the entrepreneurial orientation construct and linking it to performance. *Academy of Management Review*.

Mayrfoer, U. (2006). Marketing. Bréal.

McGraw, E., Alain, R., & Robichaud, Y. (2001). Toward the development of a measuring instrument for entrepreneurial motivation. *Journal of Developmental Entrepreneurship*, *6*(2), 189.

McMullen, J. S., & Shepherd, D. A. (2006). Entrepreneurial action and the role of uncertainty in the theory of the entrepreneur". *Academy of Management Review*, *31*(1), 132–152. doi:10.5465/amr.2006.19379628

Miller, D. (1983). The correlates of entrepreneurship in three types of firms. *Management Science*, *29*(7), 770–791. doi:10.1287/mnsc.29.7.770

Miller, D., & Toulouse, J. M. (1986). Chief executive personality and corporate strategy and structure in small firms. *Management Science*, *32*(11), 1389–1409. doi:10.1287/mnsc.32.11.1389

Mintzberg, H. (1979). *The structuring of organizations: A synthesis of the research*. University of Illinois at Urbana-Champaign's Desautels Faculty of Management.

Morin, E., Guérin, M., & Boulianne, É. (1996). Les indicateurs de performance. Academic Press.

Morris, M.-H., Mihasaki, N.-N., & Watters, C.-E. (2006). Thedilemma of growth: Understanding venture size choices of women entrepreneurs. *Journal of Small Business Management*, *44*(2), 221–244. doi:10.1111/j.1540-627X.2006.00165.x

Nambubbi, L. (2016). *Entrepreneurial Personality Traits That Affect Venture Development and Growth* [Doctoral dissertation]. United States International University-Africa.

Neely, A. (1999). The performance measurement revolution: Why now and what next? *International Journal of Operations & Production Management*, *19*(2), 205–228. doi:10.1108/01443579910247437

Okhomina.D, (2010). Entrepreneurial orientation and psychological traits: the moderating influence of supportive environment. *Journal of Behavioral Studies in Business.*

Phares, E. J. (1976). *Locus of control in personality* (Vol. 174). General Learning Press.

Pinchot, G. (1985). *Intrapreneuring: Why you don't have to leave the corporation to become an entrepreneur*. Academy for Entrepreneurial Leadership Historical Research Reference in Entrepreneurship.

Poon, J. M. L., Ainuddin, R. A., & Junit, H. S. (2006). Effects of self-concept traits and Entrepreneuriale Orientation on firm performance. *International Small Business Journal, 24*(1), 61–68. doi:10.1177/0266242606059779

Randerson, K. (2011). Orientation entrepreneuriale:uneapproche par les configurations. *7th congress of the Académie de l'Entrepreneuriat et de l'innovation*, Paris, France.

Report, G. E. M. (2009). *Global Entrepreneurship Monitor: GEM-MENA Regional Report 2009*. Middle East and North Africa.

Sadler-Smith, E., Hampson, Y., Chaston, I., & Et Badger, B. (2003). Managerialbehaviour; Entrepreneurial style, and small firm performance. *Journal of Small Business Management, 41*(1), 47–67. doi:10.1111/1540-627X.00066

Schollhammer, H. (1982). Internal corporate entrepreneurship. In Encyclopedia of entrepreneurship (pp. 209–229). Prentice Hall.

Scott, S. (2008). A leading expert in entrepreneurial activity in the United States and other. Yale University Press.

Shane, S., & Venkataraman, S. (2000). The promise of entrepreneurship as a field of research. *Academy of Management Review, 25*(01), 217–226. doi:10.5465/amr.2000.2791611

St-Pierre, J. (2005). *La gestionfinancière des PME: théoriesetpratiques*. University of Quebec Press.

St-Pierre, J., & Cadieux, L. (2009). *La conception de la performance: quel lien avec le profil entrepreneurial des propriétairesdirigeants de PME*. 6th Congress of the Académie de l'Entrepreneuriat, Sophia-Antipolis, France.

Stevenson & Jarillo. (1990). A Paradigm of Entrepreneurship: Entrepreneurial Management. *Strategic Management Journal, 15*(7), 521–536.

Walker, E., & Et Brown, A. (2004). What success factors are important to small business owners? *International Small Business Journal, 22*(6), 577–594. doi:10.1177/0266242604047411

Wiklund & Shepherd. (2003). Knowledge Based Resources, Entrepreneurial Orientation, and the Performance of Small and Medium-Sized Businesses. *Strategic Management Journal*, 24.

Wood & Bandura. (1989). Impact of conceptions of ability on self- regulatory Mechanisms and complex decision Making. *Journal of Personality and Social Psychology, 56*(3), 407-415.

Zahra, S. A. (1991). A conceptual model of entrepreneurship as firm behavior: A critique and extension. *Entrepreneurship Theory and Practice, 17*(4), 5–21. doi:10.1177/104225879301700401

Zina, A. (2022). Entrepreneurial Orientation, Organizational Culture and Business Performance in SMEs: Evidence from Emerging Economy. *Sustainability, 14*(9).

Zina, A., & Ettayib, M. (2021). The personality of the Algerian leader and Entrepreneurship: Test of analysis by structural equations (Smart PLS). *Industrial Economics Review, 11*(2).

ENDNOTES

1 http://www.mdipi.gov.dz/spip.php?page=plan

2 https://www.doingbusiness.org/content/dam/doingBusiness/country/a/algeria/DZA.pdf

3 "In general, the top managers in my firm favour a strong emphasis on R&D, technological leadership and innovation."

4 "Very many new lines of products or services."

5 "My company is radically changing its products or services."

6 "In dealing with competitors, my company normally starts activities which competitors then point react to."

7 "In dealing with competitors, my company is all the time the main business to present new products/services, regulatory procedures, operating innovations, etc."

8 "In general, the top supervisors of my company have a solid tendency to be in front of others in presenting clever ideas or products."

9 "My firm for the most part has a solid proclivity for high risk projects."

10 "My company typically takes an aggressive and bold stance to maximize the exploitation of potential opportunities."

11 "Owing to the nature of the context, striking wide-going acts are essential to accomplish the firm's objectives."

Chapter 7
Entrepreneurship Education: A Sustainable Strategy for Economic Development in Nigeria

Azeez Babatunde Adebakin
https://orcid.org/0000-0001-5963-0873
Obafemi Awolowo University, Nigeria

Adesoji Emmanuel Ayanlowo
https://orcid.org/0000-0002-7444-8508
Baptist College of Theology, Oyo, Nigeria

ABSTRACT

Every aspect of a country's economy, including education, now places a high priority on economic development. Economic development is the all-encompassing process of steadily enhancing the wellbeing of each person as well as the equitable allocation of available economic resources. No nation can surpass the caliber of its educational system, formal or informal, and education is a necessary tool for economic success. This chapter therefore presents as a crucial element of education that has a significant potential to stimulate economic growth and development through the lens of entrepreneurship education.

1.0 INTRODUCTION

Over the years, the need to continuously improve economic condition has become a growing concern among countries across the globe. It is no doubt that governments, at all levels (national, regional, and international), through their ministries, institutions and agencies are endlessly making efforts to cushion existing or imminent poor

DOI: 10.4018/978-1-6684-7127-2.ch007

economic outlook, with its far reaching and overarching consequences on growth and development. As a result, economic development has become a central agenda entrenched in the operations of every sector of a nation's economy including education. This implies that all sectoral activities must be channeled towards achieving development for the country.

Onuigbo (2021) conceived economic development as sustained and combined actions (safety, literacy, social inclusion and health) of government and citizens to promote general well-being. In other words, economic development refers to all-inclusive process of continuously improving the well-being of individual and the entire community through their active, free and meaningful participation and distribution of economic resources (Erhun, 2015). In his view, Ijere, (2014) established that it is the efforts taken to improve the quality of life which is measured with indicators such as Gross Domestic Product (GDP), life expectancy, literacy and levels of employment. This shows that economic development can be determined using different parameters.

From the economics standpoint, education stands as one of the crucial indicators for determining economic development (Valero, 2021). It is important to emphasise the central position of education in improving all sectors of the economy such as agriculture, health, finance, manufacturing, oil and gas, energy and aviation among others. This, it does through training and production of skilled manpower. Further implication to this connotes that education, formal or informal, is an indispensable tool for economic development (Chiemeka-Unogu, 2020). Hence, the justification for the popular axiom, 'no nation can rise above the quality of its educational system' (Jonathan et al., 2019).

One of the essential components of education that has great capacity for driving economic growth and development is entrepreneurship education (Adebakin & Ayanlowo, 2023). This assertion supports the idea of the Consortium of Entrepreneurship Education (CEE, USA) that entrepreneurship education is a form of education that seeks to prepare people, especially youths, to be responsible and enterprising individuals who will contribute to economic development and sustainable communities (Nwosu & Chukwudi, 2018). The central thought embedded in this definition has to do with preparation of individuals to participate in developing and sustaining the economy. This indicates that entrepreneurship education is not limited to creating business ventures, but also involves developing people to champion positive societal changes.

Stemming from the ideology on which entrepreneurship is established, it could be stated that implementing an effective entrepreneurship education is tantamount to promoting sustainable economic development. However, the situation, as observed in Nigeria in terms of poverty, unemployment, poor standard of living indicates that the nation's economy is seriously challenged and declining. Consequently, this chapter seeks to explore entrepreneurship education as an important strategy for the sustainability of economic development in Nigeria.

2.0 CONCEPT OF ENTREPRENEURSHIP EDUCATION

The concept of entrepreneurship education is majorly associated with higher leaning and education. Although, there could be some elements of skill training for students at the lower levels, yet, more advocacies for this component of education is concentrated at higher level. This is because students at higher level are prepared as skilled manpower to productively take advantage of the labour market. This view agrees with Chiemeka-Unogu (2020) who explained that entrepreneurship education is basically offered in universities. Hence, it could be inferred that entrepreneurship education essentially deals with the training offered at higher education institutions to provide individuals with skills to become self-reliant through employment creation for themselves and others after graduation.

According to Kalyoncuoğlu et al. (2017) entrepreneurship education refers to the development and transfer of entrepreneurial knowledge and skills, including technological innovation, product development, discovery and exploration of new business opportunities, leadership, creativity, negotiation and long-term business planning. It could also be described as the development of entrepreneurial competence, attitudes and behaviours. Considering this understanding, it implies that entrepreneurship education involves the acquisition of wide-range set of skills towards becoming an entrepreneurial and enterprising individual.

Entrepreneurship education also involves the acquisition of theoretical and practical entrepreneurial skills (Deveci & Seikkula-Leino, 2018). The implication of offering a combination both experiences is germane for promoting and sustaining economic growth and development. It should be noted that entrepreneurship education that is deficient of either theoretical or practical skill may fail to drive the economy in desired direction. Lending credence to this, Nwosu and Chukwudi (2018) submitted that entrepreneurship education can make significant contributions to economic growth in widening employment opportunities, when it is practically oriented. This, therefore, suggests that entrepreneurship education curriculum should be equipped with contents that support theoretical and practical learning that will allow individuals to contribute to economic growth and development.

Part of the essential components of entrepreneurship education that necessitates its practical applicability is technical and vocational training. This corroborates the position of Ebong and Nwakudu (2017) that entrepreneurship education is designed to provide graduates with sufficient training that will propel the effective use of their creative and innovative abilities, towards identifying and exploiting novel business opportunities and to be economically self-reliant. While Ebong and Nwakudu's submission may portend individual benefits of entrepreneurship education, it also has implication for the economy at large in the sense that, individual enterprise created through entrepreneurial efforts will serve as a catalyst for economic growth and development.

In addition, entrepreneurship education can be conceptualised in terms of the benefits it seeks to offer. Balogun and Olatoro (2020) asserted that entrepreneurship education is the type of education that promote poverty alleviation, stimulate innovations and foster healthy competition. In their view, Peluola et al. (2014) reviewed that entrepreneurship development, entrepreneurial intention, entrepreneurial success, creativity, innovations, wealth creation and talent development are benefits accrue to entrepreneurship education. In view of these monumental benefits, it is pertinent to suggest that entrepreneurship education should be positioned as one of the central ideas in the economic planning and developmental agenda of a nation.

Within the formal school settings, Olorundare and Kayode (2014) identified three aims which entrepreneurship education must achieve to include: learn and understand entrepreneurship, learn to acquire entrepreneurial aptitudes and learn to become an entrepreneur. These aims, first, indicate that developing an effective entrepreneurship education requires painstaking efforts of policy makers and curriculum experts to plan and design learning contents that is capable of transforming individuals to become entrepreneurial. Secondly, they underscore the need for managers and administrator of higher institutions of learning, particularly in Nigeria, to ensure that the training components of entrepreneurship education are successfully implemented.

Viewing through the lens of economic and social development, Ogundele et al. (2013) stressed that entrepreneurship education aims at achieving certain objectives which have positive implication for economic development. These objectives range from identification of business opportunities; selection of opportunities; decision on form of enterprise; allocation and distribution of resources; coordination of factors of production (land, labour and capital); planning and controlling organisational programmes and activities; mobilisation and utilisation of locally produced raw materials; risk management; employment generation; marketing activities for customer satisfaction; and innovation to meet with needs of local market.

A salient trajectory of thought to point out from the different scholarly perspectives explored above is that entrepreneurship education can be described as the training or learning that offers lifelong skills. Conceptualising entrepreneurship education from this standpoint is imperative because it is the type of education that is capable of changing the orientation and attitude of its recipients, and equipping them with requisite entrepreneurial skills, attitudes and competencies that will arouse their enterprising dispositions. Invariably, individuals who had successfully identified and initiated an enterprise through their entrepreneurial knowledge are most likely not willingly to seek paid employment any more but to remain tenacious in growing their business to sustain relevance in the market over time. When this happens, it is evident that such individual had acquired life-long skills.

3.0 RATIONALE FOR ENTREPRENEURSHIP EDUCATION

The need for entrepreneurship education cannot be overstressed simply because it has the wherewithal to drive the growth and development agenda of a nation (Osakwe, 2015). Besides, the poor and unfavourable economy, with its underlying consequences of unemployment, poverty, and poor standard of living on individuals and the state at large, has proven to be a strong justification for the inclusion of entrepreneurship education as an economic tool for development.

Ayanlowo (2021), while examining entrepreneurship education as a strategy to enhance students' employment prospects, discussed that the objectives of entrepreneurship education include: offer functional education to the youths to enable them become self-employed and self-reliant; provide adequate training for young graduates to become creative and innovative in identifying novel business opportunities; serve as a catalyst for economic growth and development of a nation; equip young graduates with adequate training in risk management; reduce poverty rate; create employment opportunities; reduce rural-urban migration; provide training and support for young graduates to establish and sustain small and/or medium-sized businesses; promote smooth transition from traditional to modern industrial economy; produce employable graduates (Akpochafo & Alika, 2018; Akpan, 2021).

To further justify the need for entrepreneurship education, Olorundare and Kayode (2014) highlighted essential skills offered in entrepreneurship training which also doubled as its objectives. They include: positive attitudes, high aptitude for rational critical thinking and timely decision making; clear vision, generation of progressive ideals, drive and passion for success; ability to convert vision to concrete reality; creativity, innovativeness, courageousness and self-confidence; ability to assume reasonable risk; mercurial ingenuity, resourcefulness, patience and/or opportunities insight; confidence and good judgement; prudence in the management of resources; willingness to learn and utilise knowledge; and hard work – an indispensable ingredient of success in business. Summarily, these skills could be considered as lifelong learning skills, capable of fostering individual and ultimately national development.

A vivid look at the objectives presupposes and provided a strong basis about why entrepreneurship education is mostly essential and required in the development of any nation. It is evident that each of them, if achieved, would directly or indirectly improve individual standard of living and stimulate economic progress at micro and macro levels. Hence, it could be argued that entrepreneurship education is a tool for economic growth and development, considering its objectives and potential positive influences on the economy. This further accentuates the need for government and all stakeholders to prioritise entrepreneurship education as a strategy for sustainable economic development.

4.0 STRATEGIES FOR PROMOTING ENTREPRENEURSHIP EDUCATION IN NIGERIA

Entrepreneurship education was introduced into the Nigerian education system, particularly for higher institutions of learning in 2006, following the directives of the Federal Government that entrepreneurship studies be integrated in the higher education curricular as a compulsory course for students (Adebakin, 2020; Agu & Ayogu, 2015; Gabadeen & Raimi, 2012). This was done with a view to equiping graduates with skills to produce goods and services that will make them job creators. As a result, higher institutions (including universities, polytechnics and colleges of education) have since then included entrepreneurial training in their different courses to become a mandatory aspect of students' coursework from 2007/2008 academic session (Akpan, 2021; Chiemeka-Unogu, 2020). This step is a laudable initiative that could be identified as the one of the strategic efforts towards promoting entrepreneurship education in the country.

The effort of individuals, institutions, agencies and government in promoting entrepreneurship education in Nigeria is worthy of note. Balogun and Olatoro (2020) emphasised that programmes and activities aimed at enhancing the knowledge, skills and attitude of individuals and groups to become entrepreneurs could be regarded as strategies that promote entrepreneurship. Thus, it is imperative to examine the different policy programmes instituted as strategies for promoting entrepreneurship education in Nigeria.

4.1 National Directorate of Employment (NDE)

According to Kanu et al. (2023), the establishment of NDE was one of the responses of the Nigerian government to combating unemployment challenge and training the youths to acquire entrepreneurial skills. This agency was set up in 1986 to implement strategies that would solve the problems of mass unemployment among Nigerians by grooming unemployed youths in entrepreneurship or business development, vocational skills, labour-based works, rural employment promotion and job placement guidance and counseling (Adebakin, 2020; Agu & Ayogu, 2015). The establishment of the NDE, with the mandate to provide unemployment solutions to youths within the formal and informal education settings, is no doubt a key strategy to promote economic growth through entrepreneurship education.

4.2 Student Industrial Working Experience Scheme (SIWES)

The SIWES is a learning arrangement facilitated to students within the formal education setting, particularly those at higher level of education. This scheme was established to enhance the practical and entrepreneurship skills of undergraduates (Adebakin, 2020; Alao et al., 2022). SIWES is a core part of the students' learning, often observed at the second or penultimate year of their studies and a major requirement for graduation. Specifically, the scheme was designed to provide students with opportunity to interact with the relevant industries to their disciplines and specific to their learning for the purpose of equipping them with practical skills that would make them employable and enterprising (Babalola & Tiamiyu, 2013). In Nigeria, SIWES is associated with learning for students in science-related courses. Other disciplines may adopt industrial attachment, industrial training, internship and teaching practice (specifically for education courses) as industrial working experience scheme for students during their studies. It is worthy of note that the scheme is a fundamental strategy to promote entrepreneurship. More so, seeing that the successful execution of the scheme is a collaborative effort of the government and the higher education institutions through policy making and implementation. It could be argued that promoting entrepreneurship education requires the painstaking contributions of all stakeholders in Nigeria.

4.3 Small and Medium Enterprises Development Agency of Nigeria (SMEDAN)

The establishment of SMEDAN could be identified as one of the strategies initiated by the Nigerian. This programme, according to Agu and Ayogu (2015), was introduced to promote the development of Small and Medium Enterprises (SMEs) within the Nigeria economy, and it has recorded tremendous success in its entrepreneurship development programmes. An example is the N200billion Small & Medium Scale Enterprises Guarantee Scheme (SMECGS) of the CBN to promote SMEs access to more credit facilities. The scheme has disbursed over N1 billion to 20 qualified applicants, with the attendant boosts in their small businesses and employment generation. On the contrary, Balogun and Olatoro (2020) stressed that SMEs have performed below expectations in Nigeria due to reasons such as frequent change in policies emanating from political instability as well as entrepreneurs' attitude. In spite of the challenges that may be associated with SMEs in the country, the advent of SMEDAN cannot be denied to have contributed to the progress of entrepreneurial activities.

4.4 Technical and Vocational Training

The Federal Republic of Nigeria (2014), through her National Policy on Education (NPE), made provision for technical and vocational training and its overlapping role in promoting entrepreneurship education in Nigeria. In line with the NPE, technical and vocational training deals with the study of technologies and related sciences and the acquisition of practical skills, attitudes, understanding and knowledge relating to occupations in various sectors of economic and social life. Examples of this type of training include electrical and electronics technology, metal work technology, mechanical/automobile technology, building technology, woodwork technology, agricultural training (cropping, livestock, forestry, fishing processing and marketing of agricultural products), ICT training, product manufacturing among others (Okoye & Arimonu, 2016). Bearing in mind the policy provision, it is no doubt that technical and vocational training brings to fore varying elements that qualifies it as a strategy that promote entrepreneurship for economic growth (Adebakin, 2020; Ubogu, 2020). To buttress this, the NPE also posited that giving training and imparting necessary skills to individuals to be economically self-reliant is one of the goals of technical and vocational training which could be adjudged to have entrepreneurship focus.

4.5 Entrepreneurship Development Centres (EDCs)

The establishment of entrepreneurship development centres (EDCs) has contributed immensely to the progress of entrepreneurship learning and education in Nigeria (Agu & Ayogu, 2015). Although, it may seem considerable benefits have not accrue to the nation from the establishment of EDCs, seeing how graduate unemployment had persisted in the country. Nonetheless, Akpan (2021) asserted that higher institutions in Nigeria have made commendable efforts for effective implementation of entrepreneurship education through the creation of EDCs to provide maximum supports to students in their entrepreneurship training.

In addition, Peluola et al. (2014) expounded the role of EDCs as it relates to achieving the objectives of entrepreneurship education to include: participating in the review and adapting the entrepreneurship curriculum to suit the various requirements and challenges of the environment; developing student with entrepreneurship spirit with relevant tools and techniques; design a framework on how to start and manage all functional areas of business enterprise for student; develop students with networking skill as contemporarily relevant for business success; producing graduates that will actualise various economic development programmes of the government; practically engaging students with product development and business management; and providing active and functional incubation centre for starters with agreed terms business friendly policies. Without mincing words, it is evident that EDCs is established as a strategy to promote full and effective implementation of entrepreneurship education in Nigeria. Therefore, it is essential for government and administrators of higher institutions to be proactive in creating and equipping these centres with requisite human, material and financial resources that will achieve their purpose of establishment.

In furtherance to understanding the strategies for promoting entrepreneurship education, these efforts (governmental programmes or schemes) are tantamount to strategies that stimulate entrepreneurial activities in Nigeria. These programmes or schemes highlighted above are few among many other efforts taken by the Nigerian government both at federal, state and local levels in developing and sustaining entrepreneurship activities for economic progress.

5.0 THEORY OF ECONOMIC DEVELOPMENT

The relevant theory to this chapter is the Human Capital Theory propounded by Schultz Theodore in 1961. This theory is crucial for economic development and holds that education is a vital instrument for improving the productivity of people by imparting them with useful knowledge and skills, thereby raising their future income and lifetime earnings. Among major ideas of the theory is its focus on strengthening the education or training given to an individual in order to satisfy the needs of skill development and specifications across all occupational strata of a nation's economy. Becker (1993) supports by arguing that Human Capital Theory deals with knowledge, information, ideas, skills, and health of individuals targeted towards enhancing economic productivity. This implies that human education is directly related to the level of individual and economic performance.

The relevance of the Human Capital Theory for economic development cannot be underestimated simply because its advocates for improving individual and economic productivity. Moreover, the theory shows the relationship between education and economic development by advocating that education should be invigorated to impart skills that would translate to economic development in terms of employment generation, increased productivity, income generation and wealth creation. In view of the theory's position, entrepreneurship education remains a vital component of the education system that is capable of promoting essential skills for economic development.

6.0 ENTREPRENEURSHIP EDUCATION AS STRATEGY FOR SUSTAINABLE ECONOMIC DEVELOPMENT IN NIGERIA

According to Onyekwere (2016), economic development refers to efforts taken to improve the standard of living and quality of life for a community by creating and/or retaining employments and supporting or growing incomes. Meanwhile, sustainable development involves judicious use and conservation of economic resources for the overall improvement in the quality of life for the present and future generations (Erhun, 2015). It could simply be described as achieving quality of life for people now and later.

The nexus between entrepreneurship education and economic development could be likened to that of a round peg in a round hole, hence, entrepreneurship education could be considered as a strategic tool for economic growth and development, considering its ability to drive creativity and innovations for product and service creation. Obviously, the benefits of entrepreneurship for the economy in terms of increased goods and services, employment generation, wealth creation, improved standard of living and increase in national income, are key elements of advocacy for sustainable economic development. With respect to the Nigerian situation, the argument of Emmanuel et al. (2016), as highlighted below, on the tangible ways by which entrepreneurship education can sustain economic development is relevant for discussion. These include:

6.1 Creation of New Technologies, Products, and Services

It is apparent that entrepreneurship promotes creativity and innovation (Okeke & Eme, 2014), being attributes that would be required of individuals to innovatively manipulate new technologies for the production of new products and services. Emmanuel et al. (2016) affirmed that invention of modern products including computers, airplanes, mobile phones et cetera can be traceable to development of entrepreneurial activities in industrial countries like Japan and USA. More so, mechanized farming involving the use of technological equipment in Europe is attributed to entrepreneurship development. Seeing how these new technologies, products and services have transformed and sustained the global economy over the years, it is imperative to note that entrepreneurship education is relevant to sustaining economic development in Nigeria as well.

6.2 Increase in Productivity

Increase in productivity is one of the essential indices of economic development that entrepreneurship seeks to continuously promote. According to Yadav and Marwah.

(2015), productivity refers to the process of creating more goods and services using minimum labor and other resources such as money and time. Entrepreneurship education increases productivity at individuals and state levels respectively through innovative, technological and managerial expertise of entrepreneurs. Olorundare and Kayode (2014) further argued that entrepreneurship education is crucial to discovering and developing talented, creative, skillful and competitive individuals that will be the nation's innovative assets towards increasing in productivity. Furthermore, Ejimonye and Eneogu (2020) assert that entrepreneurship education will increase the innovative skills of prospective entrepreneurs and the productivity of their businesses. This implies that entrepreneurship education has a significant role to play in sustaining economic development in Nigeria through increased productivity.

6.3 Enhancement of Market Competition

Entrepreneurship widens the market of goods and services, and promotes healthy competition that provides consumers with a variety of alternative products to purchase at reduced prices (Emmanuel et al., 2016). With increased productivity occasioned by entrepreneurship education, the market would be made larger to terminate monopolistic activities of any producer that may have negative implication for individuals and the economy (Dieppe, 2021). Thus, individuals will have opportunity to improve their satisfaction. Moreover, an expansion of the market would create more job opportunities and infrastructures necessary for business development such as roads, communication, power supply et cetera all of which are essential to sustaining economic development in Nigeria.

6.4 Employment Generation

One of the objectives of entrepreneurship education is to generate employment opportunities for through the establishment of business enterprises (Ayanlowo, 2021; Akpan, 2021). It is no doubt that the creation of business enterprises would encourage effective use of untapped resources and provide employment opportunities for others who are unemployed so that they can have a means of livelihood. In addition, employment generation is able to promote social wealth by curbing idleness, thuggery, drug addiction and insecurity among others (Akogwu, 2020). All these benefits associated to employment generation are germane for sustainability of economic development and could be traceable to entrepreneurship education.

6.5 Income Generation and Wealth Creation

Income and wealth creation is an important measure of economic development. This presupposes that a nation's development could be associated to the level at which she is able to generate income and create wealth through economic activities. Bearing this in mind, Chiemeka-Unogu (2020) posited that entrepreneurship education, at the macro level, stimulates economic activities, increases government revenue through taxation, increases per capita income and Gross Domestic Product (GDP) through income generation. At the micro level, entrepreneurship generates income for individuals from their employment for consumption, investments and savings. To this end, it is obvious that income and wealth creations are essential economic developmental variables that could be sustained by entrepreneurship education.

7.0 CONCLUSION

Economic development is an indispensable element of progress in any nation. Its relevance for promoting quality of life cannot be underestimated, hence, the need to ensure its sustainability. The role of entrepreneurship education as a strategy for sustaining economic development is crucial considering its ability to drive economic growth and development. This may have led to the establishment of the following initiatives to promote entrepreneurship education in Nigeria: NDE, SIWES, SMEDAN, technical and vocational training and EDCs. In spite of these laudable steps, poverty, unemployment, and poor standard of living are realities of the Nigeria economic situation. Nonetheless, it was affirmed that entrepreneurship education would suffice as a strategy to sustain the economic development in Nigeria through creation of new technologies, products and services; increase in productivity; enhancement of market competition; employment generation; and income generation and wealth creation.

REFERENCES

Adebakin, A. B. (2020). A review of measures, instances and frameworks of government policy on entrepreneurial practices in Nigeria. In C. O. Fashiku, M. A. Yusuf, S. O. Subair, O. T. Ajadi & T. L. Adepoju (Eds.), Dimensions of Politics, Policies and Thoughts in Education (pp. 72-81). Obafemi Awolowo University Press.

Adebakin, A. B., & Ayanlowo, A. E. (2023). Addressing the challenges of entrepreneurship and innovation in Nigeria: The roles of tertiary education. In M. E. A. Abdelli, N. Chemma, S. Ahlem, S. B. Maliki, & G. Singh (Eds.), *Competitive Advantage, Strategy and Innovation in Africa: Issues and Applications* (pp. 172–190). Routledge Taylor and Francis Group. doi:10.4324/9781003306405-10

Agu, E. O., & Ayogu, D. U. (2015). Assessing the prospects and problems of entrepreneurship development in Nigeria. *International Journal of Current Research and Academic Review*, *3*(10), 208–221.

Akogwu, A. P. (2020). Effects of job creation determinants on the security of Abuja Metropolis. *Gusau International Journal of Management and Social Sciences*, *3*(1), 14–14.

Akpan, O. E. (2021). Entrepreneurship studies education in tertiary institutions in Nigeria: Theories and practices. *International Journal of Vocational and Technical Education Research*, *7*(1), 35–42.

Akpochafo, G. O., & Alika, I. H. (2018). Perceived impact of entrepreneurship education on career development among undergraduates in South-South universities in Nigeria: Implication for counselling. *Journal of Education and Learning*, *7*(3), 102–108. doi:10.5539/jel.v7n3p102

Alao, O. E., Osanyinro, J. B., & Alao, P. O. (2022). Achieving the effectiveness of the Students Industrial Work Experience Scheme for sustainability of the Nigerian economy. *International Journal of Work-Integrated Learning*, *23*(3), 393–404.

Ayanlowo, A. E. (2021). *Relationship between students' employment prospects and demand for university education in Osun State, Nigeria* [Master's Dissertation]. Obafemi Awolowo University, Ile-Ife, Nigeria.

Babalola, Y. A., & Tiamiyu, R. (2013). Job creation and economic empowerment through Business education. *Information and Knowledge Management*, *3*(3), 64–67.

Balogun, B. B., & Olatoro, F. (2020). Challenges facing entrepreneurship development in Nigeria: An empirical review. *Journal of African Sustainable Development*, *19*(2), 75–82.

Becker, G. S. (1993). *Human capital: A theoretical and empirical analysis with special reference to education* (3rd ed.). University of Chicago Press. doi:10.7208/chicago/9780226041223.001.0001

Chiemeka-Unogu, C. M. (2020). Entrepreneurship education in Nigeria universities: Programmes and goals for sustainable national development. *Multidisciplinary Journal of Research Development*, *29*(1), 1–7.

Deveci, I., & Seikkula-Leino, J. (2018). A review of entrepreneurship education in teacher education. *Malaysian Journal of Learning and Instruction*, *15*(1), 105–148. doi:10.32890/mjli2018.15.1.5

Dieppe, A. (Ed.). (2021). *Global productivity: Trends, drivers, and policies*. World Bank Publications. doi:10.1596/978-1-4648-1608-6

Ebong, J. M., & Nwakudu, G. N. (2017). Managing entrepreneurship education at universities level in Rivers State in an era of economic recession. *African Journal of Educational Research and Development*, *9*(1), 10–19.

Ejimonye, J. C., & Eneogu, N. D. (2020). Productivity of innovative entrepreneurs in nigeria: Role of entrepreneurship education. *International Journal of Studies in Education*, *16*(2), 141–152.

Erhun, M. O. (2015). A sustainable approach to economic development in Nigeria: A legal perspective. *Journal of Economics and Sustainable Development*, *6*(14), 1–6.

Gabadeen, W. O., & Raimi, L. (2012). Management of entrepreneurship education in Nigerian higher institutions: Issues, challenges and way forward. *Abuja International Journal of Education and Management Sciences*, *2*, 1–26.

Ijere, T. C. (2014). The state, governance and socio-economic development realities in Nigeria. *Public Policy and Administration Research*, *4*(1), 46–49.

Jonathan, J., Daniel, V. L., & Bulus, G. (2019). The role of quality education in national development: The interface. *British Journal of Education. Learning and Development Psychology*, *2*(1), 21–30.

Kalyoncuoğlu, S., Aydıntan, B., & Göksel, A. (2017). The effect of entrepreneurship education on entrepreneurial intention: An experimental study on undergraduate business students. *Journal of Management Research*, *9*(3), 72–91. doi:10.5296/jmr.v9i3.11282

Kanu, M. C., Aja, C. E., & Umurhurhu, E. (2023). National directorate of employment trainees' ratings of their skills for employability in Anambra State. *African Journal of Educational Management. Teaching and Entrepreneurship Studies*, *9*(1), 32–43.

Nwosu, J. C., & Chukwudi, J. H. (2018). Entrepreneurship education and the challenges of graduate employability in Nigeria. *International Journal of Innovation, Management and Technology*, *9*(5), 189–193.

Ogundele, M. O., Kayode, D. J., Oduleke, F. L., & Alade, O. S. (2017). The influence of private sector involvement on entrepreneurial education of secondary schools in Kwara state, Nigeria. *MOJEM: Malaysian Online Journal of Educational Management*, *1*(1), 1–11.

Okeke, M. I., & Eme, O. I. (2014). Challenges facing entrepreneurs in Nigeria. *Singaporean Journal of Business Economics and Management Studies*, *3*(5), 18–34. doi:10.12816/0010956

Okoye, R., & Arimonu, M. O. (2016). Technical and vocational education in Nigeria: Issues, challenges and a way forward. *Journal of Education and Practice*, *7*(3), 113–118.

Olorundare, A. S., & Kayode, D. J. (2014). Entrepreneurship education in Nigerian universities: A tool for national transformation. *Asia Pacific Journal of Educators and Education*, *29*, 155–175.

Onuigbo, F. N. (2021). Human capital development and economic development in Nigeria- An analysis of the role of government. *International Journal of Innovative Social Sciences & Humanities Research*, *9*(4), 181–190.

Osakwe, R. N. (2015). Entrepreneurship education in Delta State tertiary institution as a means of achieving national growth and development. *International Journal of Higher Education*, *4*(1), 182–186. doi:10.5430/ijhe.v4n1p182

Peluola, S. B., Oyelola, T. O., Ajiboshin, I. O., Igwe, C. N., & Shokunbi, M. O. (2014). Achieving excellence in the operations of entrepreneurship development centres in Nigeria higher institutions. *Journal of Poverty. Investment and Development*, *5*, 37–41.

Schultz, T. W. (1961). Investment in human capital. *The American Economic Review*, *51*(1), 1–17.

Ubogu, R. (2020). Entrepreneurship education: Challenges and strategies towards promoting entrepreneurship in higher education in Nigeria. *Academic Journal of Interdisciplinary Studies*, *9*(5), 125–137. doi:10.36941/ajis-2020-0091

Valero, A. (2021). *Education and economic growth*. Discussion Paper No. 1764. Centre for Economic Performance, London School of Economics and Political Science.

Yadav, P., & Marwah, C. S. (2015). The concept of productivity. *International Journal of Engineering and Technical Research*, *3*(5), 192–196.

Chapter 8
A Review of the Promotion of Entrepreneurship in the Solar Water Heating Industry in Turkey

S. Ece Yilmaz
Adana Alparslan Türkeş Science and Technology University, Turkey

ABSTRACT

The integration of renewable energy and entrepreneurship concepts has the potential to foster economic growth. Despite its advantageous geographical position for solar energy utilization, Turkey's solar water heating system sector has yet to capitalize on its potential fully. Hence, there is a need to expand entrepreneurship in solar water heating systems. Consequently, attaining national and sustainable development goals can be facilitated alongside promoting regional development. This chapter examines the impact of entrepreneurship in the solar water heating system industry on economic growth, with a specific focus on Turkey's position in this sector. The evaluation is conducted by drawing upon relevant research. The chapter examines the various aspects that could potentially influence the development of entrepreneurship in the solar water heating system industry. It also proposes potential solutions to improve the prospects of solar water heating system entrepreneurship.

1. INTRODUCTION

The solar water heating system (SWHS) is a widely adopted solar energy technology that facilitates the transfer of heat from the sun's rays to a circulating medium,

DOI: 10.4018/978-1-6684-7127-2.ch008

typically water or air (Sadhishkumar & Balusamy, 2014). According to Kaygusuz & Kaygusuz (2002), these systems frequently supply hot water for domestic use in sunny coastal areas. In the present context, there is a growing trend towards its adoption due to economic factors. Consumers are compelled to seek other systems due to factors such as high volatility in currency rates and the occurrence of an energy crisis. Moreover, the increasing seriousness of environmental issues has contributed to the increased demand for these systems.

Turkey is strategically located in a geographically advantageous position to capitalize on solar, wind, and hydroelectric energy sources. Nevertheless, it has not yet attained its complete capacity. Turkey commonly utilizes SWHS, with a special focus on the Aegean and Mediterranean areas (IEA, 2021). According to Kapluhan (2021), the Mediterranean region is considered to be the highest-ranking area in terms of average annual total sunlight duration and yearly total radiation value. Research conducted on Turkey's radiation potential has revealed that the southern portion of the country exhibits higher suitability for radiation, particularly in the context of solar water heating (SWH) applications (Benli, 2016; Siampour et al., 2021). Based on data collected from the Adana Chamber of Commerce and Adana Chamber of Tradesmen and Craftsmen, it has been observed that a total of 53 enterprises operating in Adana, a Mediterranean region located in the southern part of Turkey renowned for its notable solar energy efficiency, are engaged in the production or distribution of SWHS. The current urban landscape lacks a sufficient number of enterprises that exhibit enhanced levels of production. Consequently, one may deduce that this figure is applicable even in a municipality characterized by optimal solar radiation levels and efficient infrastructure, indicating a general scarcity of firms engaged in the production of SWHS within the nation.

Furthermore, this particular case serves as evidence that the utilization of SWHS as a basis is not commonly observed in the renewable energy sector, hence indicating a deviation from usual entrepreneurial practices. Renewable energies play a crucial role in the advancement of regional development. Therefore, doing thorough research is crucial in order to identify the specific requirements and obstacles within a certain region, thereby ensuring the promotion of local development (Nalan, Murat & Nuri, 2009). Moreover, it is imperative to acknowledge that entrepreneurship plays a crucial role in fostering the development of economies at the regional, national, and global levels (Reynolds et al., 2005). According to Porter (1990), entrepreneurship is at the core of national advantage. Entrepreneurship refers to the capacity and inclination of individuals to identify and capitalize on opportunities, such as novel products and innovative manufacturing processes, and to effectively introduce their ideas to the market, even in the face of uncertainties and many impediments (Carree & Thurik, 2010). For instance, Germany in the 1990s witnessed a notable instance of a favorable correlation between entrepreneurship and regional prosperity. According to Audretsch and Fritsch (2002), it has been found that locations characterized by greater initial rates have more rapid rates of expansion. The existing body of literature highlights the substantial impact of entrepreneurship on various aspects such as economic growth, regional development, and national development. This implies that the establishment of new firms within the SWHS industry has the potential to influence economic development.

The chapter presents a range of potential solutions aimed at promoting entrepreneurship within the context of SWHS, addressing the aforementioned concerns. The potential resolutions outlined above are delineated within the context of prior research. The chapter encompasses a number of significant parts, namely an introductory section, a comprehensive review of relevant literature, the presentation of findings, an in-depth discussion, and a conclusive section.

2. LITERATURE REVIEW

The literature review part provides a comprehensive analysis of the worldwide solar thermal market, as well as an in-depth examination of the SWHS specifically in Turkey. This paper begins by examining the current state of the worldwide solar thermal market, followed by an analysis of Turkey's position within this context. The present condition of this industry and its subsequent development is being discussed.

2.1. The Global Solar Thermal Market

According to the Global Status Report, annual installations increased in 10 of the world's top 20 markets in 2018. 33.3 GWth of solar thermal capacity was added around the world. China contributed 74% of gross additions with 24.8 GWth. (Ranalder & Gibb, 2020). However, the global solar thermal market decreased in 2020, with an anticipated 25.2 GWth of capacity added globally, down 3.6% from 26.1 GWth in 2019. Nevertheless, China has demonstrated persistent growth in the year 2020 through its strategic investments in solar thermal infrastructure. The CSNP Royal Tech Urat plant, with a capacity of 100 MW, commenced its operations in China in the year 2020. The implementation of the project has resulted in an increase in the country's overall installed power capacity, reaching a total of 520 MW. This particular project boasts a thermal storage capacity of 10 hours or roughly 1,000 MWh, making it the largest concentrating solar power (CSP) facility in China (Murdock et al., 2021). Concentrating Solar Thermal Power Global Capacity has been shown in Figure 1.

China, Turkey, India, Brazil, the United States, Germany, and Australia have emerged as the leading nations in terms of new installations of glazed and unglazed

Figure 1. Concentrating solar thermal power global capacity, by country/region, 2010–2020 (Murdock, et al., 2021)

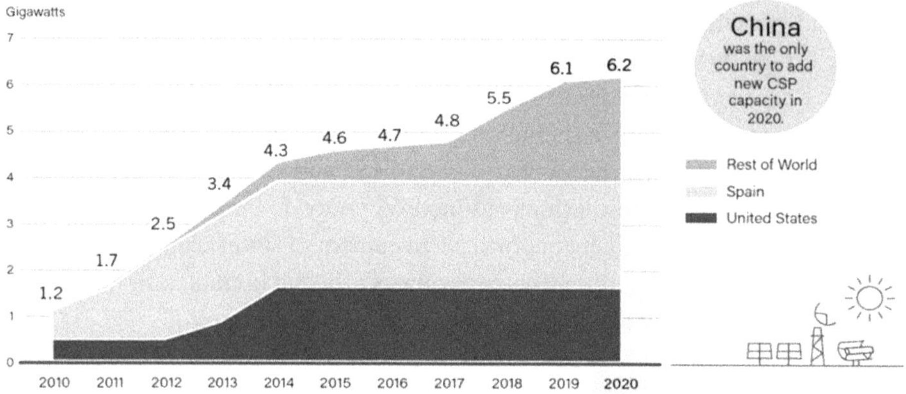

materials in 2020. China held the predominant position in the market, with a substantial share of 71% in new global sales, followed by Turkey and India. In 2020, Turkey experienced a small gain of 2 percent in its second-largest solar market for new sales, resulting in a total of 1.35 GWth of newly installed capacity (Murdock et al., 2021) (Figure 2).

Figure 2. Solar water heating collector additions, top 20 countries for capacity added, 2020 (Murdock, et al. 2021)

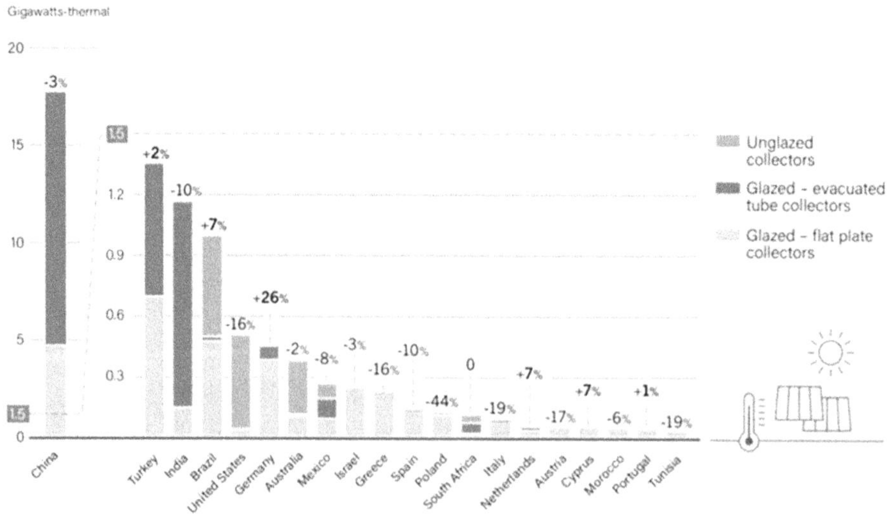

Note: Additions represent gross capacity added. For the Netherlands, the shares of flat plate and vacuum tube collectors were estimated based on actual shares in 2019. For Morocco, the share of collector types was not available.

Solar collectors play a pivotal role as the primary components of SWHS. Solar collectors are designed with the objective of transforming solar energy into thermal energy (Murdock et al., 2020). The inclusion of a collector is a crucial element inside an operational solar system. According to Hepbasli, Ulgen, & Eke (2004), there exist three primary categories of solar collectors, namely flat-plate, evacuated tube, and concentrating collectors. Flat plate collectors and vacuum tube collectors are the two predominant forms of solar collectors commonly employed in practical applications. Flat plate collectors are commonly used due to their lower cost (Şerban, Bărbuţă-Mişu, Ciucescu, Paraschiv & Paraschiv, 2016). SWH Collectors' Global Capacity is shown in Figure 3.

Figure 3. Solar water heating collectors' global capacity, 2010-2020 (Murdock, et al., 2021)

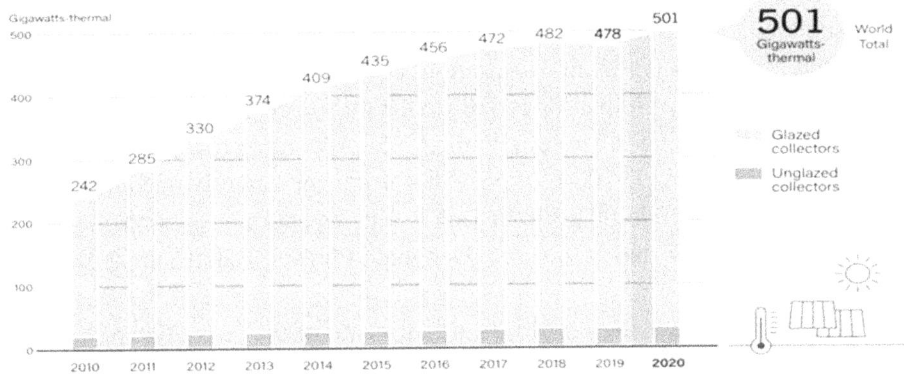

Moreover, it has been noted that cities have experienced substantial advancements as a result of advantageous legislation and incentives related to finance and taxation. For example, the implementation of SWHS has been observed in preschools and nurseries located in Kyiv. In 2018, the city of Barcelona implemented city-building laws with the intention of promoting the adoption of solar energy systems (Ranalder & Gibb, 2020). In the Netherlands in 2020, incentive schemes encompass renewable heat. The United Kingdom has recently broadened its funding initiative aimed at retrofitting buildings with heating systems that rely on renewable energy sources. Several nations have implemented bans and restrictions on the usage and distribution of fossil fuels. Several cities across Asia, North America (particularly the state of California in the United States), Europe, and Oceania have adopted measures aimed at gradually eliminating the reliance on fossil fuels for the purpose of space and water heating in both new and existing buildings (Murdock et al., 2021). Based on the findings presented, it is apparent that there is a notable deficiency in worldwide policies aimed at promoting the adoption of renewable energy sources in buildings, with a special emphasis on their utilization for heating purposes.

2.2. The Solar Water Heating Systems in Turkey

Turkey is located between 36° and 42° north latitude and 26° and 45° east longitude. The average annual total sunshine duration is 2741.07 hours in Turkey1. The SWHS industry started to operate in the 1970s and became the world's third-largest producer and fourth-largest market in the 2000s in Turkey (Erdemir & Altuntop, 2018). The production of SWHS originally began in Izmir in 1975, and it quickly expanded as the Turkish people embraced the technology (as cited in Eskin, 2006). The manufacture of SWHS was affected by a significant decline between 2015 and 2018 due to large enterprises ceasing their production activities and a rise in imports. It is stated that the growing use of natural gas also influenced this decline. The supply of natural gas for summer and winter use in many cities of the country has negatively affected the demand for SWHS (Erdemir & Altuntop, 2018).

Annual solar energy production is 828 kteo, with 65 percent of this energy going to domestic water heating in Turkey (Benli, 2016). According to a study, the annual energy required to provide 100 L of 55°C hot water for a family of four people is between 1418.69 and 1975.08 kWh. In Turkey, the payback period for a galvanized SWHS is between 2.98 and 8.24 years (Dehghan, Pfeiffer, Rakhshani & Bakhshi-Jafarabadi, 2021).

In the Mediterranean, the sun shines 300 days out of the year. According to the Turkish solar map, residents of Adana, which is situated in the Mediterranean and has high solar efficiency, obtain most of their hot water needs from solar energy. Almost every building in the city has a SWHS on the roof. SWHS powered by solar energy makes a significant contribution to energy savings. In the summer, 150 liters of water may be heated to 80 degrees for 2 hours using solar energy systems that cost between 1,000 and 3,000 Turkish liras to install in the city. With these systems installed on the roofs of the buildings, approximately 15 kW of savings are achieved per day2.

Some projects show the relevance given to SWHS in government-supported projects. By implementing these projects based on the energy industry's growth, Turkey aims to enhance employment and economic growth in the industry. There is legislation based on these projects. With this legislation, broad areas could be expected to profit from solar energy. It is envisaged to install solar energy equipment in buildings with more than 1,000 m2 floor area in Turkey. Owing to this regulation, the demand for SWHS increased in hotels, hospitals, dorms, and sports facilities. These systems are now accessible in many residences, businesses, and public structures. Even prisons are now using central solar-powered hot water systems. A total of 50 SWHS were installed in prisons in Istanbul, Ankara, Diyarbakir, and other provinces (Epp, 2020). Additionally, the Housing Development Administration's project is crucial for the spread of SWHS. For people who lost their homes in the Van earthquake, more than 15,000 new dwellings were constructed as part of this initiative, and 120-liter thermosiphon SWHS with a combined collector area of 30,646 m^2 were placed in these residences (Augsten, 2012).

3. FINDINGS

This section elucidates the correlation between entrepreneurship within the renewable energy sector and its impact on economic growth, as supported by existing research. Additionally, the factors influencing the promotion of SWHS entrepreneurship are examined in this section.

3.1. The Relationship Between Entrepreneurship in the Renewable Energy Industry and Economic Growth

A study shows that the level of entrepreneurial activity in different regions of post-Soviet Russia, as measured by the number of firms per population, has played a significant role in fostering regional growth (Berkowitz & DeJong, 2005). In addition, the Global Entrepreneurship Monitor research program conducts investigations on the subject of entrepreneurship. The research program's findings indicate a positive association between entrepreneurial activity and economic growth, as reported by Reynolds et al. (2005).

The optimal usage of renewable energy resources has played a significant role in facilitating sustainable development and economic growth (Benli, 2016). Energy is widely recognized as a crucial factor in facilitating economic and social development (Nalan et al., 2009). According to Michalena & Tripanagnostopoulos (2010), the utilization of solar energy systems on a large scale has the potential to stimulate economic growth at the local level. The utilization of a renewable energy source has the potential to positively influence economic growth. The study examined the impact of renewable energy consumption on economic growth by utilizing the "Renewable Energy Country Attractiveness Index" devised by Ernst & Young. In order to elucidate the trajectory of expansion from 1991 to 2012, the aforementioned study opted to examine a sample of 38 nations that have made the most extensive use of renewable energy sources (Bhattacharya, Paramati, Ozturk & Bhattacharya, 2016). Based on the findings, the study demonstrated that the utilization of renewable

Figure 4. The economic growth process with the SWHS

energy exhibited a notable and favorable impact on the economic productivity of 57% of the nations included in the analysis.

Economic growth can be achieved with the SWHS entrepreneurship, which is based on solar energy from renewable energy sources (see Figure 4).

The SWHS is the most critical and commercially practical solar thermal usage system (Hepbaşlı et al., 2004). The fact that it is suitable for commercialization demonstrates that it has the potential to be a valuable tool for economic development. Hot water production is a significant cost factor (Gunerhan & Hepbasli, 2007). A study on the economic analysis and feasibility of a SWH examined a techno-economic evaluation of the system. The results reveal that this system may save 182 kg of LPG, 379 liters of kerosene, 152 kilograms of charcoal, and 649 kg of fuel-wood every year, all of which are used in water heating (Saxena & Srivastava, 2012). The usage of renewable energy has an impact on economic growth, as evidenced by research in the literature.

3.2. The Factors Influencing the Promotion of SWHS Entrepreneurship

Government policies play a significant role in the growth of solar energy markets. Decision-makers in both developed and developing countries are following an incentive policy to promote solar energy to a higher level. A clear incentive policy has not been observed for SWHS in Turkey so far. However, The Department of Forestry and Village Relations has implemented an SWH project in forest settlements since 2004. This initiative aims to prevent the villagers from cutting down trees for hot water and instead give them solar collectors to meet their needs. This initiative has been running smoothly since 2004 and has produced positive outcomes. The village's hot water demands are met in their houses thanks to the project's use of the sun. In addition, there has been a paragraph about using renewable energy resources in Turkey's 10th section of energy performance in buildings regulation. This paragraph is as follows: *"Paragraph 22 (4): It is obligatory in new hotels, hospitals, dorms, and similar non-residential buildings with a usage area of more than 1,000* m^2 *and sports facilities to support the system with solar energy collectors in central heating and sanitary hot water systems"*. The government revised Section 7, paragraph 19, to keep the mandated solar energy standards in 2017. This paragraph is as follows: *It is required to plan a central sanitary hot water system in hotels, hospitals, dorms, and similar non-residential structures with a consumption area of more than 1000 m² and in sports facilities."3* Over the last few years, Turkey's laws on installing solar energy equipment in buildings with more than 1,000 m² of floor area have increased the number of centralized SWHS in prisons. As a result of this, SWHS has been built in jails in Diyarbakir, Ankara, and Istanbul (Epp, 2020). SWHS can be utilized more widely in Turkey; however, subsidies from the government are required to enforce (Üçtuğ & Azapagic, 2018).

The high cost of domestically produced goods and the dependence on imported goods for manufacturing processes could perhaps be attributed to the origins of these unfavorable occurrences. Concurrently, the manufacturing sector saw adverse effects as a result of fluctuations in exchange rates. Furthermore, it has been asserted by Erdemir & Altuntop (2018) that the industry has also been affected by fossil fuel taxes and fluctuations in prices. Mitigating the impact of fluctuations in exchange rates is of utmost importance for both customers and entrepreneurs associated with SWHS.

The optimal utilization of SWHS can be influenced by certain demographic characteristics. According to Aydin, Eichholtz & Yönder (2018), the adoption of SWHS in Turkey is significantly influenced by income, education, and geographic location. Income is a changeable characteristic that varies among individuals. Hence, it is possible that the low-income demographic may exhibit a lack of preference for it. Individuals may opt not to make purchases in places characterized by poor productivity due to their geographical location. Individuals with a higher level of education possess the ability to assess the return on investment of SWHS and take into account its ecological implications.

It is noteworthy that certain customers exhibit a reluctance towards adopting SWHS, despite the fact that these systems contribute to a reduction in fossil fuel consumption, encourage ecologically responsible consumption practices, and yield energy savings. According to the demand-supply theory, it is posited that this situation may also have an influence on output. There are several reasons why these systems are not preferred, as highlighted by Sakınç and Sözen (2010). These include aesthetic concerns regarding the unattractive facades and roof ends of the buildings, structural deterioration observed on the roofs, the potential risk of legionnaires' disease in warehouses that are not properly maintained due to neglect in material selection, and financial losses incurred as a result of poorly designed systems. The subsequent analysis presents an elucidation of the variables that could potentially influence the advancement of SWHS entrepreneurship, as derived from the existing body of literature:

- Financial support
- Legal requirement
- Regulatory rules
- Aesthetic improvements
- Public Relation (PR) activities
- Environmental impact

4. DISCUSSION

The implementation of protective regulations necessitates a procedural approach, with decision-makers commonly opting for financial subsidies as a prevalent technique to preserve renewable energy (Siampour et al., 2021). Subsidies and regulatory measures should be used to stimulate the manufacturing of SWHS, as it plays a substantial role in bolstering the economy. Policy instruments are selected and implemented based on their capacity to generate economic outcomes and their alignment with established institutional frameworks (Li, Rubin & Onyina, 2013). Tragically, the solar collector sector in Turkey has not received any subsidies. Despite the absence of incentives or legislative support, Turkey has emerged as a prominent nation in terms of SWH installations. Turkey exhibited a marginally lower number of cumulated water collection installations in 2018 compared to the United States (Weiss, Spörk-Dür & Mauthner, 2019). In order to fully harness its potential, it is fundamental that the region enhances the quality of its technology and infrastructure, considering its geographical location and favorable radiation conditions (IEA, 2021).

Initiatives should be supported in the solar energy industry, which is the primary consumer of renewable energy because of its benefits. Countries that use more renewable energy will have less of an adverse effect on the environment and have more chance for prosperous economic growth. More benefits will result from this, particularly in nations with favorable geographic locations (IEA, 2021). The government can make promotions for the widespread use and promotion of SWHS. Australia is reliant on incentives. Israel has an obligatory approach. China's local governments present a mix of mechanisms. Analyzing the different country's policies shows that there are categories of subsidies. The categories are *"collector area-based subsidies (Germany, upper Austria, Korea), collector/system performance-based subsidies (Sweden, the Netherlands, Australia), tax credits (France, USA), tax deduction (Greece), and mandatory installation (Israel, Spain)."* In markets such as Germany, Spain, and Israel, the government provides support and imposes requirements in the area of solar energy. When new buildings are being constructed in these markets, for example, it is verified to see if solar collector systems are included (Li et al. 2013). However, in Turkey, there is no such support.

In contrast, Denmark, Australia, and Germany offer incentives and low-credit financing alternatives for the installation of solar collectors. The magnitude of solar collector installations directly influences the magnitude of grants allocated in Denmark. According to Tschopp, Tian, Berberich, Fan, Perers, & Furbo (2020), in cases where the solar collector area surpasses 20m^2, the government is willing to provide a subsidy of up to 50% of the installation expenses. Solar incentives in North America and Europe are predominantly centered around the provision of inexpensive financing options and subsidies (Zhou, Matisoff, Kingsley & Brown, 2019; Huang, Fan, Furbo & Li, 2020). Incentives are equally necessary when considering the consumer's standpoint. The ultimate outcome may incur significant expenses for the consumer as a result of the importation of certain equipment utilized in the construction of solar collectors. According to Dehghan et al. (2021), the implementation of domestic production for certain equipment types can lead to a substantial reduction in expenses. Government rules and incentives have a crucial role in the augmentation of output, as substantiated by empirical research.

The implementation of various incentives and laws is necessary for the government. Providing such support to both entrepreneurs and customers will contribute to the flourishing of the industry. In Turkey, where the economic conditions are now adverse, a significant portion of the population holds the belief that SWHS are costly. Sales can be stimulated by the use of strategies such as providing credit facilities to consumers and offering interest-free deferred payment options. From an entrepreneurial standpoint, securing finance is an essential prerequisite for initiating a company venture. Entrepreneurs have the opportunity to obtain financial assistance in the form of interest-free or low-interest loans, which may also come with other favorable terms.

Furthermore, it is vital to implement new regulatory mandates that enforce the obligatory utilization of SWHS and broaden their scope of application. Consequently, Turkey has the potential to leverage this situation to its advantage and foster economic growth by diminishing its reliance on foreign sources. This can be achieved by capitalizing on its favorable geographical location for the utilization of SWHS. Currently, the industry faces challenges stemming from substantial exchange rate fluctuations and a heavy dependence on foreign suppliers for the procurement of raw materials in collector manufacturing. In order to enhance efforts, it becomes apparent that the implementation of incentives and legislative regulations is necessary.

In order for the condition to achieve widespread prevalence, it is imperative that awareness-raising programs and actions be implemented, mostly by policymakers. Due to increased awareness among individuals, it is expected that there will be a corresponding increase in demand within this particular business. The presence of demand will consequently stimulate the generation of supply, thereby establishing a conducive atmosphere for commercial enterprises. In addition to establishing an optimal working environment, firms must fulfill additional prerequisites.

The following is an illustration of the potential solutions for the promotion of SWHS entrepreneurship based on the literature:

- Financial subsidy and incentives for both entrepreneurs and consumers
- Loan opportunity for both entrepreneurs and consumers
- Legal mandate of SWHS for eligible buildings
- Concentrating on raw material manufacturing to reduce foreign dependency in terms of raw materials and encouraging entrepreneurial activitities
- Avoiding the adverse scenario that develops as a result of ongoing exchange rate swings damaging entrepreneurs and consumers.
- Applying efficient and aesthetically pleasing modifications to current designs
- Ensuring that SWHS is a sensible investment and the payback period is recognized publicly
- Providing publicity to inform regarding how much energy it saves
- Providing publicity about being eco-friendly
- Organizing training and interviews on the advantages and benefits of SWHS

5. CONCLUSION

The chapter discussed the various aspects that can potentially influence the promotion of SWHS entrepreneurship, beginning with the concern surrounding the inadequate level of SWHS entrepreneurship. Furthermore, this chapter presented several ideas that have the potential to increase entrepreneurship in SWHS.

It is evident that solar energy exerts a significant influence on the advancement of economic development. Therefore, it is imperative to draw attention to the significance of solar energy. SWHS plays a pivotal role in fostering the development of a significant sector focused on the widespread utilization of solar energy. There exist numerous advantages associated with the utilization of SWHS in comparison to conventional sources such as natural gas, electricity, or other fossil fuels, including economic and environmental aspects. The attainment of economic growth can be facilitated by the utilization of SWHS as a means of entrepreneurship. The chapter provides a comprehensive analysis of the economic growth process using the SWHS model and establishes the interconnections between various ideas, drawing upon relevant literature.

Consequently, the implementation of SWHS can play a pivotal role in the ecological development of both a country and its local region. The expansion of firms within the industry has the potential to stimulate economic growth. Nevertheless, simply promoting entrepreneurship is insufficient for the successful implementation of this procedure. In addition to implementing policies, it is recommended that the government undertake public relations campaigns to facilitate the use of solar energy and offer incentives to aspiring entrepreneurs. In addition, government-sponsored promotional activities have the potential to enhance consumer awareness. Consequently, the industry would experience a rise in demand. As a consequence, the government assumes a substantial role in the implementation of advertising, promotion, and incentive initiatives.

Future research endeavors may center on examining the influence of demographic and environmental variables through the administration of surveys among entrepreneurs affiliated with SWHS. Furthermore, the present circumstances might be further investigated in order to enhance the industry through the implementation of interviews with entrepreneurs and consumers. Furthermore, empirical research can provide insights into the prevailing market prices, the duration required for the return on investment of SWHSs, and the quantifiable reductions in energy use.

REFERENCES

Augsten, E. (2012). *Turkey: High-quality Solar Hot Water Systems across Earthquake Area*. https://solarthermalworld.org/news/turkey-high-quality-solar-hot-water-systems-across-earthquake-area/

Aydin, E., Eichholtz, P., & Yönder, E. (2018). The economics of residential solar water heaters in emerging economies: The case of Turkey. *Energy Economics*, *75*, 285–299. doi:10.1016/j.eneco.2018.08.001

Benli, H. (2016). Potential application of solar water heaters for hot water production in Turkey. *Renewable & Sustainable Energy Reviews*, *54*, 99–109. doi:10.1016/j.rser.2015.09.061

Bhattacharya, M., Paramati, S. R., Ozturk, I., & Bhattacharya, S. (2016). The effect of renewable energy consumption on economic growth: Evidence from top 38 countries. *Applied Energy*, *162*, 733–741. doi:10.1016/j.apenergy.2015.10.104

Binalarda Enerji Performansı Yönetmeliği Resmi Gazete. (2008). https://www.resmigazete.gov.tr/eskiler/2008/12/20081205-9.htm

Dehghan, M., Pfeiffer, C. F., Rakhshani, E., & Bakhshi-Jafarabadi, R. (2021). A review on techno-economic assessment of solar water heating systems in the middle east. *Energies*, *14*(16), 4944. doi:10.3390/en14164944

Epp, B. (2020). *50 new solar hot water systems at Turkish prisons in three years.* https://solarthermalworld.org/news/50-new-solar-hot-water-systems-turkish-prisons-three-years/

Erdemir, D. & Altuntop, N. (2018). Güneş Enerjisinden Sıcak Su Elde Etme Yöntemleri ve Bu Yöntemin Türkiye'deki Gelişimi. *Mühendis ve Makina,* 35-42.

Eskin, N. (2006). *Türkiye'de Güneş Enerjisi Araştırma ve Geliştirme*. Academic Press.

Gunerhan, H., & Hepbasli, A. (2007). Exergetic modeling and performance evaluation of solar water heating systems for building applications. *Energy and Building*, *39*(5), 509–516. doi:10.1016/j.enbuild.2006.09.003

Hepbasli, A., Ulgen, K., & Eke, R. (2004). Solar energy applications in Turkey. *Energy Sources*, *26*(6), 551–561. doi:10.1080/00908310490438579

Huang, J., Fan, J., Furbo, S., & Li, Q. (2020). A policy study on the mandatory installation of solar water heating systems–Lessons from the experience in China. *Solar Energy*, *206*, 614–627. doi:10.1016/j.solener.2020.06.049

IEA. (2021). *Turkey 2021 Energy Policy Review.* https://iea.blob.core.windows.net/assets/cc499a7b-b72a-466c-88de-d792a9daff44/Turkey _2021_Energy_Policy_Review.pdf

Kapluhan, E. (2021). Türkiye Güneş Enerjisinde Mevcut Durum. *Yeni Türkiye*, *27*(118), 1–39.

Kaygusuz, K., & Kaygusuz, A. (2002). Renewable energy and sustainable development in Turkey. *Renewable Energy*, *25*(3), 431–453. doi:10.1016/S0960-1481(01)00075-1

Li, W., Rubin, T. H., & Onyina, P. A. (2013). Comparing solar water heater popularization policies in China, Israel and Australia: The roles of governments in adopting green innovations. *Sustainable Development (Bradford)*, *21*(3), 160–170. doi:10.1002d.1547

Michalena, E., & Tripanagnostopoulos, Y. (2010). Contribution of the solar energy in the sustainable tourism development of the Mediterranean islands. *Renewable Energy*, *35*(3), 667–673. doi:10.1016/j.renene.2009.08.016

Murdock, H. E., Gibb, D., André, T., Sawin, J. L., Brown, A., Appavou, F., ... Mastny, L. (2020). *Renewables 2020-Global status report.* Academic Press.

Murdock, H. E., Gibb, D., Andre, T., Sawin, J. L., Brown, A., Ranalder, L., ... Brumer, L. (2021). *Renewables 2021-Global status report.* Academic Press.

Nalan, Ç. B., Murat, Ö., & Nuri, Ö. (2009). Renewable energy market conditions and barriers in Turkey. *Renewable & Sustainable Energy Reviews*, *13*(6-7), 1428–1436. doi:10.1016/j.rser.2008.09.001

Ranalder, L., & Gibb, D. (2020). *Renewables in Cities 2019 Global Status Report.* https://www.ises.org/sites/default/files/webinars/REN21%20Presentation_0.pdf

Republic of Turkey Ministry of Energy and Natural Resources. (2022). https://enerji.gov.tr/eigm-resources-en//

Reynolds, P., Bosma, N., Autio, E., Hunt, S., De Bono, N., Servais, I., Lopez-Garcia, P., & Chin, N. (2005). Global entrepreneurship monitor: Data collection design and implementation 1998–2003. *Small Business Economics*, *24*(3), 205–231. doi:10.100711187-005-1980-1

Sadhishkumar, S., & Balusamy, T. (2014). Performance improvement in solar water heating systems—A review. *Renewable & Sustainable Energy Reviews*, *37*, 191–198. doi:10.1016/j.rser.2014.04.072

Sakınç, E., & Sözen, M. Ş. (2010). Yapılarda Güneş Enerjili Su Isıtma Sistemleri Sorunsalı ve Mimari Çözüm Önerileri (Mersin Örneği). *Megaron*, *5*(1), 1–10.

Saxena, A., & Srivastava, G. (2012). Potential and economics of solar water heating. *MIT International Journal of Mechanical Engineering*, *2*(2), 97–104.

Şerban, A., Bărbuţă-Mişu, N., Ciucescu, N., Paraschiv, S., & Paraschiv, S. (2016). Economic and environmental analysis of investing in solar water heating systems. *Sustainability (Basel)*, *8*(12), 1286. doi:10.3390u8121286

Siampour, L., Vahdatpour, S., Jahangiri, M., Mostafaeipour, A., Goli, A., Shamsabadi, A. A., & Atabani, A. (2021). Techno-enviro assessment and ranking of Turkey for use of home-scale solar water heaters. *Sustainable Energy Technologies and Assessments*, *43*, 100948. doi:10.1016/j.seta.2020.100948

Tschopp, D., Tian, Z., Berberich, M., Fan, J., Perers, B., & Furbo, S. (2020). Large-scale solar thermal systems in leading countries: A review and comparative study of Denmark, China, Germany and Austria. *Applied Energy*, *270*, 114997. doi:10.1016/j.apenergy.2020.114997

Üçtuğ, F. G., & Azapagic, A. (2018). A. Environmental impacts of small-scale hybrid energy systems: Coupling solar photovoltaics and lithium-ion batteries. *The Science of the Total Environment*, *643*, 1579–1589. doi:10.1016/j.scitotenv.2018.06.290 PMID:30189574

Weiss, W., Spörk-Dür, M., & Mauthner, F. (2019). *Solar heat worldwide, Global market developments and trends in 2018, SHC-Solar Heating and Cooling Programme*. International Energy Agency.

Zhou, S., Matisoff, D. C., Kingsley, G. A., & Brown, M. A. (2019). Understanding renewable energy policy adoption and evolution in Europe: The impact of coercion, normative emulation, competition, and learning. *Energy Research & Social Science*, *51*, 1–11. doi:10.1016/j.erss.2018.12.011

ENDNOTES

1 https://enerji.gov.tr/eigm-resources-en//

2 https://www.iklimhaber.org/adananin-suyu-gunes-enerjisi-ile-isiniyor/

3 https://www.resmigazete.gov.tr/eskiler/2008/12/20081205-9.htm

Compilation of References

Abdelhadi, M., & Eddine, K. A. (2021). The Impact of Human Capital on Economic Growth in Algeria During the Period 1970-2018: Application of ARDL Approach to Cointegration. *Strategy and Development Review*, *11*(3), 554–571. doi:10.34276/1822-011-003-030

Abdelli, M., Ul-Durar, S., & Wasef Hattab, H. (2023). Entrepreneurship Ecosystems and Their Opportunities and Challenges. IGI Global. doi:10.4018/978-1-6684-7140-1

Acha, N. (2013). Accompagnement de l'Orientation entrepreneuriale par un management entrepreneurial: Une approche par les ressources. *XXII International Strategic Management Conference(AIMS)*.

Acquier, A., & Aggeri, F. (2008). Une généalogie de la penséemanagérialesur la RSE. *Revue française de gestion, 180*.

Adebakin, A. B. (2020). A review of measures, instances and frameworks of government policy on entrepreneurial practices in Nigeria. In C. O. Fashiku, M. A. Yusuf, S. O. Subair, O. T. Ajadi & T. L. Adepoju (Eds.), Dimensions of Politics, Policies and Thoughts in Education (pp. 72-81). Obafemi Awolowo University Press.

Adebakin, A. B., & Ayanlowo, A. E. (2023). Addressing the challenges of entrepreneurship and innovation in Nigeria: The roles of tertiary education. In M. E. A. Abdelli, N. Chemma, S. Ahlem, S. B. Maliki, & G. Singh (Eds.), *Competitive Advantage, Strategy and Innovation in Africa: Issues and Applications* (pp. 172–190). Routledge Taylor and Francis Group. doi:10.4324/9781003306405-10

Adeyanju, D., Mburu, J., & Mignouna, D. (2021). Youth agricultural entrepreneurship: Assessing the impact of agricultural training programmes on performance. *Sustainability (Basel)*, *13*(4), 1697. doi:10.3390u13041697

Afshan, G., Shahid, S., & Tunio, M. N. (2021). Learning experiences of women entrepreneurs amidst COVID-19. *International Journal of Gender and Entrepreneurship*.

Aghion, P. (2018). Innovation and Growth from a Schumpeterian Perspective. Dalloz. *Revue d'Économie Politique*, *128*(5), 693–711. doi:10.3917/redp.285.0693

Agu, E. O., & Ayogu, D. U. (2015). Assessing the prospects and problems of entrepreneurship development in Nigeria. *International Journal of Current Research and Academic Review*, *3*(10), 208–221.

Ajzen, I. (1987). Attitudes, traits, and actions: Dispositional prediction of behavior in personality and social psychology. *Advances in Experimental Social Psychology*, *20*(1), 1–63.

Akogwu, A. P. (2020). Effects of job creation determinants on the security of Abuja Metropolis. *Gusau International Journal of Management and Social Sciences*, *3*(1), 14–14.

Akpan, O. E. (2021). Entrepreneurship studies education in tertiary institutions in Nigeria: Theories and practices. *International Journal of Vocational and Technical Education Research*, *7*(1), 35–42.

Akpochafo, G. O., & Alika, I. H. (2018). Perceived impact of entrepreneurship education on career development among undergraduates in South-South universities in Nigeria: Implication for counselling. *Journal of Education and Learning*, *7*(3), 102–108. doi:10.5539/jel.v7n3p102

Alao, O. E., Osanyinro, J. B., & Alao, P. O. (2022). Achieving the effectiveness of the Students Industrial Work Experience Scheme for sustainability of the Nigerian economy. *International Journal of Work-Integrated Learning*, *23*(3), 393–404.

Allen, J. P. (2019). *Digital Entrepreneurship*. Routledge. doi:10.4324/9780429506567

Al-Qahtani, M., Fekih Zguir, M., Al-Fagih, L., & Koç, M. (2022). Women Entrepreneurship for Sustainability: Investigations on Status, Challenges, Drivers, and Potentials in Qatar. *Sustainability (Basel)*, *14*(7), 4091. doi:10.3390u14074091

Arabeche & Abdelli. (2021). The New Trends Technology of Entrepreneurship in the Incubators A Case Study of Cyberpark Sidi Abdallah. In *Big Data for Entrepreneurship and Sustainable Development*. Taylor and Francis.

Arabeche, Z., Soudani, A., Brahmi, M., Aldieri, L., Vinci, C. P., & Abdelli, M. E. A. (2022, April 25). Entrepreneurial Orientation, Organizational Culture and Business Performance in SMEs: Evidence from Emerging Economy. *Sustainability (Basel)*, *14*(9), 5160. Advance online publication. doi:10.3390u14095160

Armitage, C. J., & Conner, M. (2001). Efficacy of the theory of planned behaviour: A meta-analytic review. *British Journal of Social Psychology*, *40*(4), 471–499. doi:10.1348/014466601164939 PMID:11795063

Arshad, S., & Munir, K. (2017). Factor Accumulation and Economic Growth in Pakistan: Incorporating Human Capital. *International Journal of Social Economics*, *45*, 180–199.

Asenjo, M. P. F., & Barbera, J. P. (2013). Assessing the impact of higher education on entrepreneurial intention. *History and Social Communication*, *18*(11), 377–386.

Audretsch, D. B. (2009). The entrepreneurial society. *The Journal of Technology Transfer*, *34*(3), 245–254. doi:10.100710961-008-9101-3

Austin. (2006). Social and Commercial Entrepreneurship: Same, Different, or Both? *Entrepreneurship Theory and Practice, 30*(1).

Autio, E. H., Keeley, R., Klofsten, M. G. C., Parker, G., & Hay, M. (2001). Entrepreneurial intent among students in Scandinavia and in the USA. *Enterprise and Innovation Management Studies*, *2*(2), 145–160. doi:10.1080/14632440110094632

Ayanlowo, A. E. (2021). *Relationship between students' employment prospects and demand for university education in Osun State, Nigeria* [Master's Dissertation]. Obafemi Awolowo University, Ile-Ife, Nigeria.

Babalola, Y. A., & Tiamiyu, R. (2013). Job creation and economic empowerment through Business education. *Information and Knowledge Management*, *3*(3), 64–67.

Babenko, V., Kulczyk, Z., Perevosova, I., Syniavska, O., & Davydova, O. (2019). Factors of the development of international e-commerce under the conditions of globalization. In *SHS Web of Conferences* (*Vol. 65*, p. 04016). EDP Sciences. 10.1051hsconf/20196504016

Bagozzi, R. P., & Yi, Y. (1988). On the evaluation of structural equation models. *Journal of the Academy of Marketing Science*, *16*(1), 74–94. doi:10.1007/BF02723327

Balogun, B. B., & Olatoro, F. (2020). Challenges facing entrepreneurship development in Nigeria: An empirical review. *Journal of African Sustainable Development*, *19*(2), 75–82.

Bank, W. (2018). *Tech Startup Ecosystem in West Bank and Gaza: Findings and Recommendations*. World Bank. doi:10.1596/31075

Barclay, D., Higgins, C., & Thompson, R. (1995). The Partial Least Squares (PLS) approach to casual modeling: Personal computer adoption and use as an illustration. *Technology Studies, Special Issue on Research Methodology*, *2*(2), 285–309.

Bates, T., Jackson, W. E. III, & Johnson, J. H. Jr. (2007). Advancing research on minority entrepreneurship. *The Annals of the American Academy of Political and Social Science*, *613*(1), 10–17. doi:10.1177/0002716207303405

Becke, G. S. (1993). Human Capital-A Theoretical and Empirical Analysis with Special Reference to Education (3rd ed.). The University of Chicago Press.

Becker, G. S. (1993). *Human capital: A theoretical and empirical analysis with special reference to education* (3rd ed.). University of Chicago Press. doi:10.7208/chicago/9780226041223.001.0001

Belloumi, M. (2013). The relationship between Trade, FDI and Economic growth in Tunisia: An application of autoregressive distributed lag model. *Economic Systems*, 269–287.

Benyakoub, B., & Es-salmani, M. (2021). The ARDL bounds cointegration test for the verification of the. *Revue Internationale du Chercheur*, *2*(4), 1–24.

Berger, E. S. C., & Kuckertz, A. (2016). Female entrepreneurship in startup ecosystems worldwide. *Journal of Business Research*, *69*(11), 5163–5168. doi:10.1016/j.jbusres.2016.04.098

Bergeron, H. (2002). *La gestionstratégique et les mesures de la performance non financière des PME*. 6th Congrès international francophone sur la PME, Montréal, Canada.

Bezzina, F. (2010). Characteristics of the Maltese entrepreneur. *The International Journal of the Arts in Society*, *3*(7), 292–312.

Bhagchandani, R. (2017). *How India can up its startup game by bolstering student entrepreneurship*. Retrieved Date 05 September 2018 from https://yourstory.com/2017/01/india-startup-game-bolstering-student-entrepreneurship

Biggadike, R. (1979). The Risky Business of Diversification. *Harvard Business Review*, *57*(3), 103–111.

Bivona, E., & Cruz, M. (2021). Can business model innovation help SMEs in the food and beverage industry to respond to crises? Findings from a Swiss brewery during COVID-19. *British Food Journal*, *123*(11), 3638–3660. doi:10.1108/BFJ-07-2020-0643

Blank, S. (2013). Why the lean start-up changes everything. *Harvard Business Review*, *91*(5), 63–72.

Bouchaer, S. (2018). The role of business incubators in supporting and developing startups: A case study of Algeria. *Journal of Economic Bashaer*, *4*(2), 417–431.

Boyd, N. G., & Vozikis, G. S. (1994). The Influence Of Self-Efficacy On The Development Of Entrepreneurial Intentions And Actions. *Entrepreneurship Theory and Practice*, *18*(4), 63–77. doi:10.1177/104225879401800404

Bozkurt, E. (2020). Is The Entrepreneurship Still Popular as A Growth Dynamic? *Journal of Academic Value Studies*, *6*(2), 225–230. doi:10.29228/javs.42914

Breznitz, D., & Taylor, M. (2014). The communal roots of entrepreneurial–technological growth–social fragmentation and stagnation: Reflection on Atlanta's technology cluster. *Entrepreneurship and Regional Development*, *26*(3–4), 375–396. doi:10.1080/08985626.2014.918183

Brush, C. G., De Bruin, A., & Welter, F. (2009). A gender-aware framework for women's entrepreneurship. *International Journal of Gender and Entrepreneurship*, *1*(1), 8–24. doi:10.1108/17566260910942318

Bruyat, C. (1993). *Business creation: epistemological contributions and modeling*. Pierre Mendès-France-Grenoble II University.

Bunyasrie, V. (2010). THE Role of Entrepreneurship on Economic Growth. *Executive Journal*, 149-156.

Burgelman, R. A. (1983). A model of the interaction of strategic behavior, corporate context, and the concept of strategy. *Strategic Management Journal*.

Butler, E. (2020). Entrepreneurship: A Primer. American Institute for Economic Research Coppel, J. (2000). E-Commerce: Impact and policy challenges. *OECD Ec. Dep. Work. P.*, *252*, 45–60.

C, N., & Plosse, C. (1982). Trends and Random Walks in Macroeconomic Time Series: Some Evidence and Implications. *Journal of Money Economics*, 10.

Cassar, G. (2007). Money, money, money? A longitudinal investigation of entrepreneur career reasons growth preferences and achieved growth. *Entrepreneurship and Regional Development*, *19*(1), 89–107. doi:10.1080/08985620601002246

Cauvin, E., & Bescos, L. (2002). *Performance evaluation: A comparison between the practices of start-ups and traditional French and American companies. Information Technology and Management: Challenges and Impacts in Accounting, Control and Auditing.*

Chell, E. (2008). *The Entrepreneurial Personality: A Social Construction* (2nd ed.). Routledge. doi:10.4324/9780203938638

Chen, C. C., Greene, P. G., & Crick, A. (1998). Does entrepreneurial self-efficacy distinguish entrepreneurs from managers? *Journal of Business Venturing*, *13*(4), 295–316. doi:10.1016/S0883-9026(97)00029-3

Chiemeka-Unogu, C. M. (2020). Entrepreneurship education in Nigeria universities: Programmes and goals for sustainable national development. *Multidisciplinary Journal of Research Development*, *29*(1), 1–7.

Cho, Y., Li, J., & Chaudhuri, S. (2020). Women entrepreneurs in Asia: Eight country studies. *Advances in Developing Human Resources*, *22*(2), 115–123. doi:10.1177/1523422320907042

Cooper, A. C., Dunkelberg, W. C., & Woo, C. Y. (1988). Survival and failure: A longitudinal study. *Frontiers of Entrepreneurship Research*, *1*, 225-237.

Covin, J. G., & Wales, W. J. (2012). The measurement of entrepreneurial orientation. *Entrepreneurship Theory and Practice*, *36*(4), 677–702. doi:10.1111/j.1540-6520.2010.00432.x

Crant, J. M. (1996). The proactive personality scale as a predictor of entrepreneurial intentions. *Journal of Small Business Management*, *34*(3), 42–49.

Dahiya, S., Panghal, A., Sindhu, S., & Siwach, P. (2021). Organic food women entrepreneurs-TISM approach for challenges. *Journal of Enterprising Communities: People and Places in the Global Economy*.

Dane, S., Akyuz, M., & Opusunju, M. I. (2021). COVID-19 and entrepreneurship development among Nigerian women. *Journal of Research in Medical and Dental Science*, *9*, 312–318.

Daroch, B., Nagrath, G., & Gupta, A. (2021). A study on factors limiting online shopping behaviour of consumers. *Rajagiri Management Journal*, *15*(1), 39–52. doi:10.1108/RAMJ-07-2020-0038

Davidson, E., & Vaast, E. (2010). Digital Entrepreneurship and its Sociomaterial Enactment. *43rd Hawaii International Conference on System Sciences*, 1-10.

Dedehouanou, S. F. A., & Araar, A. (2020). Gender, entrepreneurship and food security in Niger. *Review of Development Economics*, *24*(3), 815–830. doi:10.1111/rode.12657

Dejardin, M. (2012). entrepreneurship and economic growth: An obvious conjunction? *CORE*.

DeNoble, A., Ehrlich, S., & Singh, G. (2007). Toward the development of a family business self-efficacy scale: A resource-based perspective. *Family Business Review*, *20*(2), 127–140. doi:10.1111/j.1741-6248.2007.00091.x

Dess, G. G., & Robinson, R. B. Jr. (1984). Measuring organizational performance in the absence of objective measures: The case of the privately-held firm and conglomerate business unit. *Strategic Management Journal*, *5*(3), 265–273. doi:10.1002mj.4250050306

Deveci, I., & Seikkula-Leino, J. (2018). A review of entrepreneurship education in teacher education. *Malaysian Journal of Learning and Instruction*, *15*(1), 105–148. doi:10.32890/mjli2018.15.1.5

Dieppe, A. (Ed.). (2021). *Global productivity: Trends, drivers, and policies*. World Bank Publications. doi:10.1596/978-1-4648-1608-6

Dollinger, M. J. (2008). *Entrepreneurship*. Marsh Publications.

Douglas, E. J., & Shepherd, A. D. (2002). Self-employment as a career choice: Attitudes, entrepreneurial intentions, and utility maximization. *Entrepreneurship Theory and Practice*, *26*(3), 81–90. doi:10.1177/104225870202600305

Douglas, E. J., & Shepherd, D. A. (2000). Entrepreneurship as a utility maximizing response. *Journal of Business Venturing*, *15*(3), 231–251. doi:10.1016/S0883-9026(98)00008-1

Drennan, J., Kennedy, J., & Renfrow, P. (2005). Impact of childhood experiences on the development of entrepreneurial intentions. *International Journal of Entrepreneurship and Innovation*, *6*(4), 231–238. doi:10.5367/000000005775179801

Drucker, P. F. (1985). *Innovation and Entrepreneurship: Practice and Principles*. Harper & Row.

Drucker, P. F. (1985). Principles of successful innovation. *Research Management*, *28*(5), 10–12. doi:10.1080/00345334.1985.11756915

Ebong, J. M., & Nwakudu, G. N. (2017). Managing entrepreneurship education at universities level in Rivers State in an era of economic recession. *African Journal of Educational Research and Development*, *9*(1), 10–19.

Ejimonye, J. C., & Eneogu, N. D. (2020). Productivity of innovative entrepreneurs in nigeria: Role of entrepreneurship education. *International Journal of Studies in Education*, *16*(2), 141–152.

Eliasson, G. (2001). Industrial policy, competence blocs and the role of science in economic development. In *Capitalism and Democracy in the 21st Century* (pp. 223–247). Springer. doi:10.1007/978-3-662-11287-8_12

Eliasson, G., & Eliasson, A. (1996). The biotechnological competence bloc. *Revue d'Economie Industrielle*, *78*(1), 7–26. doi:10.3406/rei.1996.1641

Engsted, T., & Johansen, S. (1997). *Granger's representation theorem and multi-cointegration*. Academic Press.

Erhun, M. O. (2015). A sustainable approach to economic development in Nigeria: A legal perspective. *Journal of Economics and Sustainable Development, 6*(14), 1–6.

EU. (2018). *ENTR/E4-Fuelling Digital Entrepreneurship in Europe*. Background Paper; European Commission 2018; EU Commission Strategic Policy Forum on Digital Entrepreneurship. Available online: http://ec.europa.eu/DocsRoom/documents/5313/attachments/1/translations

Fatukasi, B., Olorunleke, G. K., Olajide, G. F., & Alimi, R. S. (2015). Bounds Testing Approaches to the Analysis of Macroeconomic Relationships In Nigeria. *European Journal of Business and Management, 7*(8), 26–34.

Fayolle, A., & Cherchem, N. (2010). Culture d'entreprise, profil du dirigeant et orientation entrepreneuriale des PME: Un modèlethéorique. 10 èmecongrès international Francophone surl'entrepreneuriat et la PME, Bordeaux, France.

Fitz-Koch, S., Nordqvist, M., Carter, S., & Hunter, E. (2018). Entrepreneurship in the agricultural sector: A literature review and future research opportunities. *Entrepreneurship Theory and Practice, 42*(1), 129–166. doi:10.1177/1042258717732958

Forbes, D. P. (2005). The Effects of Strategic Decision Making on Entrepreneurial Self- Efficacy. *Entrepreneurship Theory and Practice, 29*(5), 599–626. doi:10.1111/j.1540-6520.2005.00100.x

Fornell, C., & Bookstein, F. L. (1982). Two structural equation models: LISREL and PLS applied to consumer exit-voice theory. *JMR, Journal of Marketing Research, 19*(4), 440–452. doi:10.1177/002224378201900406

Fortin, P.A. (2004). *La culture entrepreneuriale, un antidote à la pauvreté*. Collection Entreprendre.

Gabadeen, W. O., & Raimi, L. (2012). Management of entrepreneurship education in Nigerian higher institutions: Issues, challenges and way forward. *Abuja International Journal of Education and Management Sciences, 2*, 1–26.

Galindo-Martín, M. Á., Castaño-Martínez, M. S., & Méndez-Picazo, M. T. (2021). Effects of the Pandemic Crisis on Entrepreneurship and Sustainable Development. *Journal of Business Research, 137*, 345–353. doi:10.1016/j.jbusres.2021.08.053 PMID:34602680

Ghosh, S., Hughes, M., Hughes, P., & Hodgkinson, I. (2021). Corporate digital entrepreneurship: Leveraging industrial internet of things and emerging technologies. *Digital Entrepreneurship*, 183-207.

Ginsberg, A., & Guth, W. (1990). Corporate Entrepreneurship (Guest Editors' Introduction). *Strategic Management Journal, 11*, 5–15.

Gökmen, A. (2012). Virtual business operations, e-commerce & its significance and the case of Turkey: Current situation and its potential. *Electronic Commerce Research, 12*(1), 31–51. doi:10.100710660-011-9084-2

Gray, C. (2002). Entrepreneurship, resistance to change and growth in small firms. *Journal of Small Business and Enterprise Development, 9*(1), 61–72. doi:10.1108/14626000210419491

Gu, S., Ślusarczyk, B., Hajizada, S., Kovalyova, I., & Sakhbieva, A. (2021). Impact of the covid-19 pandemic on online consumer purchasing behavior. *Journal of Theoretical and Applied Electronic Commerce Research, 16*(6), 2263–2281. doi:10.3390/jtaer16060125

Hair, J. F., Black, W. C., Babin, B. J., & Anderson, R. E. (2010). *Multivariate data analysis: International version*. Pearson.

Hakima, L., Adem, H., & Abbes, B. E. (2020). Investment in education and economic growth: ARDL Model. *Economic Sciences, Management and Commercial Sciences Review, 13*(2), 39-50.

Hechavarria, D. M., & Ingram, A. (2014). A review of the entrepreneurial ecosystem and the entrepreneurial society in the United States: An exploration with the global entrepreneurship monitor dataset. *Journal of Business and Entrepreneurship, 26*(1), 1–35.

Henseler, J., Ringle, C. M., & Sinkovics, R. R. (2009). *The use of partial least squares path modeling in international marketing*. New Challenges to International Marketing. doi:10.1108/S1474-7979(2009)0000020014

Holcombe, R. G. (1998). Entrepreneurship and Economic Growth. *The Quarterly Journal of Austrian Economics, 1*(2), 45–62. doi:10.100712113-998-1008-1

Hossain, S. M., Akbar, A., Tehseen, S., Poulova, P., Haider, S. A., Sheraz, F., & Yasmin, F. (2021). Evaluation of entrepreneurs success: A special reference to women entrepreneurs in Bangladesh. *Academy of Entrepreneurship Journal, 27*, 1–13.

Hudcová, E., Chovanec, T., & Moudrý, J. (2018). Social entrepreneurship in agriculture, a sustainable practice for social and economic cohesion in rural areas: The case of the Czech Republic. *European Countryside, 10*(3), 377–397. doi:10.2478/euco-2018-0022

Hull, C. E. K., Hung, Y. T. C., Hair, N., Perotti, V., & DeMartino, R. (2007). Taking advantage of digital opportunities: A typology of digital entrepreneurship. *International Journal of Networking and Virtual Organisations, 4*(3), 290–303. doi:10.1504/IJNVO.2007.015166

Hussain, S. A., Ahmad, G., Khan, A., Hassan, A., & Shamim, M. (2022). Cognitive antecedents of the agricultural entrepreneurship intentions of Indian university students. In *Driving factors for venture creation and success in agricultural entrepreneurship* (pp. 121–140). IGI Global. doi:10.4018/978-1-6684-2349-3.ch006

Hu, X., Lin, Z., Whinston, A. B., & Zhang, H. (2004). Hope or hype: On the viability of escrow services as trusted third parties in online auction environments. *Information Systems Research, 15*(3), 236–249. doi:10.1287/isre.1040.0027

Hylleberg, S., Engle, R. F., Granger, C. W., & Yoo, B. S. (1990). Seasonal integration and cointegration. *Journal of Econometrics, 44*(1-2), 215–238. doi:10.1016/0304-4076(90)90080-D

Ijere, T. C. (2014). The state, governance and socio-economic development realities in Nigeria. *Public Policy and Administration Research, 4*(1), 46–49.

Ingalagi, S. S., Nawaz, N., Rahiman, H. U., Hariharasudan, A., & Hundekar, V. (2021). Unveiling the crucial factors of women entrepreneurship in the 21st century. *Social Sciences (Basel, Switzerland)*, *10*(5), 153. doi:10.3390ocsci10050153

Isa, F. M., Muhammad, N. M. N., Ahmad, A., & Noor, S. (2021). Effect of ICT on women entrepreneur business performance: Case of Malaysia. *Journal of Economics and Business*, *4*(1). Advance online publication. doi:10.31014/aior.1992.04.01.326

Ismail, N., Jaffar, N., & Hooi, T. S. (2013). Using EAO model to predict the self-employment intentions among the Universities' Undergraduates in Malaysia. *International Journal of Trade, Economics and Finance*, *4*(5), 282–287. doi:10.7763/IJTEF.2013.V4.302

Ivanovic Đukic, M. B., & Tamara, R. (2022). Entrepreneurship and economic growth in emerging markets: An empirical analysis. *Acta Oeconomica*, *72*(1), 65–84. doi:10.1556/032.2022.00004

J, M. J. (1991). *Critical Values for Co integration Test in Long-Run Relationships: Reading in Co integration*. Oxford University Press.

Jaim, J. (2021). Exist or exit? Women business-owners in Bangladesh during COVID-19. *Gender, Work and Organization*, *28*(S1), 209–226. doi:10.1111/gwao.12546

Jarvis, R., Curan, J., Kitching, J., & Et Lightfoot, G. (2000). The use of quantitative and qualitative criteria in the measurement of performance in small firms. *Journal of Small Business and Enterprise Development*, *7*(2), 123–134. doi:10.1108/EUM0000000006834

Jella, M., & Bouzahzah, M. (2012). Governance education and economic growth. *Munich Personal RePEc Archive*, 1-19.

Johansson, B., Lööf, H., & Savin, M. (2015). European r&d efficiency. *Economics of Innovation and New Technology*, *24*(1–2), 140–158. doi:10.1080/10438599.2014.897857

Jonathan, J., Daniel, V. L., & Bulus, G. (2019). The role of quality education in national development: The interface. *British Journal of Education. Learning and Development Psychology*, *2*(1), 21–30.

Kalyoncuoğlu, S., Aydıntan, B., & Göksel, A. (2017). The effect of entrepreneurship education on entrepreneurial intention: An experimental study on undergraduate business students. *Journal of Management Research*, *9*(3), 72–91. doi:10.5296/jmr.v9i3.11282

Kan, A., Kan, M., Dogan, H. G., Tosun, F., Ucum, I., & Solmaz, C. (2018). *Evaluatıon Of Young Farmers Project Support Program İn Terms Of Agrı-Entrepreneurshıp İn Turkey*. Academic Press.

Kanu, M. C., Aja, C. E., & Umurhurhu, E. (2023). National directorate of employment trainees' ratings of their skills for employability in Anambra State. *African Journal of Educational Management. Teaching and Entrepreneurship Studies*, *9*(1), 32–43.

Kaplan, R., & Norton, D. (1996). Linking the Balanced Scorecard to Stategy. *California Management Review*, *39*(1), 53–79. doi:10.2307/41165876

Kazanas, T. (2017). A Vector Error Correction Forecasting Model of the Greek Economy. *Hellenic Fiscal Council*, (2), 2–6.

Keen, C., Wetzels, M., De Ruyter, K., & Feinberg, R. (2004). E-tailers versus retailers: Which factors determine consumer preferences. *Journal of Business Research*, *57*(7), 685–695. doi:10.1016/S0148-2963(02)00360-0

Kenney, M., & Von Burg, U. (1999). Technology, entrepreneurship and path dependence: Industrial clustering in Silicon Valley and Route 128. *Industrial and Corporate Change*, *8*(1), 67–103. doi:10.1093/icc/8.1.67

Khalil, A., Abdelli, M. E. A., & Mogaji, E. (2022). *Do Digital Technologies Influence the Relationship between the COVID-19 Crisis and SMEs' Resilience in Developing Countries?* Academic Press.

Khalil, A., Abdelli, M. E. A., & Mogaji, E. (2022). Do Digital Technologies Influence the Relationship between the COVID-19 Crisis and SMEs' Resilience in Developing Countries? *Journal of Open Innovation*, *8*(2), 100. doi:10.3390/joitmc8020100

Khyareh, M. M., & Amini, H. (2021). Governance Quality, Entrepreneurship and Economic Growth. *Journal of Competitiveness*, *13*(2), 41–64. doi:10.7441/joc.2021.02.03

Kirton, M. (1978). Field dependence and adaption-innovation theories. *Perceptual and Motor Skills*, *47*(3), 1239–1245. doi:10.2466/pms.1978.47.3f.1239 PMID:745906

Klapper, L., Amit, R., Guillén, M. F., & Quesada, J. M. (2009). *Entrepreneurship and Firm Formation Across Countries*. Research Gate.

Koch, J., Frommeyer, B., & Schewe, G. (2020). Online shopping motives during the COVID-19 pandemic—Lessons from the crisis. *Sustainability (Basel)*, *12*(24), 10247. doi:10.3390u122410247

Kolvereid, L., & Isaksen, E. (2006). New business start-up and subsequent entry into self-employment. *Journal of Business Venturing*, *21*(6), 866–885. doi:10.1016/j.jbusvent.2005.06.008

Kolvereid, L., & Moen, Ø. (1997). Entrepreneurship among business graduates: Does a major in entrepreneurship make a difference? *Journal of European Industrial Training*, *21*(4), 154–160. doi:10.1108/03090599710171404

Kornum, N., & Bjerre, M. (Eds.). (2005). *Grocery E-Commerce: Consumer behaviour and business strategies*. Edward Elgar Publishing. doi:10.4337/9781781008317

Krajcik, V., & Formanek, I. (2015). Regional startup ecosystem. *European Business & Management*, *1*(2), 14–18.

Kraus, S., Palmer, C., Kailer, N., Kallinger, F. L., & Spitzer, J. (2019). Digital entrepreneurship: A research agenda on new business models for the twenty-first century. *International Journal of Entrepreneurial Behaviour & Research*, *25*(2), 353–375. doi:10.1108/IJEBR-06-2018-0425

Krueger, N. F., & Carsrud, A. L. (1993). Entrepreneurial intentions: Applying the theory of planned behaviour. *Entrepreneurship and Regional Development*, *5*(4), 315–330. doi:10.1080/08985629300000020

Krueger, N. F. Jr, Reilly, M. D., & Carsrud, A. L. (2000). Competing models of entrepreneurial intentions. *Journal of Business Venturing*, *15*(5&6), 411–432. doi:10.1016/S0883-9026(98)00033-0

Kuehn, K. W. (2008). Entrepreneurial intentions research: Implications for entrepreneurship education. *Journal of Entrepreneurship Education*, *11*, 87.

Kuratko Donald, F., & Audretsch David, B. (2009). Strategic Entrepreneurship: Exploring Different Perspectives of an Emerging Concept. *Entrepreneurship Theory and Practice*, *33*(1), 1–17. doi:10.1111/j.1540-6520.2008.00278.x

Kuratko, D. F., O'Connor, A., & Frederick, H. (2018). *Entrepreneurship: Theory/ Process/ Practice*. Cengage Learning Australia.

Leonard, N., Humayun, K., Haiyue, Z., & Yunjie, T. (2020). A Vector Error Correction Model (VECM) Approach in explaining the relationship between Fixed Investment and Economic Growth in Rural China. *Pacific International Journal, 3*(3), 138-145.

Lepojević, V., Đukić, M. I., & Mladenović, J. (2016). Entrepreneurship and economic development: A comparative analysis of developed and developing countries. *Economics and Organization*, *13*(1), 17–29.

Li, Y., Yao, P., Osman, S., Zainudin, N., & Sabri, M. F. (2022). A Thematic Review on Using Food Delivery Services during the Pandemic: Insights for the Post-COVID-19 Era. *International Journal of Environmental Research and Public Health*, *19*(22), 15267. doi:10.3390/ijerph192215267 PMID:36429983

Long, J. D., & Summers, H. (1991). Equipment Investment and Economic Growth. *The Quarterly Journal of Economics*, *106*(2), 445–502. doi:10.2307/2937944

Lucien, B. (2014). Entrepreneurship is not a whim, it is a necessity. *The Business Journal, 29*. https://www.lesaffaires.com/strategie-d-entreprise/entreprendre/

Lumpkin & Dess. (1996). Clarifying the entrepreneurial orientation construct and linking it to performance. *Academy of Management Review*.

Luthje, C., & Franke, N. (2003). The 'making' of an entrepreneur: Testing a model of entrepreneurial intent among engineering students at MIT. *Research Management*, *33*(2), 135–147.

Maja, I.-Đ., Tamara, R., & Talić, M. (2021). Innovative entrepreneurship and economic growth in emerging markets. *ЕКОНОМИКА*, *67*(4), 55–64.

Mamta, C. (2004). *Currency Crisis and Stock Prices in East Asian Countries:an Applicatin of Cointegratin Granger Causality*. School of Economics and Finance.

Martinho, V. J. P. D. (2020). Agricultural entrepreneurship in the European Union: Contributions for a sustainable development. *Applied Sciences (Basel, Switzerland)*, *10*(6), 2080. doi:10.3390/app10062080

Marty, O. (2002). The life of Start-up (s′) Investing in innovative companies. *Manage and Understand. Annals of Mines*, *67*, 4–15.

Mayrfoer, U. (2006). Marketing. Bréal.

McGraw, E., Alain, R., & Robichaud, Y. (2001). Toward the development of a measuring instrument for entrepreneurial motivation. *Journal of Developmental Entrepreneurship*, *6*(2), 189.

McMullen, J. S., & Shepherd, D. A. (2006). Entrepreneurial action and the role of uncertainty in the theory of the entrepreneur". *Academy of Management Review*, *31*(1), 132–152. doi:10.5465/amr.2006.19379628

Md Reza, S., Fan, H., Wang, B., Bhuiyan, M. A., & Mehedi, K. M., A. (. (2019). Trade (exports) as an opportunity for Bangladesh: A VECM analysis. *The International Trade Journal*, *33*(1), 95–110. doi:10.1080/08853908.2018.1511489

Mehta, A. M., Qamrozzaman, M., & Serfraz, A. (2022). The Effects of Finance and Knowledge on Entrepreneurship Development: An Empirical Study from Bangladesh. The Journal of Asian Finance. *Economics and Business*, *9*(2), 409–418.

Michelle, K., & Tendai, C. (2016). The association of entrepreneurship education and entrepreneurial intention among university students in the Eastern Cape Province of South Africa. *International Journal of Educational Sciences*, *12*(3), 200–211. doi:10.1080/09751122.2016.11890427

Migros Faaliyet Raporu. (2020). https://www.migroskurumsal.com/userfiles/image/pdf/migros-tr-20.pdf

Migros Yemek Basın Bülteni. (2022). https://migroskurumsalstr.blob.core.windows.net/migroskurumsalstr/migros-yemek-basin-bulteni-10-06-2022-637908068272354200.pdf

Miller, D. (1983). The correlates of entrepreneurship in three types of firms. *Management Science*, *29*(7), 770–791. doi:10.1287/mnsc.29.7.770

Miller, D., & Toulouse, J. M. (1986). Chief executive personality and corporate strategy and structure in small firms. *Management Science*, *32*(11), 1389–1409. doi:10.1287/mnsc.32.11.1389

Mintzberg, H. (1979). *The structuring of organizations: A synthesis of the research*. University of Illinois at Urbana-Champaign's Desautels Faculty of Management.

Mitchell, R. K., Busenitz, L., Lant, T., McDougall, P. P., Morse, E. A., & Smith, J. B. (2003). Toward a theory of entrepreneurial cognition: Rethinking the people side of entrepreneurship research. *Entrepreneurship Theory and Practice*, *27*(2), 93–104. doi:10.1111/1540-8520.00001

Montani, D., Gervasio, D., & Pulcini, A. (2020). Startup Company Valuation: The State of Art and Future Trends. *International Business Research*, *13*(9), 1–31. doi:10.5539/ibr.v13n9p31

Moraes, G. H. S. M. D., Iizuka, E. S., & Pedro, M. (2018). Effects of entrepreneurial characteristics and university environment on entrepreneurial intention. *RAC. Revista de Administração Contemporânea*, *22*(2), 226–248. doi:10.1590/1982-7849rac2018170133

Moriano, J. A., Gorgievski, M., Laguna, M., Stephan, U., & Zarafshani, K. (2012). A cross-cultural approach to understanding entrepreneurial intention. *Journal of Career Development*, *39*(2), 162–185. doi:10.1177/0894845310384481

Morin, E., Guérin, M., & Boulianne, É. (1996). Les indicateurs de performance. Academic Press.

Morris, M.-H., Mihasaki, N.-N., & Watters, C.-E. (2006). Thedilemma of growth: Understanding venture size choices of women entrepreneurs. *Journal of Small Business Management*, *44*(2), 221–244. doi:10.1111/j.1540-627X.2006.00165.x

Morrison, A. (2000). Entrepreneurship: What triggers it? *International Journal of Entrepreneurial Behaviour & Research*, *6*(2), 59–71. doi:10.1108/13552550010335976

Mustafa, F., Khursheed, A., Fatima, M., & Rao, M. (2021). Exploring the impact of COVID-19 pandemic on women entrepreneurs in Pakistan. *International Journal of Gender and Entrepreneurship*, *13*(2), 187–203. doi:10.1108/IJGE-09-2020-0149

Nabi, G., Liñán, F., Ertuna, Z. İ., & Gurel, E. (2011). The moderating role of higher education on entrepreneurship. *Education + Training*, *53*(5), 387–402. doi:10.1108/00400911111147703

Nachega, J.-C., & Fontaine, T. (2006). Economic Growth and Total Factor Productivity in Niger. *International Monetary Fund Working Papers*, 1-28.

Nambisan, S. (2017). Digital Entrepreneurship: Toward a Digital Technology Perspective of Entrepreneurship. *Entrepreneurship Theory and Practice*, *41*(6), 1029–1055. doi:10.1111/etap.12254

Nambubbi, L. (2016). *Entrepreneurial Personality Traits That Affect Venture Development and Growth* [Doctoral dissertation]. United States International University-Africa.

Neely, A. (1999). The performance measurement revolution: Why now and what next? *International Journal of Operations & Production Management*, *19*(2), 205–228. doi:10.1108/01443579910247437

Nguyen, T. T. H., Nguyen, N., Nguyen, T. B. L., Phan, T. T. H., Bui, L. P., & Moon, H. C. (2019). Investigating consumer attitude and intention towards online food purchasing in an emerging economy: An extended tam approach. *Foods*, *8*(11), 576. doi:10.3390/foods8110576 PMID:31731668

Nona, R. V., Ambarawati, I. G. A. A., Darmawan, D. P., & Budiasa, I. W. (2019). Realizing Regional Food Security Through Community Food Business Development in East Nusa Tenggara Province, Indonesia. *International Journal of Agriculture System*, *6*(2), 146–155. doi:10.20956/ijas.v6i2.1593

Nunnally, J. C. (1978). An overview of psychological measurement. Clinical diagnosis of mental disorders, 97-146. doi:10.1007/978-1-4684-2490-4_4

Nwosu, J. C., & Chukwudi, J. H. (2018). Entrepreneurship education and the challenges of graduate employability in Nigeria. *International Journal of Innovation, Management and Technology*, *9*(5), 189–193.

OECD. (1998). *Fostering Entrepreneurship, The OECD Jobs Strategy*. OECD.

Ogundana, O. M., Simba, A., Dana, L.-P., & Liguori, E. (2021). Women entrepreneurship in developing economies: A gender-based growth model. *Journal of Small Business Management, 59*(sup1), S42-S72.

Ogundele, M. O., Kayode, D. J., Oduleke, F. L., & Alade, O. S. (2017). The influence of private sector involvement on entrepreneurial education of secondary schools in Kwara state, Nigeria. *MOJEM: Malaysian Online Journal of Educational Management*, *1*(1), 1–11.

Okeke, M. I., & Eme, O. I. (2014). Challenges facing entrepreneurs in Nigeria. *Singaporean Journal of Business Economics and Management Studies*, *3*(5), 18–34. doi:10.12816/0010956

Okhomina.D, (2010). Entrepreneurial orientation and psychological traits: the moderating influence of supportive environment. *Journal of Behavioral Studies in Business*.

Okoye, R., & Arimonu, M. O. (2016). Technical and vocational education in Nigeria: Issues, challenges and a way forward. *Journal of Education and Practice*, *7*(3), 113–118.

Olorundare, A. S., & Kayode, D. J. (2014). Entrepreneurship education in Nigerian universities: A tool for national transformation. *Asia Pacific Journal of Educators and Education*, *29*, 155–175.

Onuigbo, F. N. (2021). Human capital development and economic development in Nigeria-An analysis of the role of government. *International Journal of Innovative Social Sciences & Humanities Research*, *9*(4), 181–190.

Osakwe, R. N. (2015). Entrepreneurship education in Delta State tertiary institution as a means of achieving national growth and development. *International Journal of Higher Education*, *4*(1), 182–186. doi:10.5430/ijhe.v4n1p182

Pahlavan, M., Wilson, E., & Worthington, A. C. (2005). Trade-GDP Nexus in Ir ade-GDP Nexus in Iran: An Application of the Autoregressive Distributed e Distributed Lag (ARDL) Model. *Social and Behavioral Sciences Commons*, 1-23.

Panda, S. (2018). Constraints faced by women entrepreneurs in developing countries: Review and ranking. *Gender in Management*, *33*(4), 315–331. doi:10.1108/GM-01-2017-0003

Passaro, R., Quinto, I., & Thomas, A. (2017). Start-up competitions as learning environment to foster the entrepreneurial process. *International Journal of Entrepreneurial Behaviour & Research*, *23*(3), 426–445. doi:10.1108/IJEBR-01-2016-0007

Peluola, S. B., Oyelola, T. O., Ajiboshin, I. O., Igwe, C. N., & Shokunbi, M. O. (2014). Achieving excellence in the operations of entrepreneurship development centres in Nigeria higher institutions. *Journal of Poverty. Investment and Development*, *5*, 37–41.

Pesaran, M. H., Shin, Y., & Smith, R. J. (1999). Bounds Testing Approaches to the Analysis of Long-run Relationships. Edinburgh School of Economics.

Peters, B. (2009). *Early Exits: Exit strategies for entrepreneurs and angel investors (but maybe not venture capitalists)*. Basil Peters.

Petrariu, R., Constantin, M., Dinu, M., Pătărlăgeanu, S. R., & Deaconu, M. E. (2021). Water, energy, food, waste nexus: Between synergy and trade-offs in Romania based on entrepreneurship and economic performance. *Energies*, *14*(16), 5172. doi:10.3390/en14165172

Phan, P. H., Wong, P. K., & Wang, C. K. (2002). Antecedents to entrepreneurship among university students in Singapore: Beliefs, attitudes and background. *Journal of Enterprising Culture*, *10*(2), 151–174. doi:10.1142/S0218495802000189

Phares, E. J. (1976). *Locus of control in personality* (Vol. 174). General Learning Press.

Pinchot, G. (1985). *Intrapreneuring: Why you don't have to leave the corporation to become an entrepreneur*. Academy for Entrepreneurial Leadership Historical Research Reference in Entrepreneurship.

Poon, J. M. L., Ainuddin, R. A., & Junit, H. S. (2006). Effects of self-concept traits and Entrepreneuriale Orientation on firm performance. *International Small Business Journal*, *24*(1), 61–68. doi:10.1177/0266242606059779

Pretheeba, P. (2014). Predicting entrepreneurial intention among business and engineering students in Sri Lanka. *Ruhuna Journal of Management and Finance*, *1*(1), 25–36.

Qin, Z., Chang, Y., Li, S., & Li, F. (2014). *E-commerce Strategy*. Springer. doi:10.1007/978-3-642-39414-0

Randerson, K. (2011). Orientation entrepreneuriale:uneapproche par les configurations. *7th congress of the Académie de l'Entrepreneuriat et de l'innovation*, Paris, France.

Rao, V. (2017). *Can Student Entrepreneurship be the answer to India's Jobless-growth problem?* Retrieved Date 05 September 2018 from https://yourstory.com/2017/07/student-entrepreneurship-sv-co

Rasel, S., Heijman, W. J., & Reinhard, S. (2022). Economic geography and entrepreneurial diversification in the agricultural sector. *Regional Studies, Regional Science*, *9*(1), 347–370. doi:10.1080/21681376.2022.2074307

Ratten, V. (2020). Coronavirus (covid-19) and entrepreneurship: Changing life and work landscape. *Journal of Small Business and Entrepreneurship*, *32*(5), 503–516. doi:10.1080/08276331.2020.1790167

Rekabet Kurumu. (2022). *Rekabet Kurulu Kararı*. https://www.rekabet.gov.tr/Karar?kararId=b6684eb6-1ca3-4551-945e-7487d0930393

Report, G. E. M. (2009). *Global Entrepreneurship Monitor: GEM-MENA Regional Report 2009*. Middle East and North Africa.

Robinson, P. B., Stimpson, D. V., Huefner, J. C., & Hunt, H. K. (1991). An attitude approach to the prediction of entrepreneurship. *Entrepreneurship Theory and Practice*, *15*(4), 13–32. doi:10.1177/104225879101500405

Rocha, E. L. C., & Freitas, A. A. F. (2014). Evaluation of entrepreneurship teaching among university students through the entrepreneurial profile. *Contemporary Administration Magazine*, *18*(4), 465–486.

Rosca, E., Agarwal, N., & Brem, A. (2020). Women entrepreneurs as agents of change: A comparative analysis of social entrepreneurship processes in emerging markets. *Technological Forecasting and Social Change*, *157*, 120067. doi:10.1016/j.techfore.2020.120067

Rozhkova, A., & Olentsova, J. (2020). *Regional support of small business in the agriculture sphere of the krasnoyarsk region.* Paper presented at the "New Silk Road: Business Cooperation and Prospective of Economic Development" (NSRBCPED 2019). 10.2991/aebmr.k.200324.151

Sadler-Smith, E., Hampson, Y., Chaston, I., & Et Badger, B. (2003). Managerialbehaviour; Entrepreneurial style, and small firm performance. *Journal of Small Business Management*, *41*(1), 47–67. doi:10.1111/1540-627X.00066

Salamzadeh, A., & Kawamorita Kesim, H. (2015). Startup companies: Life cycle and challenges. *4th International Conference on Employment, Education and Entrepreneurship (EEE).*

Sammut, S. (1996). The small business start-up process. Complexity of the management system and emergence of start-up scenarios. *Proceedings of the VI Conference of the International Association of Strategic Management.*

Saqib, N., & Shah, G. B. (2023). Business Model Innovation Through Digital Entrepreneurship: A Case of Online Food Delivery Start-Up in India. *International Journal of E-Entrepreneurship and Innovation*, *13*(1), 1–20. doi:10.4018/IJEEI.315294

Sargani, G. R., Zhou, D., Raza, M. H., & Wei, Y. (2020). Sustainable entrepreneurship in the agriculture sector: The nexus of the triple bottom line measurement approach. *Sustainability (Basel)*, *12*(8), 3275. doi:10.3390u12083275

Savastano, M., Samo, A. H., Channa, N. A., & Amendola, C. (2022). Toward a Conceptual Framework to Foster Green Entrepreneurship Growth in the Agriculture Industry. *Sustainability (Basel)*, *14*(7), 4089. doi:10.3390u14074089

Schmidt, S., & Bohnenberger, M. C. (2009). Entrepreneurial profile and organizational performance. *Contemporary Administration Magazine*, *13*(3), 450–467.

Schollhammer, H. (1982). Internal corporate entrepreneurship. In Encyclopedia of entrepreneurship (pp. 209–229). Prentice Hall.

Schultz, T. W. (1961). Investment in human capital. *The American Economic Review*, *51*(1), 1–17.

Scott, S. (2008). A leading expert in entrepreneurial activity in the United States and other. Yale University Press.

Seema, N., & Nayaran, P. K. (2004). Determinants of Demand for FIJI's Exports an Ampirical Investigation. *The Developing Economies*, 95–112.

Segal, G., Borgia, D., & Schoenfeld, J. (2005). The motivation to become an entrepreneur. *International Journal of Entrepreneurial Behaviour & Research*, *11*(1), 42–57. doi:10.1108/13552550510580834

Shahzad, A., & Munir, K. (2015). *Factor Accumulation and Economic Growth in Pakistan: Incorporating Human Capital*. Munich Personal RePEc Archive.

Shane, S., & Venkataraman, S. (2000). The promise of entrepreneurship as a field of research. *Academy of Management Review*, *25*(01), 217–226. doi:10.5465/amr.2000.2791611

Shastri, S., Shastri, S., & Pareek, A. (2019). Motivations and challenges of women entrepreneurs: Experiences of small businesses in Jaipur city of Rajasthan. *The International Journal of Sociology and Social Policy*, *39*(5/6), 338–355. doi:10.1108/IJSSP-09-2018-0146

Shepherd, D. A., Douglas, E. J., & Shanley, M. (2000). New venture survival: Ignorance, external shocks, and risk reduction strategies. *Journal of Business Venturing*, *15*(5–6), 393–410. doi:10.1016/S0883-9026(98)00032-9

Sher, A., Mazhar, S., Abbas, A., Iqbal, M. A., & Li, X. (2019). Linking entrepreneurial skills and opportunity recognition with improved food distribution in the context of the CPEC: A case of Pakistan. *Sustainability (Basel)*, *11*(7), 1838. doi:10.3390u11071838

Sinyolo, S. (2020). Technology adoption and household food security among rural households in South Africa: The role of improved maize varieties. *Technology in Society*, *60*, 101214. doi:10.1016/j.techsoc.2019.101214

Sinyolo, S., & Mudhara, M. (2018). The impact of entrepreneurial competencies on household food security among smallholder farmers in KwaZulu Natal, South Africa. *Ecology of Food and Nutrition*, *57*(2), 71–93. doi:10.1080/03670244.2017.1416361 PMID:29271664

Souitaris, V., Zerbinati, S., & Al-Laham, A. (2007). Do entrepreneurship programmes raise entrepreneurial intention of science and engineering students? The effect of learning, inspiration and resources. *Journal of Business Venturing*, *22*(4), 566–591. doi:10.1016/j.jbusvent.2006.05.002

Srivastava, S., & Misra, R. (2017). Exploring antecedents of entrepreneurial intentions of young women in India. *Journal of Entrepreneurship in Emerging Economies*, *9*(2), 181–206. doi:10.1108/JEEE-04-2016-0012

Standish-Kuon, T., & Rice, M. P. (2002). Introducing engineering and science students to entrepreneurship: Models and influential factors at six American universities. *Journal of Engineering Education, 91*(1), 33–39. doi:10.1002/j.2168-9830.2002.tb00670.x

Stefan, D., Vasile, V., Oltean, A., Comes, C.-A., Stefan, A.-B., Ciucan-Rusu, L., Bunduchi, E., Popa, M.-A., & Timus, M. (2021). Women entrepreneurship and sustainable business development: Key findings from a SWOT–AHP analysis. *Sustainability (Basel), 13*(9), 5298. doi:10.3390u13095298

Stevenson & Jarillo. (1990). A Paradigm of Entrepreneurship: Entrepreneurial Management. *Strategic Management Journal, 15*(7), 521–536.

Stock, J. H., & Watson, M. W. (1988). Testing for Common Trends. *Journal of American Statistical Association, 83.*

St-Pierre, J., & Cadieux, L. (2009). *La conception de la performance: quel lien avec le profil entrepreneurial des propriétairesdirigeants de PME.* 6th Congress of the Académie de l'Entrepreneuriat, Sophia-Antipolis, France.

St-Pierre, J. (2005). *La gestionfinancière des PME: théoriesetpratiques.* University of Quebec Press.

Taallah, L., & Chine, L. (2020). Total Factor Productivity and Sources of Economic Growth in Algeria (1970-2018) by Uusing ARDL Approach. *Revue des Réformes Economiques et Intégration En Economie Mondiale, 14*(03), 1–11.

Tajvidi, R., & Tajvidi, M. (2021). The growth of cyber entrepreneurship in the food industry: Virtual community engagement in the COVID-19 era. *British Food Journal, 123*(10), 3309–3325. doi:10.1108/BFJ-06-2020-0559

Tegtmeier. (2012). Empirical implications for promoting students entrepreneurial intentions. *Journal of Enterprising Culture, 20*(2), 151–169.

Tekin, E. (2019). *Girişimcilik ve Sosyal Sermaye.* Eğitim Yayınevi.

Thaher, L. M., Radieah, N. M., & Wan Norhaniza, W. H. (2021). The effect of microfinance services on women entrepreneurship: A case study in Jordan. The Journal of Asian Finance. *Economics and Business, 8*(5), 807–815.

Thasnimol, C. M., & Rajathy, R. (2021). Vector Error Correction Model for Distribution Dynamic State Estimation. Springer Science and Business Media Deutschland GmbH. doi:10.1007/978-981-15-8815-0_2

Ticaret Bakanlığı E-ticaret Bilgi Platformu Genel İstatistikler. (n.d.). https://www.eticaret.gov.tr/istatistikler

Tiwari, P., Bhat, A. K., & Tikoria, J. (2017). Predictors of social entrepreneurial intention: An empirical study. *South Asian Journal of Business Studies, 6*(1), 53–79. doi:10.1108/SAJBS-04-2016-0032

Torun, Akdeniz, Demireli, & Grima. (2022). Long-Term US Economic Growth and the Carbon Dioxide Emissions Nexus: A Wavelet-Based Approach. *Sustainability, 14*. doi:10.3390/su141710566

Ubogu, R. (2020). Entrepreneurship education: Challenges and strategies towards promoting entrepreneurship in higher education in Nigeria. *Academic Journal of Interdisciplinary Studies, 9*(5), 125–137. doi:10.36941/ajis-2020-0091

Urbano, D., & Aparicio, S. (2016). *Entrepreneurship capital types and economic growth: International evidence.* Science Direct.

Valero, A. (2021). *Education and economic growth.* Discussion Paper No. 1764. Centre for Economic Performance, London School of Economics and Political Science.

Van Gelderen, M., Brand, M., Van Praag, M., Bodewes, W., Poutsma, E., & Van Gils, A. (2008). Explaining entrepreneurial intentions by means of the theory of planned behaviour. *Career Development International, 13*(6), 538–559. doi:10.1108/13620430810901688

Vodwa, M., Mimouni, B., & Beniba, M. (2021). The role of business incubators in supporting and developing startups in Algeria. *Journal of Economic Growth and Entrepreneurship, 6*(4), 116–125.

Walker, E., & Et Brown, A. (2004). What success factors are important to small business owners? *International Small Business Journal, 22*(6), 577–594. doi:10.1177/0266242604047411

Wang, C. K., & Wong, P. K. (2004). Entrepreneurial interest of university students in Singapore. *Technovation, 24*(2), 163–172. doi:10.1016/S0166-4972(02)00016-0

Wiklund & Shepherd. (2003). Knowledge Based Resources, Entrepreneurial Orientation, and the Performance of Small and Medium-Sized Businesses. *Strategic Management Journal*, 24.

Wood & Bandura. (1989). Impact of conceptions of ability on self- regulatory Mechanisms and complex decision Making. *Journal of Personality and Social Psychology, 56*(3), 407-415.

World Bank. (2023). *Firms with female participation in ownership (% of firms).* Author.

Yadav, P., & Marwah, C. S. (2015). The concept of productivity. *International Journal of Engineering and Technical Research, 3*(5), 192–196.

Yang. (2013). The theory of planned behavior and prediction of entrepreneurial intention among Chinese undergraduates. *Social Behavior and Personality, 41*(3), 367–376.

Yeo, V. C. S., Goh, S. K., & Rezaei, S. (2017). Consumer experiences, attitude and behavioral intention toward online food delivery (OFD) services. *Journal of Retailing and Consumer Services, 35*, 150–162. doi:10.1016/j.jretconser.2016.12.013

Yoshida, S., Yagi, H., Kiminami, A., & Garrod, G. (2019). Farm diversification and sustainability of multifunctional peri-urban agriculture: Entrepreneurial attributes of advanced diversification in Japan. *Sustainability (Basel), 11*(10), 2887. doi:10.3390u11102887

Yule, G. (1926). Why Do We Some Times Get Nonsense-Correlations Between Time-Series? A Study in Sampling and the Nature of Time-Series. *Journal of the Royal Statistical Society*, 89.

Zaheer, H., Breyer, Y., & Dumay, J. (2019). Digital entrepreneurship: An interdisciplinary structured literature review and research agenda. *Technological Forecasting and Social Change*, *148*, 119735. doi:10.1016/j.techfore.2019.119735

Zahra, S. A. (1991). A conceptual model of entrepreneurship as firm behavior: A critique and extension. *Entrepreneurship Theory and Practice*, *17*(4), 5–21. doi:10.1177/104225879301700401

Zaki, I. M., & Rashid, N. H. (2016). Entrepreneurship Impact on Economic Growth in Emerging Countries. *The Business and Management Review*, *7*(2), 31–39.

Zhao, H., Hills, G. E., & Seibert, S. (2005). The mediating role of self-efficacy in the development of entrepreneurial intentions. *The Journal of Applied Psychology*, *90*(6), 1265–1272. doi:10.1037/0021-9010.90.6.1265 PMID:16316279

Zhou, L., Dai, L., & Zhang, D. (2007). Online shopping acceptance model-A critical survey of consumer factors in online shopping. *Journal of Electronic Commerce Research*, *8*(1).

Zina, A. (2022). Entrepreneurial Orientation, Organizational Culture and Business Performance in SMEs: Evidence from Emerging Economy. *Sustainability, 14*(9).

Zina, A., & Ettayib, M. (2021). The personality of the Algerian leader and Entrepreneurship: Test of analysis by structural equations (Smart PLS). *Industrial Economics Review, 11*(2).

Related References

To continue our tradition of advancing information science and technology research, we have compiled a list of recommended IGI Global readings. These references will provide additional information and guidance to further enrich your knowledge and assist you with your own research and future publications.

Abdul Razak, R., & Mansor, N. A. (2021). Instagram Influencers in Social Media-Induced Tourism: Rethinking Tourist Trust Towards Tourism Destination. In M. Dinis, L. Bonixe, S. Lamy, & Z. Breda (Eds.), *Impact of New Media in Tourism* (pp. 135-144). IGI Global. https://doi.org/10.4018/978-1-7998-7095-1.ch009

Abir, T., & Khan, M. Y. (2022). Importance of ICT Advancement and Culture of Adaptation in the Tourism and Hospitality Industry for Developing Countries. In C. Ramos, S. Quinteiro, & A. Gonçalves (Eds.), *ICT as Innovator Between Tourism and Culture* (pp. 30–41). IGI Global. https://doi.org/10.4018/978-1-7998-8165-0.ch003

Abtahi, M. S., Behboudi, L., & Hasanabad, H. M. (2017). Factors Affecting Internet Advertising Adoption in Ad Agencies. *International Journal of Innovation in the Digital Economy*, *8*(4), 18–29. doi:10.4018/IJIDE.2017100102

Afenyo-Agbe, E., & Mensah, I. (2022). Principles, Benefits, and Barriers to Community-Based Tourism: Implications for Management. In I. Mensah & E. Afenyo-Agbe (Eds.), *Prospects and Challenges of Community-Based Tourism and Changing Demographics* (pp. 1–29). IGI Global. doi:10.4018/978-1-7998-7335-8.ch001

Agbo, V. M. (2022). Distributive Justice Issues in Community-Based Tourism. In I. Mensah & E. Afenyo-Agbe (Eds.), *Prospects and Challenges of Community-Based Tourism and Changing Demographics* (pp. 107–129). IGI Global. https://doi.org/10.4018/978-1-7998-7335-8.ch005

Agrawal, S. (2017). The Impact of Emerging Technologies and Social Media on Different Business(es): Marketing and Management. In O. Rishi & A. Sharma (Eds.), *Maximizing Business Performance and Efficiency Through Intelligent Systems* (pp. 37–49). Hershey, PA: IGI Global. doi:10.4018/978-1-5225-2234-8.ch002

Ahmad, A., & Johari, S. (2022). Georgetown as a Gastronomy Tourism Destination: Visitor Awareness Towards Revisit Intention of Nasi Kandar Restaurant. In M. Valeri (Ed.), *New Governance and Management in Touristic Destinations* (pp. 71–83). IGI Global. https://doi.org/10.4018/978-1-6684-3889-3.ch005

Alkhatib, G., & Bayouq, S. T. (2021). A TAM-Based Model of Technological Factors Affecting Use of E-Tourism. *International Journal of Tourism and Hospitality Management in the Digital Age*, *5*(2), 50–67. https://doi.org/10.4018/IJTHMDA.20210701.oa1

Altinay Ozdemir, M. (2021). Virtual Reality (VR) and Augmented Reality (AR) Technologies for Accessibility and Marketing in the Tourism Industry. In C. Eusébio, L. Teixeira, & M. Carneiro (Eds.), *ICT Tools and Applications for Accessible Tourism* (pp. 277-301). IGI Global. https://doi.org/10.4018/978-1-7998-6428-8.ch013

Anantharaman, R. N., Rajeswari, K. S., Angusamy, A., & Kuppusamy, J. (2017). Role of Self-Efficacy and Collective Efficacy as Moderators of Occupational Stress Among Software Development Professionals. *International Journal of Human Capital and Information Technology Professionals*, *8*(2), 45–58. doi:10.4018/IJHCITP.2017040103

Aninze, F., El-Gohary, H., & Hussain, J. (2018). The Role of Microfinance to Empower Women: The Case of Developing Countries. *International Journal of Customer Relationship Marketing and Management*, *9*(1), 54–78. doi:10.4018/IJCRMM.2018010104

Antosova, G., Sabogal-Salamanca, M., & Krizova, E. (2021). Human Capital in Tourism: A Practical Model of Endogenous and Exogenous Territorial Tourism Planning in Bahía Solano, Colombia. In V. Costa, A. Moura, & M. Mira (Eds.), *Handbook of Research on Human Capital and People Management in the Tourism Industry* (pp. 282–302). IGI Global. https://doi.org/10.4018/978-1-7998-4318-4.ch014

Arsenijević, O. M., Orčić, D., & Kastratović, E. (2017). Development of an Optimization Tool for Intangibles in SMEs: A Case Study from Serbia with a Pilot Research in the Prestige by Milka Company. In M. Vemić (Ed.), *Optimal Management Strategies in Small and Medium Enterprises* (pp. 320–347). Hershey, PA: IGI Global. doi:10.4018/978-1-5225-1949-2.ch015

Aryanto, V. D., Wismantoro, Y., & Widyatmoko, K. (2018). Implementing Eco-Innovation by Utilizing the Internet to Enhance Firm's Marketing Performance: Study of Green Batik Small and Medium Enterprises in Indonesia. *International Journal of E-Business Research, 14*(1), 21–36. doi:10.4018/IJEBR.2018010102

Asero, V., & Billi, S. (2022). New Perspective of Networking in the DMO Model. In M. Valeri (Ed.), *New Governance and Management in Touristic Destinations* (pp. 105–118). IGI Global. https://doi.org/10.4018/978-1-6684-3889-3.ch007

Atiku, S. O., & Fields, Z. (2017). Multicultural Orientations for 21st Century Global Leadership. In N. Baporikar (Ed.), *Management Education for Global Leadership* (pp. 28–51). Hershey, PA: IGI Global. doi:10.4018/978-1-5225-1013-0.ch002

Atiku, S. O., & Fields, Z. (2018). Organisational Learning Dimensions and Talent Retention Strategies for the Service Industries. In N. Baporikar (Ed.), *Global Practices in Knowledge Management for Societal and Organizational Development* (pp. 358–381). Hershey, PA: IGI Global. doi:10.4018/978-1-5225-3009-1.ch017

Atsa'am, D. D., & Kuset Bodur, E. (2021). Pattern Mining on How Organizational Tenure Affects the Psychological Capital of Employees Within the Hospitality and Tourism Industry: Linking Employees' Organizational Tenure With PsyCap. *International Journal of Tourism and Hospitality Management in the Digital Age, 5*(2), 17–28. https://doi.org/10.4018/IJTHMDA.2021070102

Ávila, L., & Teixeira, L. (2018). The Main Concepts Behind the Dematerialization of Business Processes. In M. Khosrow-Pour, D.B.A. (Ed.), Encyclopedia of Information Science and Technology, Fourth Edition (pp. 888-898). Hershey, PA: IGI Global. https://doi.org/ doi:10.4018/978-1-5225-2255-3.ch076

Ayorekire, J., Mugizi, F., Obua, J., & Ampaire, G. (2022). Community-Based Tourism and Local People's Perceptions Towards Conservation: The Case of Queen Elizabeth Conservation Area, Uganda. In I. Mensah & E. Afenyo-Agbe (Eds.), *Prospects and Challenges of Community-Based Tourism and Changing Demographics* (pp. 56–82). IGI Global. https://doi.org/10.4018/978-1-7998-7335-8.ch003

Baleiro, R. (2022). Tourist Literature and the Architecture of Travel in Olga Tokarczuk and Patti Smith. In R. Baleiro & R. Pereira (Eds.), *Global Perspectives on Literary Tourism and Film-Induced Tourism* (pp. 202-216). IGI Global. https://doi.org/10.4018/978-1-7998-8262-6.ch011

Barat, S. (2021). Looking at the Future of Medical Tourism in Asia. *International Journal of Tourism and Hospitality Management in the Digital Age, 5*(1), 19–33. https://doi.org/10.4018/IJTHMDA.2021010102

Barbosa, C. A., Magalhães, M., & Nunes, M. R. (2021). Travel Instagramability: A Way of Choosing a Destination? In M. Dinis, L. Bonixe, S. Lamy, & Z. Breda (Eds.), *Impact of New Media in Tourism* (pp. 173-190). IGI Global. https://doi.org/10.4018/978-1-7998-7095-1.ch011

Bari, M. W., & Khan, Q. (2021). Pakistan as a Destination of Religious Tourism. In E. Alaverdov & M. Bari (Eds.), *Global Development of Religious Tourism* (pp. 1-10). IGI Global. https://doi.org/10.4018/978-1-7998-5792-1.ch001

Bartens, Y., Chunpir, H. I., Schulte, F., & Voß, S. (2017). Business/IT Alignment in Two-Sided Markets: A COBIT 5 Analysis for Media Streaming Business Models. In S. De Haes & W. Van Grembergen (Eds.), *Strategic IT Governance and Alignment in Business Settings* (pp. 82–111). Hershey, PA: IGI Global. doi:10.4018/978-1-5225-0861-8.ch004

Bashayreh, A. M. (2018). Organizational Culture and Organizational Performance. In W. Lee & F. Sabetzadeh (Eds.), *Contemporary Knowledge and Systems Science* (pp. 50–69). Hershey, PA: IGI Global. doi:10.4018/978-1-5225-5655-8.ch003

Bechthold, L., Lude, M., & Prügl, R. (2021). Crisis Favors the Prepared Firm: How Organizational Ambidexterity Relates to Perceptions of Organizational Resilience. In A. Zehrer, G. Glowka, K. Schwaiger, & V. Ranacher-Lackner (Eds.), *Resiliency Models and Addressing Future Risks for Family Firms in the Tourism Industry* (pp. 178–205). IGI Global. https://doi.org/10.4018/978-1-7998-7352-5.ch008

Bedford, D. A. (2018). Sustainable Knowledge Management Strategies: Aligning Business Capabilities and Knowledge Management Goals. In N. Baporikar (Ed.), *Global Practices in Knowledge Management for Societal and Organizational Development* (pp. 46–73). Hershey, PA: IGI Global. doi:10.4018/978-1-5225-3009-1.ch003

Bekjanov, D., & Matyusupov, B. (2021). Influence of Innovative Processes in the Competitiveness of Tourist Destination. In J. Soares (Ed.), *Innovation and Entrepreneurial Opportunities in Community Tourism* (pp. 243–263). IGI Global. https://doi.org/10.4018/978-1-7998-4855-4.ch014

Bharwani, S., & Musunuri, D. (2018). Reflection as a Process From Theory to Practice. In M. Khosrow-Pour, D.B.A. (Ed.), Encyclopedia of Information Science and Technology, Fourth Edition (pp. 1529-1539). Hershey, PA: IGI Global. doi:10.4018/978-1-5225-2255-3.ch132

Bhatt, G. D., Wang, Z., & Rodger, J. A. (2017). Information Systems Capabilities and Their Effects on Competitive Advantages: A Study of Chinese Companies. *Information Resources Management Journal, 30*(3), 41–57. doi:10.4018/IRMJ.2017070103

Bhushan, M., & Yadav, A. (2017). Concept of Cloud Computing in ESB. In R. Bhadoria, N. Chaudhari, G. Tomar, & S. Singh (Eds.), *Exploring Enterprise Service Bus in the Service-Oriented Architecture Paradigm* (pp. 116–127). Hershey, PA: IGI Global. doi:10.4018/978-1-5225-2157-0.ch008

Bhushan, S. (2017). System Dynamics Base-Model of Humanitarian Supply Chain (HSCM) in Disaster Prone Eco-Communities of India: A Discussion on Simulation and Scenario Results. *International Journal of System Dynamics Applications*, *6*(3), 20–37. doi:10.4018/IJSDA.2017070102

Binder, D., & Miller, J. W. (2021). A Generations' Perspective on Employer Branding in Tourism. In V. Costa, A. Moura, & M. Mira (Eds.), *Handbook of Research on Human Capital and People Management in the Tourism Industry* (pp. 152–174). IGI Global. https://doi.org/10.4018/978-1-7998-4318-4.ch008

Birch Freeman, A. A., Mensah, I., & Antwi, K. B. (2022). Smiling vs. Frowning Faces: Community Participation for Sustainable Tourism in Ghanaian Communities. In I. Mensah & E. Afenyo-Agbe (Eds.), *Prospects and Challenges of Community-Based Tourism and Changing Demographics* (pp. 83–106). IGI Global. https://doi.org/10.4018/978-1-7998-7335-8.ch004

Biswas, A., & De, A. K. (2017). On Development of a Fuzzy Stochastic Programming Model with Its Application to Business Management. In S. Trivedi, S. Dey, A. Kumar, & T. Panda (Eds.), *Handbook of Research on Advanced Data Mining Techniques and Applications for Business Intelligence* (pp. 353–378). Hershey, PA: IGI Global. doi:10.4018/978-1-5225-2031-3.ch021

Boragnio, A., & Faracce Macia, C. (2021). "Taking Care of Yourself at Home": Use of E-Commerce About Food and Care During the COVID-19 Pandemic in the City of Buenos Aires. In M. Korstanje (Ed.), *Socio-Economic Effects and Recovery Efforts for the Rental Industry: Post-COVID-19 Strategies* (pp. 45–71). IGI Global. https://doi.org/10.4018/978-1-7998-7287-0.ch003

Borges, V. D. (2021). Happiness: The Basis for Public Policy in Tourism. In A. Perinotto, V. Mayer, & J. Soares (Eds.), *Rebuilding and Restructuring the Tourism Industry: Infusion of Happiness and Quality of Life* (pp. 1–25). IGI Global. https://doi.org/10.4018/978-1-7998-7239-9.ch001

Bücker, J., & Ernste, K. (2018). Use of Brand Heroes in Strategic Reputation Management: The Case of Bacardi, Adidas, and Daimler. In A. Erdemir (Ed.), *Reputation Management Techniques in Public Relations* (pp. 126–150). Hershey, PA: IGI Global. doi:10.4018/978-1-5225-3619-2.ch007

Buluk Eşitti, B. (2021). COVID-19 and Alternative Tourism: New Destinations and New Tourism Products. In M. Demir, A. Dalgıç, & F. Ergen (Eds.), *Handbook of Research on the Impacts and Implications of COVID-19 on the Tourism Industry* (pp. 786–805). IGI Global. https://doi.org/10.4018/978-1-7998-8231-2.ch038

Bureš, V. (2018). Industry 4.0 From the Systems Engineering Perspective: Alternative Holistic Framework Development. In R. Brunet-Thornton & F. Martinez (Eds.), *Analyzing the Impacts of Industry 4.0 in Modern Business Environments* (pp. 199–223). Hershey, PA: IGI Global. doi:10.4018/978-1-5225-3468-6.ch011

Buzady, Z. (2017). Resolving the Magic Cube of Effective Case Teaching: Benchmarking Case Teaching Practices in Emerging Markets – Insights from the Central European University Business School, Hungary. In D. Latusek (Ed.), *Case Studies as a Teaching Tool in Management Education* (pp. 79–103). Hershey, PA: IGI Global. doi:10.4018/978-1-5225-0770-3.ch005

Camillo, A. (2021). *Legal Matters, Risk Management, and Risk Prevention: From Forming a Business to Legal Representation*. IGI Global. doi:10.4018/978-1-7998-4342-9.ch004

Căpusneanu, S., & Topor, D. I. (2018). Business Ethics and Cost Management in SMEs: Theories of Business Ethics and Cost Management Ethos. In I. Oncioiu (Ed.), *Ethics and Decision-Making for Sustainable Business Practices* (pp. 109–127). Hershey, PA: IGI Global. doi:10.4018/978-1-5225-3773-1.ch007

Chan, R. L., Mo, P. L., & Moon, K. K. (2018). Strategic and Tactical Measures in Managing Enterprise Risks: A Study of the Textile and Apparel Industry. In K. Strang, M. Korstanje, & N. Vajjhala (Eds.), *Research, Practices, and Innovations in Global Risk and Contingency Management* (pp. 1–19). Hershey, PA: IGI Global. doi:10.4018/978-1-5225-4754-9.ch001

Charlier, S. D., Burke-Smalley, L. A., & Fisher, S. L. (2018). Undergraduate Programs in the U.S: A Contextual and Content-Based Analysis. In J. Mendy (Ed.), *Teaching Human Resources and Organizational Behavior at the College Level* (pp. 26–57). Hershey, PA: IGI Global. doi:10.4018/978-1-5225-2820-3.ch002

Chumillas, J., Güell, M., & Quer, P. (2022). The Use of ICT in Tourist and Educational Literary Routes: The Role of the Guide. In C. Ramos, S. Quinteiro, & A. Gonçalves (Eds.), *ICT as Innovator Between Tourism and Culture* (pp. 15–29). IGI Global. https://doi.org/10.4018/978-1-7998-8165-0.ch002

Dahlberg, T., Kivijärvi, H., & Saarinen, T. (2017). IT Investment Consistency and Other Factors Influencing the Success of IT Performance. In S. De Haes & W. Van Grembergen (Eds.), *Strategic IT Governance and Alignment in Business Settings* (pp. 176–208). Hershey, PA: IGI Global. doi:10.4018/978-1-5225-0861-8.ch007

Damnjanović, A. M. (2017). Knowledge Management Optimization through IT and E-Business Utilization: A Qualitative Study on Serbian SMEs. In M. Vemić (Ed.), *Optimal Management Strategies in Small and Medium Enterprises* (pp. 249–267). Hershey, PA: IGI Global. doi:10.4018/978-1-5225-1949-2.ch012

Daneshpour, H. (2017). Integrating Sustainable Development into Project Portfolio Management through Application of Open Innovation. In M. Vemić (Ed.), *Optimal Management Strategies in Small and Medium Enterprises* (pp. 370–387). Hershey, PA: IGI Global. doi:10.4018/978-1-5225-1949-2.ch017

Daniel, A. D., & Reis de Castro, V. (2018). Entrepreneurship Education: How to Measure the Impact on Nascent Entrepreneurs. In A. Carrizo Moreira, J. Guilherme Leitão Dantas, & F. Manuel Valente (Eds.), *Nascent Entrepreneurship and Successful New Venture Creation* (pp. 85–110). Hershey, PA: IGI Global. doi:10.4018/978-1-5225-2936-1.ch004

David, R., Swami, B. N., & Tangirala, S. (2018). Ethics Impact on Knowledge Management in Organizational Development: A Case Study. In N. Baporikar (Ed.), *Global Practices in Knowledge Management for Societal and Organizational Development* (pp. 19–45). Hershey, PA: IGI Global. doi:10.4018/978-1-5225-3009-1.ch002

De Uña-Álvarez, E., & Villarino-Pérez, M. (2022). Fostering Ecocultural Resources, Identity, and Tourism in Inland Territories (Galicia, NW Spain). In G. Fernandes (Ed.), *Challenges and New Opportunities for Tourism in Inland Territories: Ecocultural Resources and Sustainable Initiatives* (pp. 1-16). IGI Global. https://doi.org/10.4018/978-1-7998-7339-6.ch001

Delias, P., & Lakiotaki, K. (2018). Discovering Process Horizontal Boundaries to Facilitate Process Comprehension. *International Journal of Operations Research and Information Systems*, *9*(2), 1–31. doi:10.4018/IJORIS.2018040101

Denholm, J., & Lee-Davies, L. (2018). Success Factors for Games in Business and Project Management. In *Enhancing Education and Training Initiatives Through Serious Games* (pp. 34–68). Hershey, PA: IGI Global. doi:10.4018/978-1-5225-3689-5.ch002

Deshpande, M. (2017). Best Practices in Management Institutions for Global Leadership: Policy Aspects. In N. Baporikar (Ed.), *Management Education for Global Leadership* (pp. 1–27). Hershey, PA: IGI Global. doi:10.4018/978-1-5225-1013-0.ch001

Deshpande, M. (2018). Policy Perspectives for SMEs Knowledge Management. In N. Baporikar (Ed.), *Knowledge Integration Strategies for Entrepreneurship and Sustainability* (pp. 23–46). Hershey, PA: IGI Global. doi:10.4018/978-1-5225-5115-7.ch002

Dezdar, S. (2017). ERP Implementation Projects in Asian Countries: A Comparative Study on Iran and China. *International Journal of Information Technology Project Management, 8*(3), 52–68. doi:10.4018/IJITPM.2017070104

Domingos, D., Respício, A., & Martinho, R. (2017). Reliability of IoT-Aware BPMN Healthcare Processes. In C. Reis & M. Maximiano (Eds.), *Internet of Things and Advanced Application in Healthcare* (pp. 214–248). Hershey, PA: IGI Global. doi:10.4018/978-1-5225-1820-4.ch008

Dosumu, O., Hussain, J., & El-Gohary, H. (2017). An Exploratory Study of the Impact of Government Policies on the Development of Small and Medium Enterprises in Developing Countries: The Case of Nigeria. *International Journal of Customer Relationship Marketing and Management, 8*(4), 51–62. doi:10.4018/IJCRMM.2017100104

Durst, S., Bruns, G., & Edvardsson, I. R. (2017). Retaining Knowledge in Smaller Building and Construction Firms. *International Journal of Knowledge and Systems Science, 8*(3), 1–12. doi:10.4018/IJKSS.2017070101

Edvardsson, I. R., & Durst, S. (2017). Outsourcing, Knowledge, and Learning: A Critical Review. *International Journal of Knowledge-Based Organizations, 7*(2), 13–26. doi:10.4018/IJKBO.2017040102

Edwards, J. S. (2018). Integrating Knowledge Management and Business Processes. In M. Khosrow-Pour, D.B.A. (Ed.), Encyclopedia of Information Science and Technology, Fourth Edition (pp. 5046-5055). Hershey, PA: IGI Global. doi:10.4018/978-1-5225-2255-3.ch437

Eichelberger, S., & Peters, M. (2021). Family Firm Management in Turbulent Times: Opportunities for Responsible Tourism. In A. Zehrer, G. Glowka, K. Schwaiger, & V. Ranacher-Lackner (Eds.), *Resiliency Models and Addressing Future Risks for Family Firms in the Tourism Industry* (pp. 103–124). IGI Global. https://doi.org/10.4018/978-1-7998-7352-5.ch005

Eide, D., Hjalager, A., & Hansen, M. (2022). Innovative Certifications in Adventure Tourism: Attributes and Diffusion. In R. Augusto Costa, F. Brandão, Z. Breda, & C. Costa (Eds.), *Planning and Managing the Experience Economy in Tourism* (pp. 161-175). IGI Global. https://doi.org/10.4018/978-1-7998-8775-1.ch009

Ejiogu, A. O. (2018). Economics of Farm Management. In *Agricultural Finance and Opportunities for Investment and Expansion* (pp. 56–72). Hershey, PA: IGI Global. doi:10.4018/978-1-5225-3059-6.ch003

Ekanem, I., & Abiade, G. E. (2018). Factors Influencing the Use of E-Commerce by Small Enterprises in Nigeria. *International Journal of ICT Research in Africa and the Middle East*, *7*(1), 37–53. doi:10.4018/IJICTRAME.2018010103

Ekanem, I., & Alrossais, L. A. (2017). Succession Challenges Facing Family Businesses in Saudi Arabia. In P. Zgheib (Ed.), *Entrepreneurship and Business Innovation in the Middle East* (pp. 122–146). Hershey, PA: IGI Global. doi:10.4018/978-1-5225-2066-5.ch007

El Faquih, L., & Fredj, M. (2017). Ontology-Based Framework for Quality in Configurable Process Models. *Journal of Electronic Commerce in Organizations*, *15*(2), 48–60. doi:10.4018/JECO.2017040104

Faisal, M. N., & Talib, F. (2017). Building Ambidextrous Supply Chains in SMEs: How to Tackle the Barriers? *International Journal of Information Systems and Supply Chain Management*, *10*(4), 80–100. doi:10.4018/IJISSCM.2017100105

Fernandes, T. M., Gomes, J., & Romão, M. (2017). Investments in E-Government: A Benefit Management Case Study. *International Journal of Electronic Government Research*, *13*(3), 1–17. doi:10.4018/IJEGR.2017070101

Figueira, L. M., Honrado, G. R., & Dionísio, M. S. (2021). Human Capital Management in the Tourism Industry in Portugal. In V. Costa, A. Moura, & M. Mira (Eds.), *Handbook of Research on Human Capital and People Management in the Tourism Industry* (pp. 1–19). IGI Global. doi:10.4018/978-1-7998-4318-4.ch001

Gao, S. S., Oreal, S., & Zhang, J. (2018). Contemporary Financial Risk Management Perceptions and Practices of Small-Sized Chinese Businesses. In I. Management Association (Ed.), Global Business Expansion: Concepts, Methodologies, Tools, and Applications (pp. 917-931). Hershey, PA: IGI Global. doi:10.4018/978-1-5225-5481-3.ch041

Garg, R., & Berning, S. C. (2017). Indigenous Chinese Management Philosophies: Key Concepts and Relevance for Modern Chinese Firms. In B. Christiansen & G. Koc (Eds.), *Transcontinental Strategies for Industrial Development and Economic Growth* (pp. 43–57). Hershey, PA: IGI Global. doi:10.4018/978-1-5225-2160-0.ch003

Gencer, Y. G. (2017). Supply Chain Management in Retailing Business. In U. Akkucuk (Ed.), *Ethics and Sustainability in Global Supply Chain Management* (pp. 197–210). Hershey, PA: IGI Global. doi:10.4018/978-1-5225-2036-8.ch011

Gera, R., Arora, S., & Malik, S. (2021). Emotional Labor in the Tourism Industry: Strategies, Antecedents, and Outcomes. In V. Costa, A. Moura, & M. Mira (Eds.), *Handbook of Research on Human Capital and People Management in the Tourism Industry* (pp. 73–91). IGI Global. https://doi.org/10.4018/978-1-7998-4318-4.ch004

Giacosa, E. (2018). The Increasing of the Regional Development Thanks to the Luxury Business Innovation. In L. Carvalho (Ed.), *Handbook of Research on Entrepreneurial Ecosystems and Social Dynamics in a Globalized World* (pp. 260–273). Hershey, PA: IGI Global. doi:10.4018/978-1-5225-3525-6.ch011

Glowka, G., Tusch, M., & Zehrer, A. (2021). The Risk Perception of Family Business Owner-Manager in the Tourism Industry: A Qualitative Comparison of the Intra-Firm Senior and Junior Generation. In A. Zehrer, G. Glowka, K. Schwaiger, & V. Ranacher-Lackner (Eds.), *Resiliency Models and Addressing Future Risks for Family Firms in the Tourism Industry* (pp. 126–153). IGI Global. https://doi.org/10.4018/978-1-7998-7352-5.ch006

Glykas, M., & George, J. (2017). Quality and Process Management Systems in the UAE Maritime Industry. *International Journal of Productivity Management and Assessment Technologies*, *5*(1), 20–39. doi:10.4018/IJPMAT.2017010102

Glykas, M., Valiris, G., Kokkinaki, A., & Koutsoukou, Z. (2018). Banking Business Process Management Implementation. *International Journal of Productivity Management and Assessment Technologies*, *6*(1), 50–69. doi:10.4018/IJPMAT.2018010104

Gomes, J., & Romão, M. (2017). The Balanced Scorecard: Keeping Updated and Aligned with Today's Business Trends. *International Journal of Productivity Management and Assessment Technologies*, *5*(2), 1–15. doi:10.4018/IJPMAT.2017070101

Gomes, J., & Romão, M. (2017). Aligning Information Systems and Technology with Benefit Management and Balanced Scorecard. In S. De Haes & W. Van Grembergen (Eds.), *Strategic IT Governance and Alignment in Business Settings* (pp. 112–131). Hershey, PA: IGI Global. doi:10.4018/978-1-5225-0861-8.ch005

Goyal, A. (2021). Communicating and Building Destination Brands With New Media. In M. Dinis, L. Bonixe, S. Lamy, & Z. Breda (Eds.), *Impact of New Media in Tourism* (pp. 1-20). IGI Global. https://doi.org/10.4018/978-1-7998-7095-1.ch001

Grefen, P., & Turetken, O. (2017). Advanced Business Process Management in Networked E-Business Scenarios. *International Journal of E-Business Research, 13*(4), 70–104. doi:10.4018/IJEBR.2017100105

Guasca, M., Van Broeck, A. M., & Vanneste, D. (2021). Tourism and the Social Reintegration of Colombian Ex-Combatants. In J. da Silva, Z. Breda, & F. Carbone (Eds.), *Role and Impact of Tourism in Peacebuilding and Conflict Transformation* (pp. 66-86). IGI Global. https://doi.org/10.4018/978-1-7998-5053-3.ch005

Haider, A., & Saetang, S. (2017). Strategic IT Alignment in Service Sector. In S. Rozenes & Y. Cohen (Eds.), *Handbook of Research on Strategic Alliances and Value Co-Creation in the Service Industry* (pp. 231–258). Hershey, PA: IGI Global. doi:10.4018/978-1-5225-2084-9.ch012

Hajilari, A. B., Ghadaksaz, M., & Fasghandis, G. S. (2017). Assessing Organizational Readiness for Implementing ERP System Using Fuzzy Expert System Approach. *International Journal of Enterprise Information Systems, 13*(1), 67–85. doi:10.4018/IJEIS.2017010105

Haldorai, A., Ramu, A., & Murugan, S. (2018). Social Aware Cognitive Radio Networks: Effectiveness of Social Networks as a Strategic Tool for Organizational Business Management. In H. Bansal, G. Shrivastava, G. Nguyen, & L. Stanciu (Eds.), *Social Network Analytics for Contemporary Business Organizations* (pp. 188–202). Hershey, PA: IGI Global. doi:10.4018/978-1-5225-5097-6.ch010

Hall, O. P. Jr. (2017). Social Media Driven Management Education. *International Journal of Knowledge-Based Organizations, 7*(2), 43–59. doi:10.4018/IJKBO.2017040104

Hanifah, H., Halim, H. A., Ahmad, N. H., & Vafaei-Zadeh, A. (2017). Innovation Culture as a Mediator Between Specific Human Capital and Innovation Performance Among Bumiputera SMEs in Malaysia. In N. Ahmad, T. Ramayah, H. Halim, & S. Rahman (Eds.), *Handbook of Research on Small and Medium Enterprises in Developing Countries* (pp. 261–279). Hershey, PA: IGI Global. doi:10.4018/978-1-5225-2165-5.ch012

Hartlieb, S., & Silvius, G. (2017). Handling Uncertainty in Project Management and Business Development: Similarities and Differences. In Y. Raydugin (Ed.), *Handbook of Research on Leveraging Risk and Uncertainties for Effective Project Management* (pp. 337–362). Hershey, PA: IGI Global. doi:10.4018/978-1-5225-1790-0.ch016

Hass, K. B. (2017). Living on the Edge: Managing Project Complexity. In Y. Raydugin (Ed.), *Handbook of Research on Leveraging Risk and Uncertainties for Effective Project Management* (pp. 177–201). Hershey, PA: IGI Global. doi:10.4018/978-1-5225-1790-0.ch009

Hawking, P., & Carmine Sellitto, C. (2017). Developing an Effective Strategy for Organizational Business Intelligence. In M. Tavana (Ed.), *Enterprise Information Systems and the Digitalization of Business Functions* (pp. 222–237). Hershey, PA: IGI Global. doi:10.4018/978-1-5225-2382-6.ch010

Hawking, P., & Sellitto, C. (2017). A Fast-Moving Consumer Goods Company and Business Intelligence Strategy Development. *International Journal of Enterprise Information Systems, 13*(2), 22–33. doi:10.4018/IJEIS.2017040102

Hawking, P., & Sellitto, C. (2017). Business Intelligence Strategy: Two Case Studies. *International Journal of Business Intelligence Research, 8*(2), 17–30. doi:10.4018/IJBIR.2017070102

Hee, W. J., Jalleh, G., Lai, H., & Lin, C. (2017). E-Commerce and IT Projects: Evaluation and Management Issues in Australian and Taiwanese Hospitals. *International Journal of Public Health Management and Ethics, 2*(1), 69–90. doi:10.4018/IJPHME.2017010104

Hernandez, A. A. (2018). Exploring the Factors to Green IT Adoption of SMEs in the Philippines. *Journal of Cases on Information Technology, 20*(2), 49–66. doi:10.4018/JCIT.2018040104

Hollman, A., Bickford, S., & Hollman, T. (2017). Cyber InSecurity: A Post-Mortem Attempt to Assess Cyber Problems from IT and Business Management Perspectives. *Journal of Cases on Information Technology, 19*(3), 42–70. doi:10.4018/JCIT.2017070104

Ibrahim, F., & Zainin, N. M. (2021). Exploring the Technological Impacts: The Case of Museums in Brunei Darussalam. *International Journal of Tourism and Hospitality Management in the Digital Age, 5*(1), 1–18. https://doi.org/10.4018/IJTHMDA.2021010101

Igbinakhase, I. (2017). Responsible and Sustainable Management Practices in Developing and Developed Business Environments. In Z. Fields (Ed.), *Collective Creativity for Responsible and Sustainable Business Practice* (pp. 180–207). Hershey, PA: IGI Global. doi:10.4018/978-1-5225-1823-5.ch010

Iwata, J. J., & Hoskins, R. G. (2017). Managing Indigenous Knowledge in Tanzania: A Business Perspective. In P. Jain & N. Mnjama (Eds.), *Managing Knowledge Resources and Records in Modern Organizations* (pp. 198–214). Hershey, PA: IGI Global. doi:10.4018/978-1-5225-1965-2.ch012

Jain, P. (2017). Ethical and Legal Issues in Knowledge Management Life-Cycle in Business. In P. Jain & N. Mnjama (Eds.), *Managing Knowledge Resources and Records in Modern Organizations* (pp. 82–101). Hershey, PA: IGI Global. doi:10.4018/978-1-5225-1965-2.ch006

James, S., & Hauli, E. (2017). Holistic Management Education at Tanzanian Rural Development Planning Institute. In N. Baporikar (Ed.), *Management Education for Global Leadership* (pp. 112–136). Hershey, PA: IGI Global. doi:10.4018/978-1-5225-1013-0.ch006

Janošková, M., Csikósová, A., & Čulková, K. (2018). Measurement of Company Performance as Part of Its Strategic Management. In R. Leon (Ed.), *Managerial Strategies for Business Sustainability During Turbulent Times* (pp. 309–335). Hershey, PA: IGI Global. doi:10.4018/978-1-5225-2716-9.ch017

Jean-Vasile, A., & Alecu, A. (2017). Theoretical and Practical Approaches in Understanding the Influences of Cost-Productivity-Profit Trinomial in Contemporary Enterprises. In A. Jean Vasile & D. Nicolò (Eds.), *Sustainable Entrepreneurship and Investments in the Green Economy* (pp. 28–62). Hershey, PA: IGI Global. doi:10.4018/978-1-5225-2075-7.ch002

Joia, L. A., & Correia, J. C. (2018). CIO Competencies From the IT Professional Perspective: Insights From Brazil. *Journal of Global Information Management, 26*(2), 74–103. doi:10.4018/JGIM.2018040104

Juma, A., & Mzera, N. (2017). Knowledge Management and Records Management and Competitive Advantage in Business. In P. Jain & N. Mnjama (Eds.), *Managing Knowledge Resources and Records in Modern Organizations* (pp. 15–28). Hershey, PA: IGI Global. doi:10.4018/978-1-5225-1965-2.ch002

K., I., & A, V. (2018). Monitoring and Auditing in the Cloud. In K. Munir (Ed.), *Cloud Computing Technologies for Green Enterprises* (pp. 318-350). Hershey, PA: IGI Global. https://doi.org/ doi:10.4018/978-1-5225-3038-1.ch013

Kabra, G., Ghosh, V., & Ramesh, A. (2018). Enterprise Integrated Business Process Management and Business Intelligence Framework for Business Process Sustainability. In A. Paul, D. Bhattacharyya, & S. Anand (Eds.), *Green Initiatives for Business Sustainability and Value Creation* (pp. 228–238). Hershey, PA: IGI Global. doi:10.4018/978-1-5225-2662-9.ch010

Kaoud, M. (2017). Investigation of Customer Knowledge Management: A Case Study Research. *International Journal of Service Science, Management, Engineering, and Technology*, *8*(2), 12–22. doi:10.4018/IJSSMET.2017040102

Katuu, S. (2018). A Comparative Assessment of Enterprise Content Management Maturity Models. In N. Gwangwava & M. Mutingi (Eds.), *E-Manufacturing and E-Service Strategies in Contemporary Organizations* (pp. 93–118). Hershey, PA: IGI Global. doi:10.4018/978-1-5225-3628-4.ch005

Khan, M. Y., & Abir, T. (2022). The Role of Social Media Marketing in the Tourism and Hospitality Industry: A Conceptual Study on Bangladesh. In C. Ramos, S. Quinteiro, & A. Gonçalves (Eds.), *ICT as Innovator Between Tourism and Culture* (pp. 213–229). IGI Global. https://doi.org/10.4018/978-1-7998-8165-0.ch013

Kinnunen, S., Ylä-Kujala, A., Marttonen-Arola, S., Kärri, T., & Baglee, D. (2018). Internet of Things in Asset Management: Insights from Industrial Professionals and Academia. *International Journal of Service Science, Management, Engineering, and Technology*, *9*(2), 104–119. doi:10.4018/IJSSMET.2018040105

Klein, A. Z., Sabino de Freitas, A., Machado, L., Freitas, J. C. Jr, Graziola, P. G. Jr, & Schlemmer, E. (2017). Virtual Worlds Applications for Management Education. In L. Tomei (Ed.), *Exploring the New Era of Technology-Infused Education* (pp. 279–299). Hershey, PA: IGI Global. doi:10.4018/978-1-5225-1709-2.ch017

Kővári, E., Saleh, M., & Steinbachné Hajmásy, G. (2022). The Impact of Corporate Digital Responsibility (CDR) on Internal Stakeholders' Satisfaction in Hungarian Upscale Hotels. In M. Valeri (Ed.), *New Governance and Management in Touristic Destinations* (pp. 35–51). IGI Global. https://doi.org/10.4018/978-1-6684-3889-3.ch003

Kożuch, B., & Jabłoński, A. (2017). Adopting the Concept of Business Models in Public Management. In M. Lewandowski & B. Kożuch (Eds.), *Public Sector Entrepreneurship and the Integration of Innovative Business Models* (pp. 10–46). Hershey, PA: IGI Global. doi:10.4018/978-1-5225-2215-7.ch002

Kumar, J., Adhikary, A., & Jha, A. (2017). Small Active Investors' Perceptions and Preferences Towards Tax Saving Mutual Fund Schemes in Eastern India: An Empirical Note. *International Journal of Asian Business and Information Management*, *8*(2), 35–45. doi:10.4018/IJABIM.2017040103

Latusi, S., & Fissore, M. (2021). Pilgrimage Routes to Happiness: Comparing the Camino de Santiago and Via Francigena. In A. Perinotto, V. Mayer, & J. Soares (Eds.), *Rebuilding and Restructuring the Tourism Industry: Infusion of Happiness and Quality of Life* (pp. 157–182). IGI Global. https://doi.org/10.4018/978-1-7998-7239-9.ch008

Lavassani, K. M., & Movahedi, B. (2017). Applications Driven Information Systems: Beyond Networks toward Business Ecosystems. *International Journal of Innovation in the Digital Economy*, *8*(1), 61–75. doi:10.4018/IJIDE.2017010104

Lazzareschi, V. H., & Brito, M. S. (2017). Strategic Information Management: Proposal of Business Project Model. In G. Jamil, A. Soares, & C. Pessoa (Eds.), *Handbook of Research on Information Management for Effective Logistics and Supply Chains* (pp. 59–88). Hershey, PA: IGI Global. doi:10.4018/978-1-5225-0973-8.ch004

Lechuga Sancho, M. P., & Martín Navarro, A. (2022). Evolution of the Literature on Social Responsibility in the Tourism Sector: A Systematic Literature Review. In G. Fernandes (Ed.), *Challenges and New Opportunities for Tourism in Inland Territories: Ecocultural Resources and Sustainable Initiatives* (pp. 169–186). IGI Global. https://doi.org/10.4018/978-1-7998-7339-6.ch010

Lederer, M., Kurz, M., & Lazarov, P. (2017). Usage and Suitability of Methods for Strategic Business Process Initiatives: A Multi Case Study Research. *International Journal of Productivity Management and Assessment Technologies*, *5*(1), 40–51. doi:10.4018/IJPMAT.2017010103

Lee, I. (2017). A Social Enterprise Business Model and a Case Study of Pacific Community Ventures (PCV). In V. Potocan, M. Üngan, & Z. Nedelko (Eds.), *Handbook of Research on Managerial Solutions in Non-Profit Organizations* (pp. 182–204). Hershey, PA: IGI Global. doi:10.4018/978-1-5225-0731-4.ch009

Leon, L. A., Seal, K. C., Przasnyski, Z. H., & Wiedenman, I. (2017). Skills and Competencies Required for Jobs in Business Analytics: A Content Analysis of Job Advertisements Using Text Mining. *International Journal of Business Intelligence Research*, *8*(1), 1–25. doi:10.4018/IJBIR.2017010101

Levy, C. L., & Elias, N. I. (2017). SOHO Users' Perceptions of Reliability and Continuity of Cloud-Based Services. In M. Moore (Ed.), *Cybersecurity Breaches and Issues Surrounding Online Threat Protection* (pp. 248–287). Hershey, PA: IGI Global. doi:10.4018/978-1-5225-1941-6.ch011

Levy, M. (2018). Change Management Serving Knowledge Management and Organizational Development: Reflections and Review. In N. Baporikar (Ed.), *Global Practices in Knowledge Management for Societal and Organizational Development* (pp. 256–270). Hershey, PA: IGI Global. doi:10.4018/978-1-5225-3009-1.ch012

Lewandowski, M. (2017). Public Organizations and Business Model Innovation: The Role of Public Service Design. In M. Lewandowski & B. Kożuch (Eds.), *Public Sector Entrepreneurship and the Integration of Innovative Business Models* (pp. 47–72). Hershey, PA: IGI Global. doi:10.4018/978-1-5225-2215-7.ch003

Lhannaoui, H., Kabbaj, M. I., & Bakkoury, Z. (2017). A Survey of Risk-Aware Business Process Modelling. *International Journal of Risk and Contingency Management, 6*(3), 14–26. doi:10.4018/IJRCM.2017070102

Li, J., Sun, W., Jiang, W., Yang, H., & Zhang, L. (2017). How the Nature of Exogenous Shocks and Crises Impact Company Performance?: The Effects of Industry Characteristics. *International Journal of Risk and Contingency Management, 6*(4), 40–55. doi:10.4018/IJRCM.2017100103

Lopez-Fernandez, M., Perez-Perez, M., Serrano-Bedia, A., & Cobo-Gonzalez, A. (2021). Small and Medium Tourism Enterprise Survival in Times of Crisis: "El Capricho de Gaudí. In D. Toubes & N. Araújo-Vila (Eds.), *Risk, Crisis, and Disaster Management in Small and Medium-Sized Tourism Enterprises* (pp. 103–129). IGI Global. doi:10.4018/978-1-7998-6996-2.ch005

Mahajan, A., Maidullah, S., & Hossain, M. R. (2022). Experience Toward Smart Tour Guide Apps in Travelling: An Analysis of Users' Reviews on Audio Odigos and Trip My Way. In R. Augusto Costa, F. Brandão, Z. Breda, & C. Costa (Eds.), *Planning and Managing the Experience Economy in Tourism* (pp. 255-273). IGI Global. https://doi.org/10.4018/978-1-7998-8775-1.ch014

Malega, P. (2017). Small and Medium Enterprises in the Slovak Republic: Status and Competitiveness of SMEs in the Global Markets and Possibilities of Optimization. In M. Vemić (Ed.), *Optimal Management Strategies in Small and Medium Enterprises* (pp. 102–124). Hershey, PA: IGI Global. doi:10.4018/978-1-5225-1949-2.ch006

Malewska, K. M. (2017). Intuition in Decision-Making on the Example of a Non-Profit Organization. In V. Potocan, M. Ünğan, & Z. Nedelko (Eds.), *Handbook of Research on Managerial Solutions in Non-Profit Organizations* (pp. 378–399). Hershey, PA: IGI Global. doi:10.4018/978-1-5225-0731-4.ch018

Maroofi, F. (2017). Entrepreneurial Orientation and Organizational Learning Ability Analysis for Innovation and Firm Performance. In N. Baporikar (Ed.), *Innovation and Shifting Perspectives in Management Education* (pp. 144–165). Hershey, PA: IGI Global. doi:10.4018/978-1-5225-1019-2.ch007

Marques, M., Moleiro, D., Brito, T. M., & Marques, T. (2021). Customer Relationship Management as an Important Relationship Marketing Tool: The Case of the Hospitality Industry in Estoril Coast. In M. Dinis, L. Bonixe, S. Lamy, & Z. Breda (Eds.), Impact of New Media in Tourism (pp. 39-56). IGI Global. https://doi.org/doi:10.4018/978-1-7998-7095-1.ch003

Martins, P. V., & Zacarias, M. (2017). A Web-based Tool for Business Process Improvement. *International Journal of Web Portals*, *9*(2), 68–84. doi:10.4018/IJWP.2017070104

Matthies, B., & Coners, A. (2017). Exploring the Conceptual Nature of e-Business Projects. *Journal of Electronic Commerce in Organizations*, *15*(3), 33–63. doi:10.4018/JECO.2017070103

Mayer, V. F., Fraga, C. C., & Silva, L. C. (2021). Contributions of Neurosciences to Studies of Well-Being in Tourism. In A. Perinotto, V. Mayer, & J. Soares (Eds.), *Rebuilding and Restructuring the Tourism Industry: Infusion of Happiness and Quality of Life* (pp. 108–128). IGI Global. https://doi.org/10.4018/978-1-7998-7239-9.ch006

McKee, J. (2018). Architecture as a Tool to Solve Business Planning Problems. In M. Khosrow-Pour, D.B.A. (Ed.), Encyclopedia of Information Science and Technology, Fourth Edition (pp. 573-586). Hershey, PA: IGI Global. doi:10.4018/978-1-5225-2255-3.ch050

McMurray, A. J., Cross, J., & Caponecchia, C. (2018). The Risk Management Profession in Australia: Business Continuity Plan Practices. In N. Bajgoric (Ed.), *Always-On Enterprise Information Systems for Modern Organizations* (pp. 112–129). Hershey, PA: IGI Global. doi:10.4018/978-1-5225-3704-5.ch006

Meddah, I. H., & Belkadi, K. (2018). Mining Patterns Using Business Process Management. In R. Hamou (Ed.), *Handbook of Research on Biomimicry in Information Retrieval and Knowledge Management* (pp. 78–89). Hershey, PA: IGI Global. doi:10.4018/978-1-5225-3004-6.ch005

Melian, A. G., & Camprubí, R. (2021). The Accessibility of Museum Websites: The Case of Barcelona. In C. Eusébio, L. Teixeira, & M. Carneiro (Eds.), *ICT Tools and Applications for Accessible Tourism* (pp. 234–255). IGI Global. https://doi.org/10.4018/978-1-7998-6428-8.ch011

Mendes, L. (2017). TQM and Knowledge Management: An Integrated Approach Towards Tacit Knowledge Management. In D. Jaziri-Bouagina & G. Jamil (Eds.), *Handbook of Research on Tacit Knowledge Management for Organizational Success* (pp. 236–263). Hershey, PA: IGI Global. doi:10.4018/978-1-5225-2394-9.ch009

Menezes, V. D., & Cavagnaro, E. (2021). Communicating Sustainable Initiatives in the Hotel Industry: The Case of the Hotel Jakarta Amsterdam. In F. Brandão, Z. Breda, R. Costa, & C. Costa (Eds.), *Handbook of Research on the Role of Tourism in Achieving Sustainable Development Goals* (pp. 224-234). IGI Global. https://doi.org/10.4018/978-1-7998-5691-7.ch013

Menezes, V. D., & Cavagnaro, E. (2021). Communicating Sustainable Initiatives in the Hotel Industry: The Case of the Hotel Jakarta Amsterdam. In F. Brandão, Z. Breda, R. Costa, & C. Costa (Eds.), *Handbook of Research on the Role of Tourism in Achieving Sustainable Development Goals* (pp. 224-234). IGI Global. https://doi.org/10.4018/978-1-7998-5691-7.ch013

Mitas, O., Bastiaansen, M., & Boode, W. (2022). If You're Happy, I'm Happy: Emotion Contagion at a Tourist Information Center. In R. Augusto Costa, F. Brandão, Z. Breda, & C. Costa (Eds.), *Planning and Managing the Experience Economy in Tourism* (pp. 122-140). IGI Global. https://doi.org/10.4018/978-1-7998-8775-1.ch007

Mnjama, N. M. (2017). Preservation of Recorded Information in Public and Private Sector Organizations. In P. Jain & N. Mnjama (Eds.), *Managing Knowledge Resources and Records in Modern Organizations* (pp. 149–167). Hershey, PA: IGI Global. doi:10.4018/978-1-5225-1965-2.ch009

Mokoqama, M., & Fields, Z. (2017). Principles of Responsible Management Education (PRME): Call for Responsible Management Education. In Z. Fields (Ed.), *Collective Creativity for Responsible and Sustainable Business Practice* (pp. 229–241). Hershey, PA: IGI Global. doi:10.4018/978-1-5225-1823-5.ch012

Monteiro, A., Lopes, S., & Carbone, F. (2021). Academic Mobility: Bridging Tourism and Peace Education. In J. da Silva, Z. Breda, & F. Carbone (Eds.), *Role and Impact of Tourism in Peacebuilding and Conflict Transformation* (pp. 275-301). IGI Global. https://doi.org/10.4018/978-1-7998-5053-3.ch016

Muniapan, B. (2017). Philosophy and Management: The Relevance of Vedanta in Management. In P. Ordóñez de Pablos (Ed.), *Managerial Strategies and Solutions for Business Success in Asia* (pp. 124–139). Hershey, PA: IGI Global. doi:10.4018/978-1-5225-1886-0.ch007

Murad, S. E., & Dowaji, S. (2017). Using Value-Based Approach for Managing Cloud-Based Services. In A. Turuk, B. Sahoo, & S. Addya (Eds.), *Resource Management and Efficiency in Cloud Computing Environments* (pp. 33–60). Hershey, PA: IGI Global. doi:10.4018/978-1-5225-1721-4.ch002

Mutahar, A. M., Daud, N. M., Thurasamy, R., Isaac, O., & Abdulsalam, R. (2018). The Mediating of Perceived Usefulness and Perceived Ease of Use: The Case of Mobile Banking in Yemen. *International Journal of Technology Diffusion*, *9*(2), 21–40. doi:10.4018/IJTD.2018040102

Naidoo, V. (2017). E-Learning and Management Education at African Universities. In N. Baporikar (Ed.), *Management Education for Global Leadership* (pp. 181–201). Hershey, PA: IGI Global. doi:10.4018/978-1-5225-1013-0.ch009

Naidoo, V., & Igbinakhase, I. (2018). Opportunities and Challenges of Knowledge Retention in SMEs. In N. Baporikar (Ed.), *Knowledge Integration Strategies for Entrepreneurship and Sustainability* (pp. 70–94). Hershey, PA: IGI Global. doi:10.4018/978-1-5225-5115-7.ch004

Naumov, N., & Costandachi, G. (2021). Creativity and Entrepreneurship: Gastronomic Tourism in Mexico. In J. Soares (Ed.), *Innovation and Entrepreneurial Opportunities in Community Tourism* (pp. 90–108). IGI Global. https://doi.org/10.4018/978-1-7998-4855-4.ch006

Nayak, S., & Prabhu, N. (2017). Paradigm Shift in Management Education: Need for a Cross Functional Perspective. In N. Baporikar (Ed.), *Management Education for Global Leadership* (pp. 241–255). Hershey, PA: IGI Global. doi:10.4018/978-1-5225-1013-0.ch012

Nedelko, Z., & Potocan, V. (2017). Management Solutions in Non-Profit Organizations: Case of Slovenia. In V. Potocan, M. Üngan, & Z. Nedelko (Eds.), *Handbook of Research on Managerial Solutions in Non-Profit Organizations* (pp. 1–22). Hershey, PA: IGI Global. doi:10.4018/978-1-5225-0731-4.ch001

Nedelko, Z., & Potocan, V. (2017). Priority of Management Tools Utilization among Managers: International Comparison. In V. Wang (Ed.), *Encyclopedia of Strategic Leadership and Management* (pp. 1083–1094). Hershey, PA: IGI Global. doi:10.4018/978-1-5225-1049-9.ch075

Nedelko, Z., Raudeliūnienė, J., & Črešnar, R. (2018). Knowledge Dynamics in Supply Chain Management. In N. Baporikar (Ed.), *Knowledge Integration Strategies for Entrepreneurship and Sustainability* (pp. 150–166). Hershey, PA: IGI Global. doi:10.4018/978-1-5225-5115-7.ch008

Nguyen, H. T., & Hipsher, S. A. (2018). Innovation and Creativity Used by Private Sector Firms in a Resources-Constrained Environment. In S. Hipsher (Ed.), *Examining the Private Sector's Role in Wealth Creation and Poverty Reduction* (pp. 219–238). Hershey, PA: IGI Global. doi:10.4018/978-1-5225-3117-3.ch010

Obicci, P. A. (2017). Risk Sharing in a Partnership. In *Risk Management Strategies in Public-Private Partnerships* (pp. 115–152). Hershey, PA: IGI Global. doi:10.4018/978-1-5225-2503-5.ch004

Obidallah, W. J., & Raahemi, B. (2017). Managing Changes in Service Oriented Virtual Organizations: A Structural and Procedural Framework to Facilitate the Process of Change. *Journal of Electronic Commerce in Organizations, 15*(1), 59–83. doi:10.4018/JECO.2017010104

Ojo, O. (2017). Impact of Innovation on the Entrepreneurial Success in Selected Business Enterprises in South-West Nigeria. *International Journal of Innovation in the Digital Economy, 8*(2), 29–38. doi:10.4018/IJIDE.2017040103

Okdinawati, L., Simatupang, T. M., & Sunitiyoso, Y. (2017). Multi-Agent Reinforcement Learning for Value Co-Creation of Collaborative Transportation Management (CTM). *International Journal of Information Systems and Supply Chain Management, 10*(3), 84–95. doi:10.4018/IJISSCM.2017070105

Olivera, V. A., & Carrillo, I. M. (2021). Organizational Culture: A Key Element for the Development of Mexican Micro and Small Tourist Companies. In J. Soares (Ed.), *Innovation and Entrepreneurial Opportunities in Community Tourism* (pp. 227–242). IGI Global. doi:10.4018/978-1-7998-4855-4.ch013

Ossorio, M. (2022). Corporate Museum Experiences in Enogastronomic Tourism. In R. Augusto Costa, F. Brandão, Z. Breda, & C. Costa (Eds.), Planning and Managing the Experience Economy in Tourism (pp. 107-121). IGI Global. https://doi.org/doi:10.4018/978-1-7998-8775-1.ch006

Ossorio, M. (2022). Enogastronomic Tourism in Times of Pandemic. In G. Fernandes (Ed.), *Challenges and New Opportunities for Tourism in Inland Territories: Ecocultural Resources and Sustainable Initiatives* (pp. 241–255). IGI Global. https://doi.org/10.4018/978-1-7998-7339-6.ch014

Özekici, Y. K. (2022). ICT as an Acculturative Agent and Its Role in the Tourism Context: Introduction, Acculturation Theory, Progress of the Acculturation Theory in Extant Literature. In C. Ramos, S. Quinteiro, & A. Gonçalves (Eds.), *ICT as Innovator Between Tourism and Culture* (pp. 42–66). IGI Global. https://doi.org/10.4018/978-1-7998-8165-0.ch004

Pal, K. (2018). Building High Quality Big Data-Based Applications in Supply Chains. In A. Kumar & S. Saurav (Eds.), *Supply Chain Management Strategies and Risk Assessment in Retail Environments* (pp. 1–24). Hershey, PA: IGI Global. doi:10.4018/978-1-5225-3056-5.ch001

Palos-Sanchez, P. R., & Correia, M. B. (2018). Perspectives of the Adoption of Cloud Computing in the Tourism Sector. In J. Rodrigues, C. Ramos, P. Cardoso, & C. Henriques (Eds.), *Handbook of Research on Technological Developments for Cultural Heritage and eTourism Applications* (pp. 377–400). Hershey, PA: IGI Global. doi:10.4018/978-1-5225-2927-9.ch018

Papadopoulou, G. (2021). Promoting Gender Equality and Women Empowerment in the Tourism Sector. In F. Brandão, Z. Breda, R. Costa, & C. Costa (Eds.), Handbook of Research on the Role of Tourism in Achieving Sustainable Development Goals (pp. 152-174). IGI Global. https://doi.org/ doi:10.4018/978-1-7998-5691-7.ch009

Papp-Váry, Á. F., & Tóth, T. Z. (2022). Analysis of Budapest as a Film Tourism Destination. In R. Baleiro & R. Pereira (Eds.), *Global Perspectives on Literary Tourism and Film-Induced Tourism* (pp. 257-279). IGI Global. https://doi.org/10.4018/978-1-7998-8262-6.ch014

Patiño, B. E. (2017). New Generation Management by Convergence and Individual Identity: A Systemic and Human-Oriented Approach. In N. Baporikar (Ed.), *Innovation and Shifting Perspectives in Management Education* (pp. 119–143). Hershey, PA: IGI Global. doi:10.4018/978-1-5225-1019-2.ch006

Patro, C. S. (2021). Digital Tourism: Influence of E-Marketing Technology. In M. Dinis, L. Bonixe, S. Lamy, & Z. Breda (Eds.), *Impact of New Media in Tourism* (pp. 234-254). IGI Global. https://doi.org/10.4018/978-1-7998-7095-1.ch014

Pawliczek, A., & Rössler, M. (2017). Knowledge of Management Tools and Systems in SMEs: Knowledge Transfer in Management. In A. Bencsik (Ed.), *Knowledge Management Initiatives and Strategies in Small and Medium Enterprises* (pp. 180–203). Hershey, PA: IGI Global. doi:10.4018/978-1-5225-1642-2.ch009

Pejic-Bach, M., Omazic, M. A., Aleksic, A., & Zoroja, J. (2018). Knowledge-Based Decision Making: A Multi-Case Analysis. In R. Leon (Ed.), *Managerial Strategies for Business Sustainability During Turbulent Times* (pp. 160–184). Hershey, PA: IGI Global. doi:10.4018/978-1-5225-2716-9.ch009

Perano, M., Hysa, X., & Calabrese, M. (2018). Strategic Planning, Cultural Context, and Business Continuity Management: Business Cases in the City of Shkoder. In A. Presenza & L. Sheehan (Eds.), *Geopolitics and Strategic Management in the Global Economy* (pp. 57–77). Hershey, PA: IGI Global. doi:10.4018/978-1-5225-2673-5.ch004

Pereira, R., Mira da Silva, M., & Lapão, L. V. (2017). IT Governance Maturity Patterns in Portuguese Healthcare. In S. De Haes & W. Van Grembergen (Eds.), *Strategic IT Governance and Alignment in Business Settings* (pp. 24–52). Hershey, PA: IGI Global. doi:10.4018/978-1-5225-0861-8.ch002

Pérez-Uribe, R. I., Torres, D. A., Jurado, S. P., & Prada, D. M. (2018). Cloud Tools for the Development of Project Management in SMEs. In R. Perez-Uribe, C. Salcedo-Perez, & D. Ocampo-Guzman (Eds.), *Handbook of Research on Intrapreneurship and Organizational Sustainability in SMEs* (pp. 95–120). Hershey, PA: IGI Global. doi:10.4018/978-1-5225-3543-0.ch005

Petrisor, I., & Cozmiuc, D. (2017). Global Supply Chain Management Organization at Siemens in the Advent of Industry 4.0. In L. Saglietto & C. Cezanne (Eds.), *Global Intermediation and Logistics Service Providers* (pp. 123–142). Hershey, PA: IGI Global. doi:10.4018/978-1-5225-2133-4.ch007

Pierce, J. M., Velliaris, D. M., & Edwards, J. (2017). A Living Case Study: A Journey Not a Destination. In N. Silton (Ed.), *Exploring the Benefits of Creativity in Education, Media, and the Arts* (pp. 158–178). Hershey, PA: IGI Global. doi:10.4018/978-1-5225-0504-4.ch008

Pipia, S., & Pipia, S. (2021). Challenges of Religious Tourism in the Conflict Region: An Example of Jerusalem. In E. Alaverdov & M. Bari (Eds.), *Global Development of Religious Tourism* (pp. 135-148). IGI Global. https://doi.org/10.4018/978-1-7998-5792-1.ch009

Poulaki, P., Kritikos, A., Vasilakis, N., & Valeri, M. (2022). The Contribution of Female Creativity to the Development of Gastronomic Tourism in Greece: The Case of the Island of Naxos in the South Aegean Region. In M. Valeri (Ed.), *New Governance and Management in Touristic Destinations* (pp. 246–258). IGI Global. https://doi.org/10.4018/978-1-6684-3889-3.ch015

Radosavljevic, M., & Andjelkovic, A. (2017). Multi-Criteria Decision Making Approach for Choosing Business Process for the Improvement: Upgrading of the Six Sigma Methodology. In J. Stanković, P. Delias, S. Marinković, & S. Rochhia (Eds.), *Tools and Techniques for Economic Decision Analysis* (pp. 225–247). Hershey, PA: IGI Global. doi:10.4018/978-1-5225-0959-2.ch011

Radovic, V. M. (2017). Corporate Sustainability and Responsibility and Disaster Risk Reduction: A Serbian Overview. In M. Camilleri (Ed.), *CSR 2.0 and the New Era of Corporate Citizenship* (pp. 147–164). Hershey, PA: IGI Global. doi:10.4018/978-1-5225-1842-6.ch008

Raghunath, K. M., Devi, S. L., & Patro, C. S. (2018). Impact of Risk Assessment Models on Risk Factors: A Holistic Outlook. In K. Strang, M. Korstanje, & N. Vajjhala (Eds.), *Research, Practices, and Innovations in Global Risk and Contingency Management* (pp. 134–153). Hershey, PA: IGI Global. doi:10.4018/978-1-5225-4754-9.ch008

Raman, A., & Goyal, D. P. (2017). Extending IMPLEMENT Framework for Enterprise Information Systems Implementation to Information System Innovation. In M. Tavana (Ed.), *Enterprise Information Systems and the Digitalization of Business Functions* (pp. 137–177). Hershey, PA: IGI Global. doi:10.4018/978-1-5225-2382-6.ch007

Rao, Y., & Zhang, Y. (2017). The Construction and Development of Academic Library Digital Special Subject Databases. In L. Ruan, Q. Zhu, & Y. Ye (Eds.), *Academic Library Development and Administration in China* (pp. 163–183). Hershey, PA: IGI Global. doi:10.4018/978-1-5225-0550-1.ch010

Ravasan, A. Z., Mohammadi, M. M., & Hamidi, H. (2018). An Investigation Into the Critical Success Factors of Implementing Information Technology Service Management Frameworks. In K. Jakobs (Ed.), *Corporate and Global Standardization Initiatives in Contemporary Society* (pp. 200–218). Hershey, PA: IGI Global. doi:10.4018/978-1-5225-5320-5.ch009

Rezaie, S., Mirabedini, S. J., & Abtahi, A. (2018). Designing a Model for Implementation of Business Intelligence in the Banking Industry. *International Journal of Enterprise Information Systems*, *14*(1), 77–103. doi:10.4018/IJEIS.2018010105

Richards, V., Matthews, N., Williams, O. J., & Khan, Z. (2021). The Challenges of Accessible Tourism Information Systems for Tourists With Vision Impairment: Sensory Communications Beyond the Screen. In C. Eusébio, L. Teixeira, & M. Carneiro (Eds.), *ICT Tools and Applications for Accessible Tourism* (pp. 26–54). IGI Global. https://doi.org/10.4018/978-1-7998-6428-8.ch002

Rodrigues de Souza Neto, V., & Marques, O. (2021). Rural Tourism Fostering Welfare Through Sustainable Development: A Conceptual Approach. In A. Perinotto, V. Mayer, & J. Soares (Eds.), *Rebuilding and Restructuring the Tourism Industry: Infusion of Happiness and Quality of Life* (pp. 38–57). IGI Global. https://doi.org/10.4018/978-1-7998-7239-9.ch003

Romano, L., Grimaldi, R., & Colasuonno, F. S. (2017). Demand Management as a Success Factor in Project Portfolio Management. In L. Romano (Ed.), *Project Portfolio Management Strategies for Effective Organizational Operations* (pp. 202–219). Hershey, PA: IGI Global. doi:10.4018/978-1-5225-2151-8.ch008

Rubio-Escuderos, L., & García-Andreu, H. (2021). Competitiveness Factors of Accessible Tourism E-Travel Agencies. In C. Eusébio, L. Teixeira, & M. Carneiro (Eds.), *ICT Tools and Applications for Accessible Tourism* (pp. 196–217). IGI Global. https://doi.org/10.4018/978-1-7998-6428-8.ch009

Rucci, A. C., Porto, N., Darcy, S., & Becka, L. (2021). Smart and Accessible Cities?: Not Always – The Case for Accessible Tourism Initiatives in Buenos Aries and Sydney. In C. Eusébio, L. Teixeira, & M. Carneiro (Eds.), *ICT Tools and Applications for Accessible Tourism* (pp. 115–145). IGI Global. https://doi.org/10.4018/978-1-7998-6428-8.ch006

Ruhi, U. (2018). Towards an Interdisciplinary Socio-Technical Definition of Virtual Communities. In M. Khosrow-Pour, D.B.A. (Ed.), Encyclopedia of Information Science and Technology, Fourth Edition (pp. 4278-4295). Hershey, PA: IGI Global. doi:10.4018/978-1-5225-2255-3.ch371

Ryan, L., Catena, M., Ros, P., & Stephens, S. (2021). Designing Entrepreneurial Ecosystems to Support Resource Management in the Tourism Industry. In V. Costa, A. Moura, & M. Mira (Eds.), *Handbook of Research on Human Capital and People Management in the Tourism Industry* (pp. 265–281). IGI Global. https://doi.org/10.4018/978-1-7998-4318-4.ch013

Sabuncu, I. (2021). Understanding Tourist Perceptions and Expectations During Pandemic Through Social Media Big Data. In M. Demir, A. Dalgıç, & F. Ergen (Eds.), *Handbook of Research on the Impacts and Implications of COVID-19 on the Tourism Industry* (pp. 330–350). IGI Global. https://doi.org/10.4018/978-1-7998-8231-2.ch016

Safari, M. R., & Jiang, Q. (2018). The Theory and Practice of IT Governance Maturity and Strategies Alignment: Evidence From Banking Industry. *Journal of Global Information Management, 26*(2), 127–146. doi:10.4018/JGIM.2018040106

Sahoo, J., Pati, B., & Mohanty, B. (2017). Knowledge Management as an Academic Discipline: An Assessment. In B. Gunjal (Ed.), *Managing Knowledge and Scholarly Assets in Academic Libraries* (pp. 99–126). Hershey, PA: IGI Global. doi:10.4018/978-1-5225-1741-2.ch005

Saini, D. (2017). Relevance of Teaching Values and Ethics in Management Education. In N. Baporikar (Ed.), *Management Education for Global Leadership* (pp. 90–111). Hershey, PA: IGI Global. doi:10.4018/978-1-5225-1013-0.ch005

Sambhanthan, A. (2017). Assessing and Benchmarking Sustainability in Organisations: An Integrated Conceptual Model. *International Journal of Systems and Service-Oriented Engineering*, *7*(4), 22–43. doi:10.4018/IJSSOE.2017100102

Sambhanthan, A., & Potdar, V. (2017). A Study of the Parameters Impacting Sustainability in Information Technology Organizations. *International Journal of Knowledge-Based Organizations*, *7*(3), 27–39. doi:10.4018/IJKBO.2017070103

Sánchez-Fernández, M. D., & Manríquez, M. R. (2018). The Entrepreneurial Spirit Based on Social Values: The Digital Generation. In P. Isaias & L. Carvalho (Eds.), *User Innovation and the Entrepreneurship Phenomenon in the Digital Economy* (pp. 173–193). Hershey, PA: IGI Global. doi:10.4018/978-1-5225-2826-5.ch009

Sanchez-Ruiz, L., & Blanco, B. (2017). Process Management for SMEs: Barriers, Enablers, and Benefits. In M. Vemić (Ed.), *Optimal Management Strategies in Small and Medium Enterprises* (pp. 293–319). Hershey, PA: IGI Global. doi:10.4018/978-1-5225-1949-2.ch014

Sanz, L. F., Gómez-Pérez, J., & Castillo-Martinez, A. (2018). Analysis of the European ICT Competence Frameworks. In V. Ahuja & S. Rathore (Eds.), *Multidisciplinary Perspectives on Human Capital and Information Technology Professionals* (pp. 225–245). Hershey, PA: IGI Global. doi:10.4018/978-1-5225-5297-0.ch012

Sarvepalli, A., & Godin, J. (2017). Business Process Management in the Classroom. *Journal of Cases on Information Technology*, *19*(2), 17–28. doi:10.4018/JCIT.2017040102

Saxena, G. G., & Saxena, A. (2021). Host Community Role in Medical Tourism Development. In M. Singh & S. Kumaran (Eds.), *Growth of the Medical Tourism Industry and Its Impact on Society: Emerging Research and Opportunities* (pp. 105–127). IGI Global. https://doi.org/10.4018/978-1-7998-3427-4.ch006

Saygili, E. E., Ozturkoglu, Y., & Kocakulah, M. C. (2017). End Users' Perceptions of Critical Success Factors in ERP Applications. *International Journal of Enterprise Information Systems*, *13*(4), 58–75. doi:10.4018/IJEIS.2017100104

Saygili, E. E., & Saygili, A. T. (2017). Contemporary Issues in Enterprise Information Systems: A Critical Review of CSFs in ERP Implementations. In M. Tavana (Ed.), *Enterprise Information Systems and the Digitalization of Business Functions* (pp. 120–136). Hershey, PA: IGI Global. doi:10.4018/978-1-5225-2382-6.ch006

Schwaiger, K. M., & Zehrer, A. (2021). The COVID-19 Pandemic and Organizational Resilience in Hospitality Family Firms: A Qualitative Approach. In A. Zehrer, G. Glowka, K. Schwaiger, & V. Ranacher-Lackner (Eds.), *Resiliency Models and Addressing Future Risks for Family Firms in the Tourism Industry* (pp. 32–49). IGI Global. https://doi.org/10.4018/978-1-7998-7352-5.ch002

Scott, N., & Campos, A. C. (2022). Cognitive Science of Tourism Experiences. In R. Augusto Costa, F. Brandão, Z. Breda, & C. Costa (Eds.), Planning and Managing the Experience Economy in Tourism (pp. 1-21). IGI Global. https://doi.org/ doi:10.4018/978-1-7998-8775-1.ch001

Seidenstricker, S., & Antonino, A. (2018). Business Model Innovation-Oriented Technology Management for Emergent Technologies. In M. Khosrow-Pour, D.B.A. (Ed.), Encyclopedia of Information Science and Technology, Fourth Edition (pp. 4560-4569). Hershey, PA: IGI Global. doi:10.4018/978-1-5225-2255-3.ch396

Selvi, M. S. (2021). Changes in Tourism Sales and Marketing Post COVID-19. In M. Demir, A. Dalgıç, & F. Ergen (Eds.), *Handbook of Research on the Impacts and Implications of COVID-19 on the Tourism Industry* (pp. 437–460). IGI Global. doi:10.4018/978-1-7998-8231-2.ch021

Senaratne, S., & Gunarathne, A. D. (2017). Excellence Perspective for Management Education from a Global Accountants' Hub in Asia. In N. Baporikar (Ed.), *Management Education for Global Leadership* (pp. 158–180). Hershey, PA: IGI Global. doi:10.4018/978-1-5225-1013-0.ch008

Sensuse, D. I., & Cahyaningsih, E. (2018). Knowledge Management Models: A Summative Review. *International Journal of Information Systems in the Service Sector, 10*(1), 71–100. doi:10.4018/IJISSS.2018010105

Seth, M., Goyal, D., & Kiran, R. (2017). Diminution of Impediments in Implementation of Supply Chain Management Information System for Enhancing its Effectiveness in Indian Automobile Industry. *Journal of Global Information Management, 25*(3), 1–20. doi:10.4018/JGIM.2017070101

Seyal, A. H., & Rahman, M. N. (2017). Investigating Impact of Inter-Organizational Factors in Measuring ERP Systems Success: Bruneian Perspectives. In M. Tavana (Ed.), *Enterprise Information Systems and the Digitalization of Business Functions* (pp. 178–204). Hershey, PA: IGI Global. doi:10.4018/978-1-5225-2382-6.ch008

Shaqrah, A. A. (2018). Analyzing Business Intelligence Systems Based on 7s Model of McKinsey. *International Journal of Business Intelligence Research, 9*(1), 53–63. doi:10.4018/IJBIR.2018010104

Sharma, A. J. (2017). Enhancing Sustainability through Experiential Learning in Management Education. In N. Baporikar (Ed.), *Management Education for Global Leadership* (pp. 256–274). Hershey, PA: IGI Global. doi:10.4018/978-1-5225-1013-0.ch013

Shetty, K. P. (2017). Responsible Global Leadership: Ethical Challenges in Management Education. In N. Baporikar (Ed.), *Innovation and Shifting Perspectives in Management Education* (pp. 194–223). Hershey, PA: IGI Global. doi:10.4018/978-1-5225-1019-2.ch009

Sinthupundaja, J., & Kohda, Y. (2017). Effects of Corporate Social Responsibility and Creating Shared Value on Sustainability. *International Journal of Sustainable Entrepreneurship and Corporate Social Responsibility*, *2*(1), 27–38. doi:10.4018/IJSECSR.2017010103

Škarica, I., & Hrgović, A. V. (2018). Implementation of Total Quality Management Principles in Public Health Institutes in the Republic of Croatia. *International Journal of Productivity Management and Assessment Technologies*, *6*(1), 1–16. doi:10.4018/IJPMAT.2018010101

Skokic, V. (2021). How Small Hotel Owners Practice Resilience: Longitudinal Study Among Small Family Hotels in Croatia. In A. Zehrer, G. Glowka, K. Schwaiger, & V. Ranacher-Lackner (Eds.), *Resiliency Models and Addressing Future Risks for Family Firms in the Tourism Industry* (pp. 50–73). IGI Global. doi:10.4018/978-1-7998-7352-5.ch003

Smuts, H., Kotzé, P., Van der Merwe, A., & Loock, M. (2017). Framework for Managing Shared Knowledge in an Information Systems Outsourcing Context. *International Journal of Knowledge Management*, *13*(4), 1–30. doi:10.4018/IJKM.2017100101

Sousa, M. J., Cruz, R., Dias, I., & Caracol, C. (2017). Information Management Systems in the Supply Chain. In G. Jamil, A. Soares, & C. Pessoa (Eds.), *Handbook of Research on Information Management for Effective Logistics and Supply Chains* (pp. 469–485). Hershey, PA: IGI Global. doi:10.4018/978-1-5225-0973-8.ch025

Spremic, M., Turulja, L., & Bajgoric, N. (2018). Two Approaches in Assessing Business Continuity Management Attitudes in the Organizational Context. In N. Bajgoric (Ed.), *Always-On Enterprise Information Systems for Modern Organizations* (pp. 159–183). Hershey, PA: IGI Global. doi:10.4018/978-1-5225-3704-5.ch008

Steenkamp, A. L. (2018). Some Insights in Computer Science and Information Technology. In *Examining the Changing Role of Supervision in Doctoral Research Projects: Emerging Research and Opportunities* (pp. 113–133). Hershey, PA: IGI Global. doi:10.4018/978-1-5225-2610-0.ch005

Stipanović, C., Rudan, E., & Zubović, V. (2022). Reaching the New Tourist Through Creativity: Sustainable Development Challenges in Croatian Coastal Towns. In M. Valeri (Ed.), *New Governance and Management in Touristic Destinations* (pp. 231–245). IGI Global. https://doi.org/10.4018/978-1-6684-3889-3.ch014

Tabach, A., & Croteau, A. (2017). Configurations of Information Technology Governance Practices and Business Unit Performance. *International Journal of IT/Business Alignment and Governance*, *8*(2), 1–27. doi:10.4018/IJITBAG.2017070101

Talaue, G. M., & Iqbal, T. (2017). Assessment of e-Business Mode of Selected Private Universities in the Philippines and Pakistan. *International Journal of Online Marketing*, *7*(4), 63–77. doi:10.4018/IJOM.2017100105

Tam, G. C. (2017). Project Manager Sustainability Competence. In *Managerial Strategies and Green Solutions for Project Sustainability* (pp. 178–207). Hershey, PA: IGI Global. doi:10.4018/978-1-5225-2371-0.ch008

Tambo, T. (2018). Fashion Retail Innovation: About Context, Antecedents, and Outcome in Technological Change Projects. In I. Management Association (Ed.), Fashion and Textiles: Breakthroughs in Research and Practice (pp. 233-260). Hershey, PA: IGI Global. https://doi.org/ doi:10.4018/978-1-5225-3432-7.ch010

Tantau, A. D., & Frăţilă, L. C. (2018). Information and Management System for Renewable Energy Business. In *Entrepreneurship and Business Development in the Renewable Energy Sector* (pp. 200–244). Hershey, PA: IGI Global. doi:10.4018/978-1-5225-3625-3.ch006

Teixeira, N., Pardal, P. N., & Rafael, B. G. (2018). Internationalization, Financial Performance, and Organizational Challenges: A Success Case in Portugal. In L. Carvalho (Ed.), *Handbook of Research on Entrepreneurial Ecosystems and Social Dynamics in a Globalized World* (pp. 379–423). Hershey, PA: IGI Global. doi:10.4018/978-1-5225-3525-6.ch017

Teixeira, P., Teixeira, L., Eusébio, C., Silva, S., & Teixeira, A. (2021). The Impact of ICTs on Accessible Tourism: Evidence Based on a Systematic Literature Review. In C. Eusébio, L. Teixeira, & M. Carneiro (Eds.), *ICT Tools and Applications for Accessible Tourism* (pp. 1–25). IGI Global. doi:10.4018/978-1-7998-6428-8.ch001

Trad, A., & Kalpić, D. (2018). The Business Transformation Framework, Agile Project and Change Management. In M. Khosrow-Pour, D.B.A. (Ed.), Encyclopedia of Information Science and Technology, Fourth Edition (pp. 620-635). Hershey, PA: IGI Global. https://doi.org/ doi:10.4018/978-1-5225-2255-3.ch054

Trad, A., & Kalpić, D. (2018). The Business Transformation and Enterprise Architecture Framework: The Financial Engineering E-Risk Management and E-Law Integration. In B. Sergi, F. Fidanoski, M. Ziolo, & V. Naumovski (Eds.), *Regaining Global Stability After the Financial Crisis* (pp. 46–65). Hershey, PA: IGI Global. doi:10.4018/978-1-5225-4026-7.ch003

Trengereid, V. (2022). Conditions of Network Engagement: The Quest for a Common Good. In R. Augusto Costa, F. Brandão, Z. Breda, & C. Costa (Eds.), *Planning and Managing the Experience Economy in Tourism* (pp. 69-84). IGI Global. https://doi.org/10.4018/978-1-7998-8775-1.ch004

Turulja, L., & Bajgoric, N. (2018). Business Continuity and Information Systems: A Systematic Literature Review. In N. Bajgoric (Ed.), *Always-On Enterprise Information Systems for Modern Organizations* (pp. 60–87). Hershey, PA: IGI Global. doi:10.4018/978-1-5225-3704-5.ch004

Vargas-Hernández, J. G. (2017). Professional Integrity in Business Management Education. In N. Baporikar (Ed.), *Management Education for Global Leadership* (pp. 70–89). Hershey, PA: IGI Global. doi:10.4018/978-1-5225-1013-0.ch004

Varnacı Uzun, F. (2021). The Destination Preferences of Foreign Tourists During the COVID-19 Pandemic and Attitudes Towards: Marmaris, Turkey. In M. Demir, A. Dalgıç, & F. Ergen (Eds.), *Handbook of Research on the Impacts and Implications of COVID-19 on the Tourism Industry* (pp. 285–306). IGI Global. https://doi.org/10.4018/978-1-7998-8231-2.ch014

Vasista, T. G., & AlAbdullatif, A. M. (2017). Role of Electronic Customer Relationship Management in Demand Chain Management: A Predictive Analytic Approach. *International Journal of Information Systems and Supply Chain Management, 10*(1), 53–67. doi:10.4018/IJISSCM.2017010104

Vieru, D., & Bourdeau, S. (2017). Survival in the Digital Era: A Digital Competence-Based Multi-Case Study in the Canadian SME Clothing Industry. *International Journal of Social and Organizational Dynamics in IT, 6*(1), 17–34. doi:10.4018/IJSODIT.2017010102

Vijayan, G., & Kamarulzaman, N. H. (2017). An Introduction to Sustainable Supply Chain Management and Business Implications. In M. Khan, M. Hussain, & M. Ajmal (Eds.), *Green Supply Chain Management for Sustainable Business Practice* (pp. 27–50). Hershey, PA: IGI Global. doi:10.4018/978-1-5225-0635-5.ch002

Vlachvei, A., & Notta, O. (2017). Firm Competitiveness: Theories, Evidence, and Measurement. In A. Vlachvei, O. Notta, K. Karantininis, & N. Tsounis (Eds.), *Factors Affecting Firm Competitiveness and Performance in the Modern Business World* (pp. 1–42). Hershey, PA: IGI Global. doi:10.4018/978-1-5225-0843-4.ch001

Wang, C., Schofield, M., Li, X., & Ou, X. (2017). Do Chinese Students in Public and Private Higher Education Institutes Perform at Different Level in One of the Leadership Skills: Critical Thinking?: An Exploratory Comparison. In V. Wang (Ed.), *Encyclopedia of Strategic Leadership and Management* (pp. 160–181). Hershey, PA: IGI Global. doi:10.4018/978-1-5225-1049-9.ch013

Wang, J. (2017). Multi-Agent based Production Management Decision System Modelling for the Textile Enterprise. *Journal of Global Information Management, 25*(4), 1–15. doi:10.4018/JGIM.2017100101

Wiedemann, A., & Gewald, H. (2017). Examining Cross-Domain Alignment: The Correlation of Business Strategy, IT Management, and IT Business Value. *International Journal of IT/Business Alignment and Governance, 8*(1), 17–31. doi:10.4018/IJITBAG.2017010102

Wolf, R., & Thiel, M. (2018). Advancing Global Business Ethics in China: Reducing Poverty Through Human and Social Welfare. In S. Hipsher (Ed.), *Examining the Private Sector's Role in Wealth Creation and Poverty Reduction* (pp. 67–84). Hershey, PA: IGI Global. doi:10.4018/978-1-5225-3117-3.ch004

Yablonsky, S. (2018). Innovation Platforms: Data and Analytics Platforms. In *Multi-Sided Platforms (MSPs) and Sharing Strategies in the Digital Economy: Emerging Research and Opportunities* (pp. 72–95). Hershey, PA: IGI Global. doi:10.4018/978-1-5225-5457-8.ch003

Yaşar, B. (2021). The Impact of COVID-19 on Volatility of Tourism Stocks: Evidence From BIST Tourism Index. In M. Demir, A. Dalgıç, & F. Ergen (Eds.), *Handbook of Research on the Impacts and Implications of COVID-19 on the Tourism Industry* (pp. 23–44). IGI Global. https://doi.org/10.4018/978-1-7998-8231-2.ch002

Yusoff, A., Ahmad, N. H., & Halim, H. A. (2017). Agropreneurship among Gen Y in Malaysia: The Role of Academic Institutions. In N. Ahmad, T. Ramayah, H. Halim, & S. Rahman (Eds.), *Handbook of Research on Small and Medium Enterprises in Developing Countries* (pp. 23–47). Hershey, PA: IGI Global. doi:10.4018/978-1-5225-2165-5.ch002

Zacher, D., & Pechlaner, H. (2021). Resilience as an Opportunity Approach: Challenges and Perspectives for Private Sector Participation on a Community Level. In A. Zehrer, G. Glowka, K. Schwaiger, & V. Ranacher-Lackner (Eds.), *Resiliency Models and Addressing Future Risks for Family Firms in the Tourism Industry* (pp. 75–102). IGI Global. https://doi.org/10.4018/978-1-7998-7352-5.ch004

Zanin, F., Comuzzi, E., & Costantini, A. (2018). The Effect of Business Strategy and Stock Market Listing on the Use of Risk Assessment Tools. In *Management Control Systems in Complex Settings: Emerging Research and Opportunities* (pp. 145–168). Hershey, PA: IGI Global. doi:10.4018/978-1-5225-3987-2.ch007

Zgheib, P. W. (2017). Corporate Innovation and Intrapreneurship in the Middle East. In P. Zgheib (Ed.), *Entrepreneurship and Business Innovation in the Middle East* (pp. 37–56). Hershey, PA: IGI Global. doi:10.4018/978-1-5225-2066-5.ch003

About the Contributors

Mohammed El Amine Abdelli is a member of the Laboratory of Economics and Management of the West-LEGO (France) and a visiting researcher at the University of Salamanca (Spain). Mohammed El Amine's research interests focus on Entrepreneurship, Innovation. He has ten years of professional experience and three years of academic experience. He is the editor and author of several books and has published 20 articles and chapters. He was a guest editor of several quality journals. He is a member of the committee of several international conferences. He is a member of the editorial board of several indexed journals.

Naima Bentouir is a finance lecturer with a Ph.D. in Finance and Business Management from Ain Temouchent University. With over four years of teaching experience, she is a valued member of the Markets, Employment, Legislation, and Simulation in the Maghreb Countries Laboratory at Ain Temouchent University and an associate researcher at the Economic Research Forum (ERF) in Egypt. Dr. Bentouir's research interests include finance, international finance, financial engineering, financial economics, and applied economics. Her work has been published in nationally and internationally indexed journals by Scopus and Springer publishers, and she has reviewed numerous manuscripts for various publishers such as IGI Global and Taylor and Francis. Dr. Bentouir is a permanent reviewer for several national journals, and from 2019 to 2021, she was an academic visitor at Brighton University in the United Kingdom.

* * *

Atilla Akbaba is a professor at the Faculty of Tourism at İzmir Katip Çelebi University (İzmir, Turkey). He received his M.Sc. from Florida International University and his Ph.D. from Dokuz Eylul University with a major in Tourism Management. He teaches hospitality and tourism-related courses. His areas of specialization include service quality, organizational culture, and management of tourism businesses. He has published widely in his areas of specialization at national and international levels.

Adesoji Emmanuel Ayanlowo is an Administrative Officer at the Baptist College of Theology, Oyo, Nigeria. He holds a Master's degree from the Obafemi Awolowo University, Ile-Ife, Nigeria. Mr. Ayanlowo is an Erasmus+ Scholar. He is a member of Teachers Registration Council of Nigeria and the Nigerian Institute of Management (Chartered).

Alper Işın, Assoc. Prof. Dr., works as an academician at the Department of Gastronomy and Culinary Arts at İzmir Kâtip Çelebi University, Turkey. His research interests include tourism, gastronomy, food & beverage management, and also destination marketing.

Akinyo Ola is a Lecturer in Management at the University of Bristol School of Management. He is an ACCA Chartered Accountant and a Project Management Professional with diverse experiences in the private and public sectors. In addition to his teaching responsibilities, he also consults on business development, entrepreneurship, performance management and business sustainability. Akinyo is very excited about building new relationships and collaborating with researchers from other disciplines and his research interest is in Project Management, Improving Organisational Performance, and Internal Control.

Yaşar Asu Tabanlı received her undergraduate degree from İzmir Katip Çelebi University, Faculty of Tourism, Department of Gastronomy and Culinary Arts in 2022. She continues her master's degree at Izmir Katip Celebi University, Institute of Social Sciences, Department of Gastronomy and Culinary Arts.

S. Ece Yilmaz completed her undergraduate studies at Çukurova University, specializing in Business Administration with a focus on the English language in 2015. In the year 2018, she successfully completed her master's degree in the field of management and organization. In 2023, she successfully obtained a PhD in Management and Organization. Currently, she is actively engaged as a researcher in several projects funded by the European Union. Additionally, she offers career training services in line with her 3-year career expert position at Adana Alparslan Türkeş Science and Technology University.

Arabeche Zina is professor at Ahmed Zabana University of Relizane, Algeria.

Index

L

P

S

T

V

W

www.ingramcontent.com/pod-product-compliance
Lightning Source LLC
LaVergne TN
LVHW081322300926
849161LV00008B/1846